Intu

Method

By

Dr. William Kalatsky

Dedication

This book is dedicated to everyone seeking to use and enhance their intuition, as well as those who are already on their intuitive journey. It's dedicated to the empaths who have felt overwhelmed and until now couldn't be in crowds and to those who want to master their inborn skills and abilities as the gifts that they are. This is for you.

It is for those who are ready to embrace their truth, knowing that their awareness shapes the future. For those who believe in miracles and energy healing, but didn't realize they have the power to access them. For those who have always wished to see auras and simply needed the right guidance.

This is dedicated to those who uplift humanity and all living things by investing their time, their practice, and their efforts into uplifting themselves.

A special dedication to the 9, 15, and 18-year-old versions of myself who wished this book existed when they wanted to learn. Here it is. Learn it now, master it by my age, and write the next version.

With heartfelt gratitude,

Dr. William Kalatsky

Acknowledgments

I have deep gratitude for all those who have supported and inspired me throughout the writing of this book. To my family and friends, your unwavering support, encouragement, and belief in me have been invaluable. Thank you.

To my mentors and teachers, your guidance, wisdom, and insights have profoundly shaped my understanding and practice. I am forever grateful for your contributions to my growth.

To my patients, students, and clients: For your trust and willingness to explore healing and your intuitive abilities. Your responses to my questions have been invaluable. You became part of my study of energy and consciousness. I learned more every time we worked together.

A special thanks to my mom for reading my drafts, for letting me know when concepts were confusing or unclear and for your proofreading. Your love and dedication mean the world to me. To my dad, for always asking how the book is coming along and for sharing your enthusiasm for many of my dreams.

To my brother, Dr. Daniel Kalatsky, one of my teachers and one of the great healers on the planet today. Your levels of awareness and teachings have been pivotal in my journey.

To all who have in some way contributed to this project through conversations that led to insights. Thank you.
With heartfelt appreciation,

Dr. William Kalatsky

About the author

Dr. William Kalatsky is a chiropractor and expert in consciousness development who has dedicated his career to exploring the profound connections between the mind and body. His journey into consciousness and energy healing began with a deep fascination with how these two aspects of human experience are intertwined. Over the years, he has developed a unique ability to sense the energy fields surrounding the human body, allowing him to detect and clear distortions that often manifest as physical pain, particularly migraines and chronic headaches.

Dr. William's innovative methods have earned widespread recognition for their effectiveness in addressing the root causes of these conditions in the field of consciousness. His approach goes beyond conventional methods, offering a holistic method that often is the catalyst for transformative healing.

In addition to his virtual healing work, Dr. Kalatsky is the author of "Piranha Yama and the Art of Non-Biting," a children's adventure book that teaches mindfulness and self-control. His upcoming book, "The Healer's Chronicles," is a compilation that shares the secrets of many healers and their experiences, guiding you on where to turn when you need help and don't have the answer. He also offers the Intuition Method Online Course, which empowers individuals to unlock their intuitive potential and enhance their overall well-being.

Dr. Kalatsky's diverse offerings and unwavering dedication to guiding others towards greater awareness and healing continue to make a significant impact in the field of consciousness development and holistic wellness. Through his work, he helps individuals achieve a deeper understanding of their own healing potential and leads them on a path to improved health and vitality.

Contents

Part 3

Your Invitation to New Awareness

Hi, I'm Dr. William Kalatsky. Welcome to *The Intuition Method,* the book and course on awakening your abilities to master your intuition and all that it encompasses, including your abilities as an empath, as a healer, and as the creator or manifestor of what you want in your life.

I'm thrilled to share this book with you because if there's one skill that's revolutionized my life and the lives of countless others, it's the power of intuition—those flashes of insight that defy logic and guide us toward our true path. Along with the mastery of energy and its intricate dance with manifestation, this journey promises to be nothing short of transformative.

At its core, this book is about dismantling the barriers that keep us from accessing our innate gifts and potential encoded within our DNA and consciousness from the moment we are born. My goal is to help you break free from limiting beliefs and blockages, empowering you to take some simple steps and witness the magic unfold in your life firsthand.

Reflecting on my life's journey, I've been privileged to learn from a diverse array of individuals—from those facing profound challenges to master energy healers, intuitive and manifestors. And you know what I've discovered? Despite our diverse backgrounds, we all share a common thread of human experience. Being human has plenty of challenges, especially because there has been no guide book to show us how to use our innate gifts. Often, we can feel inadequate even while others see us as way more than we feel we could be. Even with this lack of trust in our inner voice or a sense of disconnection from it, we all can agree that we want more clarity and a sense of purpose.

Through this book, I've had the privilege of guiding individuals toward unlocking their inner potential, tapping into their innate wisdom, and harnessing the power of manifestation. And I want to assure you, the journey is worth every step.

Let me tell you a story about intuition… I was driving along the Jackie Robinson Parkway in NY on the way to see a client when a vision of the flooded highway flashed into my mind as I was going a little too fast entering a big, blind curve. The vision took over my whole mental screen. It was as if my eyes were rewired and were seeing what was in my mind instead of the road in front of me. I slammed on the brakes and snapped out of it just as fast as it happened. There was no flood. I had about 2 seconds to wonder if I was going crazy until I went around the curve. The road was flooded. If I hadn't braked seconds in advance, I would have gone full speed into it, lost control, and been taken right off the parkway into the trees.

"When you unlock the power of intuition, you gain the clarity to uncover answers and find unexpected guidance."

By choosing to delve into this book, you've taken a courageous step toward unlocking your full potential. I've crafted this book with bite-sized insights, allowing you to absorb and practice at your own pace. Whether you're a skeptic or a believer, this journey promises to expand your horizons and deepen your understanding of the mysteries of intuition and manifestation.

So many already believe that Intuition, psychic abilities, and the ability to manifest exist and are available to them at certain seemingly random times. For those who don't believe, it's less likely you are reading this book, but if you are, you know there are some unexplained phenomena that you have considered quite amazing and have probably wondered what the heck just happened. Of those who believe, some think others have these gifts while they, themselves, don't. On the other hand, you may have had intuitive or psychic experiences at times without knowing how they have happened. You may even think that it was simply coincidence, or perhaps you imagine or tell yourself that there is more to it. If you do, you are correct! This book will put all of those thoughts to bed because *you* will be learning to make all of these experiences available to *you*. I'm excited about this for you because I know what life is like when you tap into the gifts that you've always had but never learned to use properly. It's like living a part two of your life. ***Life 2.0***

In this book, you are going to learn my latest discoveries and breakthroughs, with new information on manifestation and how to use the present moment, including Deja vú, inner voice, breath, and intentional meditation to create your life.

You will learn how to become sensitive and feel energy, be an empath and feel peoples' emotions, see auras, heal people, and do all the things that have been available to you as life skills if you were only to find some guidance so you could learn.

You may feel like you don't know how to activate these abilities yet, or maybe you know you have them and will be amazing once you practice. It may even lead to a new career path for you. Still, I had one thing to add to this version of the book and to The Intuition Method online course that I've discovered about manifestation when my intuition showed me the way to manifest even better. I had to share it with you here.

You are about to lift and turbo-boost your life, your experiences, and your awesomeness to the next level. You will never be bored again when you can sit and practice seeing auras or read other people whenever you feel like it.

You will begin to notice the moments that we call intuitive or psychic moments and soon realize they are what you do automatically when you are *not* paying attention to that part of your mind. Once you learn to pay attention and what to pay attention to, you will know that you have had the ability all along.

So, buckle up and get ready to elevate your life to new heights. With each page read, understood and practiced, you're one step closer to unleashing more of your true brilliance and embracing the magic that lies within. Welcome to *The Intuition Method*—where your untapped abilities seamlessly integrate into your daily life, and the mystical becomes a powerful tool you can leverage, direct, and even shape according to your desires.

The separation between the subconscious mind and the conscious mind is like being in a swimming pool with a rope separating the shallow from the deep end. You are in the shallow end, and even when you don't cross to the other side, the water from the deep end flows into the shallow side, and the shallow water flows to the deep side under the surface. The whole time, you remain physically in the same space, not noticing this. That's how information passes from your Intuition to your conscious, awake mind.

Part One

Chapter One
Let's Start with Intuition

Imagine what it might be like if you could access your Intuition and know when it is sending you messages at almost any time.

How would it change your life if you suddenly knew that some of the greatest circumstances in your life that seemed to be what you would call "lucky" at the time were not luck at all, but that you were being guided by a deeper part of your mind that is always there, always on, and always working for you? You usually aren't paying attention to this part of your mind, because you have not been trained to find it or shown how to use it.

Sure, some of the messages from deeper parts of what we call the Quantum Mind, Layer One Mind, or Universal Intelligence float up to the surface so you can receive the message, but you tend to notice it only when your mind is quiet enough inside as the message is released into your awareness. At times, an emergency message forces its way to your conscious mind to give you important news, like the image of that flooded highway that saved me from a car accident, but the truth is that the gentle message that was telling you that there is a gift waiting for you was completely missed because your mind didn't shout it loudly at you.

Now, there is a way to connect to the wealth of information that is floating in the depths of your mind, where your ideas and your whole life are created. Your subconscious, your higher self, your spirit, and even part of your conscious self that is the 'you' reading this right now, are waiting for you to learn it, savor it, and use it for your greatest benefit. These different parts of you sit back like they are behind a screen, just like you sit back when you watch a movie on the screen. When you are watching the actors getting closer to finding what they most want and need, you begin to get excited for them. The actor doesn't know they are just around the corner from reaching their goal, and they certainly don't know you are watching them and cheering them on, just like you don’t know the parts of yourself watching you.

Here is a simple way to look at it:

Imagine there is a huge bank account overflowing with money with your name on it, but no-one told you it existed. You just found out that it exists right now while reading this book! It's real and legitimate, and it's assigned to you, but you have to find it. That's the rule. What would you do to get it? How much easier is it already now that you know all of your financial issues are taken care of once you find that bank account? With the internet, it won't take too long to find. You might even hire someone who has done it before to show you where it is. Someone who found theirs already could show you the steps. The hardest part is finding out it exists, and that part is already done.

Now imagine it's not hidden from you at all. You only had to find the secret note in your pocket. The reason you didn't have access to it is because no one told you it was there. No one told you because they didn't know either. It was just there waiting to be found.

Now imagine you never reached into your pocket and found the note with the bank information. Life would stay the same for you. But luckily you found the note, and if you are honest with yourself, you didn't believe it at first. Wouldn’t you question a winning lottery ticket for a minute? So you did some detective work and found out the note was real and it's your inheritance! Some might quit their job to be a detective until they found that bank account. I know I would!

That's exactly what you have in the deeper layers of your mind. Your consciousness is a massive facility that connects to all the levels of life, from your body to your thoughts, your feelings, and everything you treasure, desire, crave, and dream about. This includes running your heartbeat twenty-four-seven while awake or asleep, keeping your lungs breathing and pumping for you. It runs digestion, keeps your hormones in check, cleans your blood—and those are just the jobs it does without you needing to even be consciously aware of it.

That health programming, with few exceptions, is in you at birth. There are many other programs in your DNA that have never developed. These are some of the programs that seem like magic to most because so few people have learned to awaken them and use them. They aren't magic, but they seem like magic because the training we receive for much of our lives tells us these kinds of experiences are either random luck or fantasy.

Have you heard of Wim Hof? He has taught thousands of people to control their breathing to access levels of consciousness that allow them to withstand and even enjoy freezing temperatures. He climbed Mount Everest while it was snowing… in shorts and shirtless. This isn't fantasy. It's controlling a part of your DNA and subconscious programming. It comes from doing specific practices that don't at all seem connected to the result you want, but the practices are ways of accessing the underlying software and programs in your mind's control room.

Using the Wim Hof Technique as an example, consider where you are in your life right now. Many things that you did led you here. You overcame many things that took a lot of effort and sometimes felt like you would never get through it, but you did, and maybe you were helped by luck, or the right prayer. This is the same principle as doing specific things or practices that lead you to a destination, even if you didn't know it was connected at the time. You can only recognize the connections that led you here in hindsight or if you are properly trained and learn to use your own abilities to make it happen. When you do it knowingly, it's still mystical and mysterious, but you recognize that you steered the boat and navigated the river using your heart, mind and gifts to do it.

It does seem like the skills you will be learning are mystical, until you learn how to do them. Once you know how you do it, it feels like it's always been a part of you, but I can tell you that it is still hard to explain to someone else who hasn't learned yet.

When you mix up ingredients for a cake and put it in the oven, if it was your first time doing it, you wouldn't know the end result was going to be a beautiful fluffy cake, but you have done it so many times, you do know if the ingredients are right, the temperature is right, and the amount of time is right, you get a fluffy cake.

We are going to make a beautiful cake here by following the recipe.

Here is another story: I was telling someone about my client and now friend, who was paralyzed and now can walk. He severed his spinal cord in a bike accident. He wasn't given any hope by the doctors, but he has an amazing and supportive family. His wife, Rachael, who believed that traditional doctors did not have the final answer if the answers were not the ones she wanted and needed, started to reach out to friends who knew of people who had miracles happen. She flew him down to Florida and started a program and protocol of healing. In less than a year, his spinal cord was healed, and he was walking. Is it a miracle? It is. But why is it a miracle? It's a miracle because people don't know the protocol that was used is available. If everyone knew, then his healing would be considered a normal response using this protocol, and these kinds of injuries would be things we expected to heal from. It's not a miracle if a painkiller helps someone with the pain of a broken leg, but it would be a miracle to someone with severe pain who didn't know painkillers existed. They would certainly think it was magic or miraculous when their pain was gone.

This is what learning to use your intuition and subconscious is. What you can begin to know, do, and create will seem like a miracle, and then after a while, it will seem like it's still a miracle but an expected miracle. Yes, becoming adept at using intuition and manifestation abilities will make you seem like the luckiest person around for those who don't know what you know, so it's up to you to share when you are ready and when they are ready.

I know you have had many hints, signs, and tastes of these Layer One formulas and techniques in your mind at the times when you wanted something, and it suddenly, miraculously happened. You felt so blessed. How about when you showed up somewhere, and the most amazing **luck**, **coincidence,** or even **Déjà vu** happened. These strange occurrences are all tools for you to delve deeper into your mind and abilities if you are curious enough. After a time, if paying proper attention, you will recognize that these tools are something special.

You are about to find out what they are and how to use them.

So, here is where you are now. You have a way to gain access to and use the mind system. Now you know what you are going to learn here. While you read this book, think about it, talk about it and sit with it in silence so your mind absorbs it. Do the exercises. Read before sleep so the information is closer to being processed by your subconscious mind. Then, follow the instructions, practice, and repeat. Repetition is key here because this will override and reprogram your current programs. You are the computer and the programmer. Together, we can write the new program that works for you to make your life what you want it to be.

You are part of the lucky group, the one that has the abilities available to you that many thought were only available to a different group of lucky few. You have had some psychic and intuitive experiences already, but either didn't know that you could make it happen at will by pushing the right keys on your mind's keyboard, or you just didn't know what keys needed to be pushed in what order.

That's this book. Awakening your birthright, your natural abilities that you were never taught to use, and in doing so, becoming a more empowered human so you can live up to your true potential. Do it. You are worth it and worthy of it.

In this latest version of *The Intuition Method*, I've added much more on what I've learned about creating the life you want. It's called MANIFESTATION. You have heard of it. It's one hundred percent real. Here, I'm going to teach you exactly how to do it.

Immersion in an experience will allow you to have a fast change, which can be for massive growth and learning or a negative outcome (and also learning). There are a number of ways this can happen. One way that happens too often is trauma. Trauma is so immersive and experiential at that moment that it can create a pattern immediately. If someone is bitten by a dog one time, they may develop a lifetime fear of dogs. Repetition works well to change a pattern and replace it with something you do want without trauma. Immersion works even better. Repetition and immersion, along with a positive experience, can lead to major growth.

1.1 So, What Exactly Is The Intuition Method?

The Intuition Method has evolved from the beginning as a method of learning to access intuition, empathic abilities, and hidden gifts to now, a much more detailed level of mastery of specific aspects of your consciousness, such as your hidden awareness and abilities.

It is a simple way to learn to understand and direct the part of your mind that I call Layer One Mind, which has been hidden from you behind a black, soundproof curtain while going about your day. It's always there, but it's purposely well hidden. It has to be. You must learn the tools and formulas so you understand your capabilities and how they work, safely practicing and honoring what you learn until you achieve it.

Here is an example.

Try to have a dream while you're wide awake and in a natural state. Don't just remember a dream, but actually be in the dream, like when you are asleep. Most people can't do this, and I haven't met anyone healthy who can. It's as if there's a locked door between being awake and being in a dream that can't be opened without the correct combination code. You have to first pass the curtain or the veil into the other part of your mind to get into that world.

The Intuition Method is the code to unlock that door. It allows you to bridge the gap between your conscious-awake mind and your subconscious, where your Intuition, psychic abilities, and manifesting powers are transmitted. These subtle abilities are closer to what happens in twilight sleep than a wide-awake state. The *Intuition Method* gives you techniques to connect these two states so you can access your potential.

By reading this book or taking the *Intuition Method* Course, you'll discover how to control aspects of your life you never thought possible. Each chapter and lesson will teach you about the incredible way you process information and how you can use your Intuition, empath-y, energy skills, and manifesting abilities. Once you've learned these secrets, you can harness them to unlock more of your human potential and live your best life.

It doesn't take much time or practice to develop these skills, but it does take some dedication. Do it, and you shape your life, making it richer and more fulfilling than you ever imagined.

This book is full of tips, shares, and reminders sprinkled in different places to plant seeds in your mind. This book is the fertile soil and plant food for your mind to work with, so it opens the curtains, veils, and doors for you to a more magical, mystical world where you can be guided by your inner voice and manifest what you want for yourself.

The reason you have Intuition or sudden inner guidance when you are about to have certain kinds of trauma, like a car accident, is because you have a special mechanism in your body that awakens your pineal gland. The pineal gland is what's known in mysticism as the third eye, which brings a non-physical seeing and knowing of great insights. It may slow time, as often happens in a car accident, and give you an immediate solution in an emergency if you have been trained in how to use it.

If you have ever been in a car accident and you've seen the other car coming at you before the collision, you may remember that you took a deep breath and held it. You may also remember that you clenched up your buttocks muscles and tightened your body.

When all of this happens at once, your spinal fluid is pumped at the base of the spine and pumped upwards through the spinal cord. You also held your breath and tightened your body, which continued to move the spinal fluid up your body like mercury moving up a thermometer to hit your pineal gland in the back center of your brain, activating it. This is a biological emergency failsafe mechanism. This is why clenching the perineum and intrinsic muscles down there is done during certain yogic breathing practices. It is a way to practice awakening the pineal gland. This knowledge is thousands of years old. This is part of your hidden brilliance. Imagine how much more there is that you don't yet know.

1.2 Reasons

There are many valuable reasons to read this book, but these are the ones that have come up the most in workshops and discussions.

People who read this book are already intuitive or think they probably are, but they know how powerful it would be to *multiply their ability* and *access it at will.*

This book is for you if you want to learn the signals of when Intuition is messaging you instead of realizing your Intuition already told you about a situation while it's happening. It's helpful to know you intuited this while in the middle of the situation, but it's more helpful to know in advance, so you don't miss out on being able to prepare for it (more on this when I cover Deja vú).

The book is for people who get déjà vu. Déjà vu and Intuition are directly related, and this course will teach you how to use your déjà vu to increase your Intuition.

It's for you if you want to understand how your mind works, so Intuition and creating with your consciousness makes sense to you in a real way.

The *Intuition Method* is for you if you want more positivity and more luck in your life. Luck, Intuition, and being psychic are in the same basket, and later, I will explain how they are actually all parts of each other. As you become more intuitive and more in touch with your consciousness sensitivities, you get luckier, and as you become luckier, you become more intuitive and aware. This automatically leads to feeling more fulfilled. I will explain how it all works. This all leads to creating and manifesting, which is the pinnacle because it's consciously making your physical world dreams a reality using your non-physical world, Layer One Mind.

If you want to know how to communicate with your subconscious to get more cosmic knowledge or just get more insight and answers about people, places, situations, and life, you will get it here.

You will learn how to program yourself for success in the different areas that you want to change.

If you have taken the Intuition Test on IntuitionMethod.com, then you have already answered some of these questions, but answer it here, too, in your journal.

Don't have a journal yet? I created one that is rich in subconscious messaging, so every time you write in it, positive messaging is affecting your mind. Even though you can't see the messages easily, your subconscious sees them subliminally and acts as if it's a positive instruction for it to follow.

Has this happened to you? Intuitive and psychic people often think of someone, and then their phone lights up, and it's the same person they just thought of. At this point the question is- why didn't you know they were going to text you when the person popped into your mind? Why didn't you associate it? (You will.) Fortunately, this situation happens so often for so many people that it is easy to track. As you find these moments and track them in your journal, they become much more obvious.

Why do so many people have so many missed intuitive messages if they are important to receive? What if your phone was always on silent? Would you miss more messages than if the ringer was on? What if you were always playing loud music? What about the vibration setting? You might get more messages from a ring than vibrations if the room is quiet. Your mind notices certain types of intuitive or psychic alerts more easily than others, too.

You will learn here how your subconscious mind speaks to you. With practice, you might find that it's more fun to call the person who just called you when you know they are about to call and let them tell you that they were just about to call you.

In Layer One Mind, like the quantum, there is no time like the present. This is a common phrase that means to enjoy the moment you are in, but it has another meaning. ***There is no time.*** *(Time does not exist the way you think it does.)* ***Like the present.*** *(Find joy and festivity in the present moment. Take this as a strong suggestion without needing to know why at the moment. We will cover it in detail later, but in short, it is because the feelings and frequency will vibrate into all aspects of your life and your future.*

If you want to develop your empathic skills to be able to *feel what others feel*, if you want to see auras, feel energy with your hands, *get glimpses of the future*, create and manifest the future you want, and be in touch with your inner knowing to **go behind the curtain of how your mind and intuition work** and then put it to use to make your life better, *this book will open all of your eyes.*

Before we go further, what is the Layer One Mind?

The Layer One Mind has a number of different names. I call it the Layer One Mind or Super Mind. Some call it the Quantum or the Void. Some call it Source or God Consciousness. All of these names are correct and interchangeable. The name - *Layer One Mind* makes it more personal and accessible to me in some ways.

The Layer One Mind is where we go to create. We live our outward lives on Layer Two and Layer Three Mind.

Here is an example. A highway is made of asphalt. Let's call asphalt Layer One. The driver is Layer two. The driver can drive a car, a bike, or a motorcycle on the highway. The vehicle is Layer Three. It was built for travel on the highway. Each one is built on the other, and they all need Layer One to get anywhere.

So, Layer One Mind is the layer we have to connect with. Like the highway, it waits to be used by a driver or consciousness. How Layer One Mind got there is very mysterious, and I don't believe I could try to answer it in spoken words. We know the highway was built by someone, and we use it without knowing who built it. Layer One Mind is the same.

The Super Mind has the same meaning as the Layer One Mind. It is the energy of the mind that is everywhere at once on all levels. It is always available to you. You just have to connect with it. When you do, miracles happen. Now mind you, you are always connected to it like you are always plugged into the earth's electrical field, but you can do things to increase voltage and draw more power, too.

Now that the basic definition is out of the way, let's continue so we can learn how to connect to Layer One and our innate abilities.

Every moment is a crystal ball; every moment, the answers are here. It's all right here, right now. It's available if you learn the language and how to pay attention.

1.3 Access To More

Let's quickly cover some of the reasons that it is worthwhile to have access to more Intuition and empathic abilities.

Everyone has their own reason for wanting to increase their abilities, and some individuals have no interest at all. Even these people would want it if the potential was properly explained to them. For those who do want to learn and enhance their abilities, in my experience, the reasons are generally one or more of those listed below.

1. You want more information (higher awareness, life, making money, relationship, truth).

2. You want to feel a greater connection to your higher self, spirit, or consciousness.

3. You are looking for answers.

4. You want to know when someone or something is right or wrong for you.

5. You have a yearning or quest for knowledge.

6. You want to prove there is "more" out there than just the physical.

7. You want to live using more of your potential.

8. You want to know what people think or feel, for better or worse.

9. You want to help more people.

10. You want to better prepare for the future.

What is your reason? Write it in your journal, and if it's not listed here, please send me an email letting me know what it is. *William@intuitionmethod.com*

When I was practicing as a doctor and energy healer full time, I would sometimes see clients whose energy was blocked in a certain area. If I saw them enough times, I could tell them that a big shift for more healing and wholeness was waiting to happen for them.

For example, a person's shoulder was holding an emotional, energetic charge that was causing other problems for them, but if the person really wanted to keep feeling angry and hold onto the emotion related to their tight shoulder, their subconscious was going to do its job to release it for them at some point...

In a sense, for this client, something was going to happen the easy way or in a way that was still unknown... The person could have chosen to make a change, but something was going to happen even if they didn't. Not choosing was still choosing. The next thing I knew, the person came in with their arm in a sling. They damaged their shoulder when they slipped and fell. Their subconscious, a part of the Intuition level of the mind, made sure a change happened in how they used that shoulder. The energy needed to be released for healing to happen, and they consciously weren't going to do it, so their inner guide had to take over.

1.4 What You Will Learn

In the book, like the online course, we will cover valuable topics. What you learn will be with you for the rest of your life.

They are:

- The concepts of mind and consciousness, so your conscious mind knows firsthand that different abilities exist and can be put to use.
- The development of your Foundational Breath Technique will allow you to always have intuition available at any time, as well as the basis for it to grow into full-blown intuition and manifestation skills.
- Mind stillness and meditative breath techniques to make room for a more intuitive awareness of all of your abilities, including manifestation.
- A simple, intuitive gauge to know if something is right or wrong for you.
- How the language of your feelings becomes more dominant and helps determine the messages you receive.
- A basic five-minute-a-day seated meditation skill for intuition and psychic enhancement.

- An easy and fun-moving meditation for those who think they can't sit still.
- Feeling energy with your hands and with your mind.
- Use your sleep to make your dreams come true by putting your subconscious to work for you.
- Feeling the energy of another person and finding areas of tension in their body without touch.
- Sending love from a distance using the hand-heart amplification technique.
- Understanding how it all works and changing your view of reality.
- Feel radar from a radar detector, high-powered wires, Wi-Fi, and microwaves.
- Seeing auras.
- Non-medical energy diagnosis of the body using a visual scan.
- How do you really manifest your life using your mind? Manifesting is not the same as creating. It's much better.
- Downloads and uploads of information and consciousness.
- Much more… tuning forks, cloud melting, direct knowing, photo reading, using energy to clear headaches and pains, and more.

1.5 Additional Uses and Examples of Intuition.

There are many skills and traits under the umbrella of the Intuition Method that you will experience once you start practicing. I mention some of them here so you recognize them and mentally file them in a category of **Intuition**, **psychic**, **empathic**, or **manifestation abilities**. It's extremely helpful to have a little bell or alert go off for you when you have an experience so you become familiar with it when it's happening.

You will learn to alert yourself so you notice those experiences and put them in a container, labeling them every time they happen. This will solidify it for you, so it's not a forgotten random occurrence.

You will be reminded to label it in your mind and write it in your journal. Once you recognize the pattern, you'll see it happening all the time. At that point, as it happens, you will become aware of why it happens. From there, you will begin to realize it was actually a part of you doing it all along.

I recommend journaling because it allows you to look back on how many of these experiences you have and how often you have them. Like a dream, memories of these moments fade quickly because you have not trained yourself to remember. The natural state is to forget these seemingly random situations because they are not relevant in your life, but they have a higher level of relevance that hasn't shown itself yet. You are less likely to remember something if it has no value to you. Assign it a value, so you'll do your best to remember. When you remember enough times, you enter a pattern-recognizing mode. The pieces come together, and you recognize the state you are in when the magic moments happen. The system, the ego program, doesn't want you to know these states unless you're ready to be there. If you're reading this book and you do the exercises every day, you are ready. Not everyone will do the exercises, but those that do will change their life forever.

Moments of Natural Strangeness

There are some strange and pretty awesome experiences in your life that wow you and amaze you, but then you forget they happened. I call these experiences moments of "natural strangeness." They are actually Intuition and psychic creations that you, yourself, are creating. You started a process at birth and even before birth, when you opened the door to participate in your subconscious mind's work and became a co-creator, but now, by reading this book and doing the exercises, you're taking control of the steering wheel, instead of letting your subconscious project the life you have been living until now onto the screen called "your reality." Remember to pay attention to anything that seems weird, strange, or out of the ordinary, even if it doesn't seem like it's ESP or intuition-related. There's always a message in the strange or unusual. Your mind is noticing something for you.

When you notice it, grab your journal. It will be your path to tracking what you usually forget. It also leads to you remembering more because when you have a moment of natural strangeness, you immediately think you need to write in your journal, so it gives you an anchor to notice that you just had an intuition or déjà vu or that you saw an aura without meaning to.

Here are some quick definitions to file away in your mind.

- **Intuition.** The overall term for what you are doing when you glimpse the future, see auras, feel energy, or know things without knowing how you know.
- **Glimpses.** Glimpses are flashes or feelings that immediately translate to knowing. Future, present, or past.
- **Direct downloads.** A way of getting information without a physical source.
- **Uploads.** What you do before, during and after downloads. It's you creating or uploading your reality. What you put in and focus on is what you create.
- **Coincidence.** You went somewhere at a given time, and a fortunate, exciting event occurred between you and someone else. By now, you may know I'm going to tell you that **this is not random.** It's how luck works, too.
- **Luck.** Your subconscious knows your wants and needs, even when you don't know it consciously. It directs you to do something without you knowing that it's taking you to a place that luck is waiting for you. Think of having a driver who puts you in the car, and you arrive somewhere where there is a gift waiting for you. The driver knew, but you didn't know. The driver is another part of your mind.

- **Déjà vu.** Time traveling with information. Bridging the past to the future and future to the past.
- **The Present Moment.** Call it by its true and hidden name, the Pre-sent Moment. You don't have to work to be in the pre-sent moment; you are always in it. What you do with it is important. As you read this, you already sent this moment that you are in to be here waiting for you when you arrive. This came from a different level of consciousness and emotional frequency where time doesn't exist in a straight line, meaning time doesn't happen in order. So, if you sent in advance this situation of you reading this book to make a better life for yourself, from a time in the past to this moment now, then without you knowing it with your conscious mind, you sent it in advance. You pre-sent it! You are in a pre-sent moment. This means that at this moment that you are now in, you are also pre-sending your vibration, frequency, state of mind, and emotions to create your future. You are always pre-sending what you vibrate or resonate with to the future, where it is waiting for you to arrive in your physical timeline. Much more on this topic later related to manifestation and déjà vu. This is why manifesting is different from just creating and why the present moment is so important for manifesting in your life.
- **Manifestation.** Manifestation is the ability to speak the subconscious and hearts language to create from. It's done with a **festive** mindset and feeling so it can vibrate across the Super Mind and consciousness to be assembled and waiting for you when you arrive.
- **Touching and knowing.** Touch someone or something and immediately know something about them.
- **Photo reading.** Look at a picture and know about someone's life.
- **Psychic abilities.** Psychic abilities are advanced and well-developed forms of Intuition. Anyone trained in Intuition will

be viewed as at least partially psychic by those who haven't learned the tools and techniques to become intuitive.

1.6 About Your Teacher

My name is William Kalatsky. I've been working in the fields of healing, energy, awareness, and consciousness for over twenty-five years. And I've been meditating even longer. I am a Doctor of Chiropractic and an energy healer with a Master Practitioner Certification in NLP. I've studied many modalities and techniques since I first stepped into the space, including The Silva Method, which I am happy to say is now regaining popularity.

Some of my special skills: I'm a strong empath with strong pattern recognition skills. I'm a healer with a high chemical sensitivity, so I know that foods and products we use for cleaning or makeup can be a problem. All the extreme sensitives I have been given brought me the opportunity to notice things many would miss, like walking in a room where there was a fight minutes earlier and feeling a strong residue or frequency, or knowing if a cleaning product is toxic from quickly being affected by the smell.

I'm an extrovert who is often introverted, but I become an extrovert again for good energy, conversation, learning and teaching.

Like so many other intuitive psychics and empaths, until I was thirteen, I had a fear of the dark, and I bit my fingernails. I saw and felt many unexplainable things. Today, I understand most of it.

I always knew there was more to being a human than being in a physical body. At twelve, I read Dr. Strange comic books. Sci-fi, mysticism, and *Psychology Today* magazine got me closer to quenching my thirst for information on how the mind works and the "secret" abilities some had and others didn't. As a child, I used any extra money I had to order books on meditation, hypnosis, and psychic abilities from the back of psychology magazines. The books, sometimes homemade and held together with staples, gave me ideas but offered little help, because I had no proof they worked, so I didn't put in the time needed to do the months of meditation exercises. I needed a step-by-step, easy guide, and I needed a teacher.

What if you were never told it existed or was possible?

I was taken to an energy healer/chiropractor when I was about twelve for a potentially serious medical condition. He helped me to heal. His name was Donnie Epstein, Creator of Network Spinal Analysis. It was then that I had proof that the mind, consciousness, and energy healing were real. This was a huge step in the right direction. At that age, healing something "experts" said was not healable was a big deal. It's a big deal any day of the week. Donnie had incredible abilities. I always believed those abilities were real, but now I had proof. The stories written in books and on TV about heroes with abilities were seeds planted and waiting to grow within me by higher consciousness, but most of us never train to learn how to use these natural abilities and talents. The reason is that they are hidden in a very gentle way. They are hidden so gently that very few would know to look for them. These traits and abilities have names like "legend," "myth," "fantasy fiction," and "science fiction," which tell the thinking mind that they aren't real. After having the gift of being worked on by a master for so many years, I saw and perceived everything differently. Life would never be the same.

What if no one ever told you that certain amazing things were possible for you if you trained your mind? Would you ever think to try to do these fictional things? What if it was so far out of the spectrum of possibility, like healing headaches for others over a video call? Have you tried that? You probably never thought to try it. I didn't either, until someone asked. Now I do it regularly, and as you will see, you can do it, too.

As a doctor, I have seen thousands of patients for over twenty years. In seeing enough people and paying enough attention, I found patterns. The patterns showed me when my Intuition gave me messages. I found the place in the mind where physical senses crossed over into intuitive senses. It's similar to the place you pass through, from being wide awake to getting tired to finally crossing the curtain into sleep. All of these sensitivities later helped develop the techniques that became the ***Intuition Method.***

I've been meditating since I was a teenager. For years at a time, I stuck with one system; Silva Mind Control, Transcendental Meditation, binaural beats to entrain brainwaves, visualization techniques, and, more recently, because of its vast research, mindfulness, tai chi, and Joe Dispenza's work. Each meditation style has taught me something different and given me new information that has added to my life and this book and course.

1.7 The Order Of The Book.

In what I would call the informational or the lecture part of the book, you are meant to become familiar with this information in your conscious mind before you reach the first exercise and the more advanced levels.

I want you to understand the concepts so they become real to you before you learn how to do it all. Why? Because your subconscious believes what you train it to believe, so the concepts should make sense to you on a rational level, too. Then, it becomes even easier.

The first exercise is to learn the basics of what it's like to feel energy. That will help you discover something that is always happening for you but that you rarely notice. It will bring your attention to the place inside you where you are sensitive to energy so you can have a reference point. It then becomes familiar to you as it happens. It's also the perfect time for your mind to see firsthand that there can be something right in front of you that you still weren't aware of until you were shown it was there.

Learning skills that aren't based on physical senses will enhance your intuition because you are getting to practice and know the more subtle energy fields. The first time you do the exercises, you may think you are imagining what you are experiencing as you feel or see something you may not have seen before. Then, after you experience it a few times, you will know with certainty that you are having intuitive, psychic, and empathic experiences.

This is why journaling is so valuable. Imagine for a moment that you went to the grocery store, and the different kinds of fresh tomatoes were all located in the same tomato area of the produce aisle. That's what you expect. They're all in the same area or the same category. Now imagine that the tomatoes were mixed in the section with the cereal, with the cleaning supplies, and with the water. It would be harder to remember where they were and which types of tomatoes were in which section of the store. You need sections or categories for each experience so you can recognize, store, and reference it later. It will take much longer to remember what a feeling or sense means to you without having a category or a label.

For example, if you eat something spicy, you immediately know it's spicy because you have a category in your mind where you store all things that remind you of spicy. You are going to do this when experiencing different kinds of intuitive and energy experiences, too.

Close your eyes and think about the color blue. Right now, you know the color blue because you have a reference point or category in your mind for the color blue that makes it familiar to you. You have seen blue so many times with your physical eyes that you now have the ability to see not only one shade of blue but many shades of blue. You still know blue, even if it's different from the original blue you learned. You expanded your awareness of blue by becoming familiar with it. You are now an expert at seeing blue. You don't even have to think about it to know it's blue.

Your intuitive abilities work the same way. When something strange and awesome happens, you will know you are having an intuitive moment. You get to reward yourself with a gold star for being aware of it. Then, you will put the experience in a category in your mind and write it down in your journal. You knew it was Intuition, and you also recognized that it was a slightly different type of intuition experience than the last time. Your awareness of the mystical is expanding.

The reason you can notice it's different is because you've stretched your awareness each time it happened. You already have a foundation to work with, and once the cement foundation has dried, you can build on top of it. That applies to every level of Intuition and psychic ability. Baby steps start small and build on a solid foundation, so you can then go big as fast as you want to.

You may have already had some experience feeling energy from other people or from your pets or plants. Feeling energy is simple because there's a physical sensation, even if it's a different physical sensation than you're used to. Feeling energy is a gateway because, when realizing the feeling is available, it makes sense that there must also be more feelings than just this feeling. It's like tasting something sweet and knowing there must be something sweeter that exists, too.

Suppose you were to only use your ability to feel energy for curiosity and not take it further. In that case, it's fun to enjoy and a good conversation starter, but it's just the tip of the iceberg. When you learn to develop it further, there are many other opportunities available. It's like learning to walk. You learn to walk for a much greater reason than just knowing you can walk. You can walk to get to many places, to do many things. Becoming good at walking and feeling energy both lead to much, much more.

Next, you'll learn the **Foundational Breath Technique** to allow you to take the first step in the language of making Intuition conscious. Using your breath this way becomes a conscious intuition technique for you that naturally develops into knowing things intuitively.

The Foundational Breath Technique gives you the ability to be your own oracle, giving you the Yes or No answers as they are needed. You can generate a lot of information by asking the right questions, and that's just the beginning. Then, depending on which you most connect with, you will learn **five options of stillness and meditation techniques** that quiet the mind and allow you to perceive time differently. This allows you to turn down the volume of your thoughts and quiet the noise in your mind so you can hear the whispers of intuition and psychic messages much louder than your chattery, busy thoughts. This way, you can **"hear" the messages** from your subconscious that are always bubbling up and landing gently on the doorstep of your conscious mind, which is the part of you that is reading this now.

1.8 The Techniques Are Coming Soon.

I want to get to them already, but the concepts I'm sharing are part of the groundwork to get your mind ready for the exercises, so they have fertile soil to grow and build upon.

Once you know and **practice the Foundational Breath Technique for two minutes at a time, in three sets for a few days**, your subconscious will put the pieces in place for you. It will build for you. You will notice synchronicities and manifestations in your life appearing more frequently. Your abilities will take on a life of their own, and it will be part of you that is sprouting and growing your new traits and abilities, even though it may seem like it's just happening on its own.

I remember when I started sprouting. Growing sprouts is a pretty amazing experience. If you've done it before, you know what I'm talking about. Some plants can take months or years to grow. It can happen so slowly that when you check on the plant, it seems like nothing is happening. But sprouts, like those stringy fluffy alfalfa sprouts you see in the clear containers in the market, you know the ones- You can grow them in little jars or dishes. Just add water and rinse them, then sit them in the sunlight during the day and then in the darkness at night. In the morning, you're like, "What happened?" Little sprouts are growing out of the seeds everywhere.

By day two, they look like a curly-haired wig of sprouts. By day three, they are fully grown and they're ready to eat. Somehow, it has massive amounts of enzymes and nutrition in it, just from air, water, and the programming in its DNA.

Here is the thing: if you don't give them the right balance of sun and darkness, you don't get the best results. They need specific information in a specific order for a very specific amount of time. Sunlight is information. It has different wavelengths of light, just like the wavelengths of light you see when you look at your phone or TV. Your body absorbs the sun's light, and you create vitamin D, testosterone, skin pigmentation, energy, sweat, happy endorphins, and plenty of other things. You don't even realize all that is happening because your subconscious mind does for you.

Consider a car. There's always something happening under the hood. The car isn't driving anywhere if what's under the hood isn't turning on and everything starts in the right order. The hood keeps it all protected. What you see on the outside doesn't show you what's happening under the hood in the car's programming.

So you have a system inside of you. Your body is a housing or a vehicle for your consciousness to live in. Once you know the easiest way to turn on some of the deeper levels and to use them, **you will notice moments you normally call intuitive and/or psychic moments and recognize that many are simply what you do for yourself while you're not paying attention.** After you finish Section 1 of this book, your new skills in Intuition, awareness, and your discovered abilities will be ready for the more advanced information and techniques in Parts 2 and 3 of this book and course.

Like the sprouts, each concept we cover is the perfect balance of sunlight and dark to get you to maximum growth. **You will notice the growth within days** if you do the exercises. I promise you that it's worth it, but you have to do it. A higher level of awareness doesn't come by luck. Desire and luck got you here. Now, you can do the work and become a more conscious director of your destiny.

After the techniques **connect your conscious awareness to the subconscious layer of your mind,** you will learn to move through these states of consciousness as simply as shifting a car from park to drive.

Next, you will learn the secret to **reverse engineering of Intuition.** You will see and know the place in your mind where intuitive and most psychic messages are given to you. They are directly attached to the stillness exercises. Each exercise builds on the one before, and when we cover one topic, you will use it to build on the next topics in the book and in your life. Then you will learn three **exercises to refine your physical senses**.

When your physical senses are more refined, it means you're increasing your sensitivity. Most things you're aware of are due to you processing your five senses. As you learn to become aware of the tiniest sensations using the five physical senses, you become sensitive to the sensation next to that one, which is even tinier. You will feel the energy of something smaller than your physical senses. If you felt a grain of sand and next felt a piece of dust, you recognize that they are both solid, but sand is easier to feel. They both have mass, but the dust is so small you can't feel it. But what if it gets in your nose? It tickles, and you sneeze! You can feel it if you are sensitive and use the right part of your awareness.

1.9 Intuition Is Your Early Warning Awareness System And Your Guidance System.

Survive and Thrive

Your senses tell you what to run from and what to run toward. They keep you from pain, warn you of pain, or lead you to pleasure. They let you hear or feel that a river flows nearby where you can relax or quench your thirst. Living within a mostly safe community, you don't need your personal warning system very often… But there was a time when you did.

How do your senses help you survive and thrive? Early warning senses start from far away and move closer, like **smelling** smoke from a long distance, **hearing** a wild animal roar from a closer distance, **seeing** the wild animal from five hundred feet away, and the one you never want to happen, **feeling** the wild animal breathing above you. You must pay attention to the senses that speak to you using distance so you have ample warning of danger.

Intuition is the sense that precludes all of these, and it shortcuts all of the physical senses.

- *Intuition is Your First Sense*
- *Intuition is your inner knowing.*

- *With it, no obvious external event is needed to gain information.*
- *No smoke is needed to warn you of fire.*
- *No thunder is needed to tell you a storm is coming.*
- *Your inner knowing is your first sense.*
- *It connects you with the world without needing a physical sense experience.*
- *It is always your 'backup' and your leverage to keep you safe and put you in the right place at the right time if you know how to listen.*
- *For your best life, it is vital to be closer to it and learn to use it.*

1.10 Where Does Intuition Come From?

Intuition, until now, has mostly been something that happened to you and for you instead of from you. When it happened, you either noticed the thought, feeling, or message, and then it likely faded away as if it had never been there. If you were quiet enough, you may have been aware that your Intuition was speaking to you. If you got the message and sensed that it was important, you may have made a mental or written note of it for later.

Most people miss the message completely, not even noticing it was there.

Your subconscious is like a radar system scanning the world for you. It grabs on or attracts the messages that pertain to you and hands them to the part of you that can receive them. Once you discover the message waiting, it opens like a surprise gift. Sometimes, it's for something immediate, and sometimes it's getting you prepared for what's coming, even if you don't know what's coming.

To intuit information implies that you are actively doing something to get it.

Intuiting, or being intuitive, actually means *"Noticing a deeper level of mind's message in the present moment that will give a glimpse of something unknowable with the five senses now, from in the past or in the future."*

You can receive one hundred messages, but if you don't hear the knock at the door to know it was dropped off for you, you miss it. Suppose you somehow remember you heard the knock and remembered the message later on. In that case, you end up with regret because you missed the early delivery and the message was time sensitive, (which can sometimes lead to Déjà vu.)

Your subconscious has been sending messages like bubbles coming up in a fish tank. Your conscious mind, what you think of as the YOU that is reading this, either notices or doesn't notice it when the bubbles pop at the entrance of your conscious mind. Being intuitive is the noticing of the messages. Intuition carries the message to you.

Becoming aware of your Intuition's messages is one of your higher-level consciousness jobs on planet Earth because when you get the message, you are being directed on the path to manifest your life purpose.

Intuition is guidance to your life purpose.
It tells you to take one step to the right without telling you why. Then, a step this way. Then, a step that way. When you listen, you end up where you are meant to be.

An Intuition Tip

Take a shower. It's a shortcut to becoming aware of your Intuition's messages.

I used to listen to podcasts in the shower. I don't anymore. The reason is the shower is one of the easiest places to have intuitive insights and epiphanies. You remember forgotten things, you have brilliant ideas, and you solve problems. Why does it happen? I'm sharing this early in the book so you know the value of a good shower, especially as you learn to quiet your mind.

Besides the obvious, getting clean in the shower, you are also cleaning your mind. How? When you are in the shower, you enter a state of feeling. You feel the sensation of warm or hot water hitting your body constantly. It massages you. You feel it on your hair and skin. You are in a complete feeler mode, and you leave your thoughts behind. That's why if you play any music, podcasts, or news in the shower, it must be very positive. I'd opt toward something you want to learn or something amazing like a Neville Goddard book like *The Feeling is the Secret*.

When you are in a deep *feeling* state, you are out of your head and out of your thoughts. What this means is *inner quiet*. Inner quiet allows the bubbles of thought messages from your subconscious to rise to the surface where you can hear them. They've been waiting for you, and since there's quiet due to your mind being distracted by the water's sensation on your skin, the thought bubbles are loud enough for you to hear them.

So, take lots of showers without noise, and you will prime your mind to notice the inner feelings, intuition, and manifestation of what's coming in this course.

1.11 Intuition and Empathic Skills In Relationships. The Upside And The Downside.

For a conscious person, it's all an upside. Whether it's with family or in the dating world, Intuition has a very important role in your relationships.

Your Intuition and empathic skills will often allow you to finish others' sentences. You will sense, very literally feel, or know someone's words, mood, or deeper unspoken feelings. Your skills will allow you to know who or what circumstance is right or wrong for you.

Long ago, I had an opportunity to test this situation. My inner guidance rarely screams at me if it's not an immediate emergency, but there it was, screaming at me not to go do something. I had time to think about it, and I was so curious about what could be that bad. Because of the insight, I went with great caution and an escape plan in mind. I'm glad I went because when I finally got out of that extremely stressful situation, I knew I'd never have to wonder what would happen if I didn't listen to it again.

When you've developed your inner knowing enough to know if someone is being honest or dishonest, you also develop a feeling of certainty. It may not make you feel better to know the person you care about is lying, but at least you know.

Intuition in personal or intimate relationships can make the relationship even better, but it doesn't always make it easy. There are so many pros to having good Intuition and empathic abilities in relationships. You'll have a better understanding of your partner and make healthier choices. You may know they want something and bring it for them as a surprise. And you become the best gift giver ever.

The con is you may have to make harder choices because you have more knowledge or awareness than the other person about certain things. If you care about yourself and them, you want to do the right thing, which isn't always easy. It might mean having difficult topics of conversation to work through the issues that are being kept hidden.

As tempting as it is in the trials of today's dating world, be careful with how you use what you learn here. The more intuitive and in touch with your inner self you become, the more you can overstep boundaries and take advantage of someone, which means the faster the laws of karma affect you.

Being aware that the laws of karma will affect you is good because your moral compass keeps you doing the right thing, or on the other side of the coin, you don't want the pain of an equal experience, so you act more nobly, more loving, and less judgemental.

If karma comes at you fast, appreciate it. It means you are closer to being the person you want to become. The energy of cause and effect isn't taking a year to teach you. It's right there in that block of time, so you learn quickly to make changes. It means you are moving up!

1.12 So What About These Abilities In A Business Setting?

When you have access to your intuition in business, you'll waste less time on people and ventures that will take up your valuable time. You'll also sense when someone is a good business partner or not. Veteran business people and deal makers develop their intuitive senses.

I spent some time in the movie business and would carefully examine how movie producers could smell who would give them money for their movies. They were sharks smelling someone with a paper cut in the ocean. It amazed me how honed in they were on who to go after. It seemed surreal that they just knew the frequency of someone who would part with their money. They developed the sense over years of being in that system. I had the privilege to watch it happen from an energetic standpoint.

Knowing things intuitively doesn't mean you will make the right choices. Your emotions of greed or hope or wanting to do something to help someone can override your intuitive inner guide's messages to you, so you have to train yourself to say no. That's not easy for many empaths when you want to give a YES that makes everyone feel good- except you.

You don't jump into a pro sport or a big-dollar poker game without a lot of training because you will lose before you start. Start training your Intuition now and practice now so you are ready when the big opportunities show themselves.

When you trust yourself enough to read someone's intentions and know you are on the same page, you'll feel more trusting about your work with them and have less concern.

As you learn to tap your Intuition, it will feed you so much information that you will be an unending creative force of new concepts and possibilities in your work and in life in general.

This book and course were made because my Intuition and higher self-spoke to me. I was nudged more than a few times. *"Why aren't you sharing this information? People need to know this. It should be available to people outside of your immediate circle."*

Here it is years later in its second incarnation, written and then rewritten with so much more information.

What do your Intuition, psychic messaging, and manifestation abilities have in store for your life?

Once you are deeply in touch with it, it's going to guide and direct you, and I assure you, it's going to be amazing.

As you read this book and do the exercises, I will be sprinkling in small tips and instructions to get you started on Intuition and manifestation, as well as all of the other skills you will be learning.

Once again, I need to cover the conscious instruction before I get into the exercises, but some simpler tips will prepare and sensitize your mind for deeper and more intricate learning.

If you ordered the journal I created, you may have noticed the messages hidden within the pages to stimulate your awareness and awaken faster each time you write in it or when you go to read what you have already journaled. Use it often for the best results in tracking your history, growth path, and how you connect to your subconscious.

This is one of the simple processes you can do.

Binaural Beats

Beta brainwaves happen when you are in a state of concentration.

Alpha brainwaves happen when you are relaxed on the way to day dreaming and falling into twilight sleep. It's one of the places where you will get flashes of insight and remote viewing happen as you slip to deeper alpha. Theta brainwaves are deeper than alpha, and they are the place where the magic of manifestation and creation happens.

Of course, it's not magic, though. It's the conscious part of you interacting with the part of your mind below the veil or partition that connects to Layer One Mind, which connects to the field of consciousness of the universe. You are already a part of the field of consciousness of everything in the universe, but you have to get inner quiet to get in the driver's seat.

Binaural beats are sounds or frequencies made to entrain or attract your brainwaves to different speeds, cycles, or hertz. Binaural beats are a good meditation helper because if you sit with headphones on and your eyes closed, they will do some of the work for you. Binaural beats are a great tool to gain the ability to recognize when you are in a different brainwave state.

Each brainwave category feels different. You can find a pure binaural beat of beta, alpha, and theta on YouTube, although I don't know if the beats are as accurate as they claim, or you can go to *IntuitionMethod.com's* website and get the bundle that is there when they are ready.

Using each one for just 5 minutes a day for a couple of weeks will teach you what your mind feels like in each one of these brainwave states. You don't need to do this, but it is a benefit to be able to calibrate your mind, so you know what level you are in as you meditate and as intuition's messages come in, or when you feel energy or see auras or manifest something awesome.

This allows you to drop into that state more easily to reproduce it when you want to.

It's part of the ability to recognize patterns of a new feeling internally.

You will quickly become aware of what state your mind is in, and it will help you create your life faster, so get started with this as you read on.

1.13 Is Intuition Born Or Learned?

Think about this for a moment. I've asked so many people this question. Can you become intuitive, or must you be born with it? The answer is both. That's probably why you are reading this book.

You already know it exists, but want to use it as powerfully as you can.

You are born with it. Everyone is born with it, but it also has to be developed like any skill, including crawling, walking, and speaking. Almost everyone is born with the capacity for those physical abilities. You've had parents and teachers who showed you how to read, write, and walk. They coached you and kept working with you until you walked like an expert. You never quit, and you were not allowed to quit.

What if your parents knew how important it was to discover their inner voice and ability to attract anything to their lives? What if they taught you how to do the same when you were in the easiest learning phase of your life? Where would you be today in terms of your Intuition, manifestation abilities, and your life path if teaching it was taken as seriously as speaking or even throwing a ball? If you are dedicated, you are going to get caught up on the life skills you are meant to have.

1.14 Intuition In The Dictionary: Did You Know?

The word tuition has a few meanings, according to the Merriam-Webster Dictionary.

1. The price of or payment for instruction
2. The act or profession of teaching: instruction pursued his studies under private tuition
3. Archaic: custody, guardianship

We usually think of tuition as payment for school.

Using the third definition, which is the old definition, intuition is the inner guardianship that watches over us.

I knew a woman who had a rescue dog. She actually found this dog on the beach. She fed it and petted it until she was able to make it hers. They became great friends. The dog looked like a mix of a pit bull and a Rottweiler. She could practically walk down the street at night with her eyes closed. Her dog cleared a path for her, and it led her. She knew she was protected. It was as if she had a bodyguard in front of her. It was her guardian. It kept her safe by just following its nature and programming.

But what if she didn't feed it, befriend it, and nurture it. It probably wouldn't have stayed with her. Once it was on her side, she had to learn to use proper language to command it. She trained it to understand her, so it sat at her side and only stood up to protect her when it was needed, but if she spent the time, she could have trained it much further. It would have taken more effort, but it could have been doing advanced things like jumping and spinning or bringing her a towel to the beach.

This is exactly what happens when you learn the language of your Intuition. You connect to your inner guardian so it can do its job for you, which is to protect you and enhance you. It's the perfect tool to lead you to your purpose. It always does a great job. To know how great it's doing, you have to learn to get quiet so you can see, hear, feel, and get the messages.

1.15 Adrenaline Happens, And So Does Intuition.

Let's talk about the unconscious process of adrenaline.

If you saw someone about to get hit by a car and you moved at lightning speed to save them, a part of your mind and body was activated that you don't use under normal circumstances.

An adrenaline response happens as a fight-or-flight response. You tend to remember it because it kept you or someone else alive. It's very surreal and, thankfully, rare.

When in a frightening or shocking situation, you don't ask for or expect adrenaline to kick in like a turbocharger. It just does. You go into super hero mode. You have this capability all the time. It's your subconscious doing its job to protect you. Your nervous system antenna reads that there is danger, and it activates. Consider that adrenaline is a physical form of Intuition or psychic ability. Intuition works the same way, but its message is quiet and gentle. If it's an emergency, then Intuition may shout at you in a way that you will hear it fairly easily, but it's worthwhile to tune in to the quieter messages, too.

You don't directly control your adrenaline with your conscious mind, but you do have a lot of control over it. You can get an adrenaline rush from watching a thrilling movie or from deeply imagining something exciting or scary. This mind hack to access the adrenaline system programming is overseen by your subconscious. By hacking or sneaking into your subconscious when viewing a horror movie, you gain entry. The system wants to let you in, but the entry you want is not due to a movie that causes you feelings of horror or fear. The door does want to be opened, and when watching movies, you stumble upon a key code for entry. And you probably guessed it, you can hack positive emotions for better health, too. Start by watching uplifting movies that make you feel good and choose uplifting thoughts. This connects with your ability to manifest, too. Watch a handful of movies about people who got well from illness, and your mind will create a stronger program that knows this is now possible for you, too.

Intuition works the same way. You can't access it directly by saying, "Intuition, I command you to do this" (at least not in a full waking brainwave state). There is a process to get its attention, and it's not done by being direct (unless it's at certain times before sleep, and we will cover that later.) It's much like going on a first date. You aren't going to kiss your date on the lips when you first meet them. It's too direct. There are steps you take in a specific order that will get you there.

When you first start learning the process, you are flirting with your subconscious and not being too obvious. You don't want it to notice you. Just the same way you mostly haven't noticed it when it speaks to you. You have to do the dance. You don't want it to notice you staring at the entrance of its gate because you want the "guardians of the gate" to stay relaxed and at ease. Do you know how guarded your mind is? Very guarded.

Here is an example to see how protected your mind is once a belief is installed. Try changing an eating habit when you really want to. Start intermittent fasting when you have never done it before. You will notice that until you get in the right frame of mind, you will feel compelled to keep eating the exact way that you want to NOT eat! The mind is guarded, which is fantastic when the right beliefs are there but not too great when you want to make a quick evolutionary change from a behavior you have done for years.

It takes effort to change. You can change through repetition, by putting the guards at ease, or by opening a side door and sneaking in. Here is an example of a side door. You want to play with your new baby nephew. Your nephew ignores you no matter what you do. So, you pull out a sparkly disco ball and roll it around. Now, your nephew looks at you. He even comes over to you and asks if he can play with the ball. You opened a side door. You found a way past the conscious programming into the subconscious. Your nephew changed his mind without realizing his guard relaxed.

This is why some of the best programming is done through TV and movies. They tell a story about things that have happened or can happen. Mainstream TV may program you with all the possible fears and negative emotions. Sometimes something positive gets added, too. Because of the many negative influences out there, and with your mind being a master creator, it has to protect you from yourself so you don't make the negative feelings that you feel inside of you real in your physical life.

Then there is the repetition. Zombie TV shows over and over will affect how you see the world and affect your mood. Your mind will perceive metaphors within the story that easily sneak in a side door to alter perceptions. You will resonate at the frequency that the actors are experiencing, and when you understand manifestation, you will know why you DO NOT want to watch these shows. Seeing hordes of mindless people in the TV show will connect your mind to the way you see big crowds. Your mind's guardian won't let you into the master control center of your reality too easily until you learn the safety rules because it's where you create from, and although it's part of how the formula for creating works, you really don't want to create while you are in a bad mood. In the meantime, the media has learned how to access your control room, so get moving and take back your power.

Alert:

Your control room has been opened too many times while in a negative state of mind. This created less than optimal situations in your life. You are now going to have the chance to change it.

Side topic:

When was the last time you remember having an intuition? Take a minute and think about it. Write it down in your journal. If you don't remember any right now, remember the next one that happens. Because of your focus and intention with this book, it will be soon. Journaling is important for tracking so you can track your progress.

1.16 Trusting Your Intuition? How Do You Know It's Correct?

I think we all know that the most used phrases in all of Intuition are:

TRUST YOUR INTUITION, or I TRUST MY INTUITION

To trust it, you have to learn how to recognize it so you know that it is Intuition communicating with you and not just a belief. You can know Intuition is trying to get your attention when something strange and unusual happens. For example, when you have a déjà vu. This part of your Intuition makes you very aware that there is a shift in the feeling of the moment. It's like you have an imprint that this scene or experience has happened already. It can even be a little disorienting. Many people don't realize that Intuition sends them a message until an event happens (a pre-sent moment), and THEN they remember they had a flash or feeling about it earlier in the day, week, or year. You may even remember it from a dream you had. Maybe you noticed a sign on the side of the road, and you read it wrong, and then later something happened, and it related to what you misread in the sign. I call these Moments of Natural Strangeness.

They are moments that are natural to all of us and part of daily life, so we forget that they happen, even though they are often very cool and strange.

You might sometimes wonder, did you have an intuition about an upcoming moment or event? Or did you manifest it?

I won't give it away yet here, but we will get to it in the manifestation cycle formula.

So, what is not Intuition? Let's cover that first.

If you are analyzing a thought and deciding what to do, then it's not Intuition. Intuition doesn't happen in the analytical mind until you have developed your ability and both sides of your brain work in a balanced state. If you are analyzing an idea, then what you are thinking is your thoughts based on a viewpoint or belief.

If a partner is cheating on you and you just feel it, then you may be correct. Intuition is the feeling that tells you that you are right, but it just gives you awareness without the emotional charge. The emotional charge may come after that message comes in. When you learn how to communicate with your intuition, it quietly slides the message in between your thoughts. If you feel angry, even if you have a good reason to be angry, you will easily miss your intuition message because the strong emotion of anger will override the quiet, neutral state needed to notice the message. Anger doesn't put you in a receiving state. It is an "extro" or outer state, not an "intro" or inner noticing state.

1.17 Trust Your Intuition? Extro And Intro States Of Being

In the early stages of learning intuition, it is very "Intro," as in "introverted." You are taking IN information. As skills develop, you will be able to go "Extro," as in "Extrovert," or "Export" information and share thoughts, feelings, energy, and frequency with others. You will learn the intro/extro cloud melting technique, which you may read about in some books.

Cloud Melting shows you how your consciousness can affect the 3D world. You will be able to experience how you are working Intro, *within your mind and self,* to get results that are Extro or *outside of 'you' results* to affect a cloud. We will get to this later after you learn the sensitivities and subtle feelings so you can shift your states at will.

So.. How do you develop trust in Intuition? First, you recognize it. Then, find a quiet place inside yourself. Then, practice a stillness exercise. There are a number of stillness exercises you will learn here. Some are seated meditation, some are visualization and feeling, and one is standing with movement in case you have a difficult time with traditional seated meditation.

What if you don't want to do a stillness exercise? Some people don't want to. Some say they can't. In actuality, someone who says this is saying it because they don't know its real value. They believe the payoff isn't real or fast enough. If one could be still for just 1 meditative second and get an important intuitive message, everyone would do it. And you can and will do that once you are trained. If anyone could lift weights one time or do 30 seconds of yoga to get in shape, it wouldn't be an achievement. We grow from challenges. We build new pathways in the brain and in the body. We work for what we want, and we win because of it. That's part of the human condition and the human formula for growth.

But for those who can only get quiet for a second, The Foundational Breath Technique makes it easy to connect with your Intuition. Doing the meditation exercises will make everything happen faster and deeper, and it's important to train your mind, but this technique will hand you your Intuition on a platter as you practice it. As you learn to use it, you will learn about how it feels to interact with light and gentle states of consciousness, and this will pull your curiosity and give you a craving to meditate and learn more about this state of stillness.

1.18 Passive Attention. Let's get Intuit!

Much of what we all learn in life is from the natural state of paying attention, but there is much more we learn from what I call passive attention and pattern recognition. Let me explain.

Once you learn how to use your passive attention ability on a conscious level, you will become aware of a wide scope of what I call "noticings" or "awareness." These "noticings" will expand your awareness even further.

They are called "noticings" because they happen in the background, and they are not what you are paying attention to. At first, you *notice* them only a little bit because your attention is on the activity you are doing. Next, you become sensitive to the background or periphery and notice things while they are happening, even while you are busy doing something else. Finally, you notice them right away when they begin and can keep a part of your attention on them, even while you are doing something else. This will lead to new discoveries and you will discover the causes of what you are noticing. What you discover becomes a "Formula" that shows you that when a certain thing happens, then something else will likely happen, too. Everything has a formula. A <u>form</u>ula is the order of things that allows something to take its <u>form</u>. Every miracle and every "thing" that happens has a formula that leads to it. There is always a cause to every effect, even if you don't see it, understand it, or consciously know it yet. We will be covering Passive Attention over and over because it's so important.

A formula is the order of things that allows something to take its form.

1.19 Intuition Gives You Cheat Codes To Get Ahead

Intuition includes a broad range of phenomena and abilities that humans naturally have at one level or another.

Intuition as a skill is the ability to be acutely aware of your connection to your subconscious, its messages, inner knowing, and a scope of psychic abilities. It can be used as a tool to "know" things that you wouldn't be able to know under normal physical sense experiences.

Once you recognize intuition's messages, you get shortcuts or "cheat codes," some of which are what, until now, you have called Coincidence, Luck, and Déjà vu. Intuition makes you conscious of these situations with the new understanding that these experiences themselves are Intuition sending you a message.

Access to your Intuition is a 2-way street where you can send messages to your subconscious mind, too. In the past, due to life experiences, many people mostly sent negative messages to themselves because of negative programming or negatively programmed people around them. If you haven't learned to send positive messages, that is perfect because you will enjoy it even more now that you know what to do with it to manifest your life. Whatever you put out or resonate, good or bad, will appear in your life. This is called creation or uploading. It's like mani**fest**ation but without the **fest**ive part.

1.20 10,000 Times

Why is information repeated in this course?

It is repeated because we learn through repetition. This course teaches you to be intuitive, empathic, psychic, and a trained manifestor. It gives you access to your subconscious as well as a large range of abilities. It teaches you to be a rockstar on the inside where YOU know what you know, and very few others know until they put in the time and have trained in it. When a lesson is repeated, read it again as if you haven't read it before. Be curious. Try to see it from a different angle. Take the time to remember when you may have experienced a similar situation and look back at it in your mind to see if you can find something new in your awareness about it.

In Martial Arts, there is a saying. "I'm not afraid to fight a man who knows 10,000 different punches. I am to fight the man who knows 1 punch and has practiced it 10,000 times." Repetition makes us masters. It makes us invincible in our skills. Your subconscious mind learns the 10,000th punch for you so well that when you need it, your mind and memory throw the punch for you. It's the same with training your mind to master your higher awareness abilities. In the beginning, you think about it as you do it. Later, it happens without thought.

So meditate 10,000 times, and do The Foundational Breath 10,000 times. See auras and feel others' emotions 10,000 times. It will be as common and normal as walking or riding a bike. You will become aware of it when you are walking or sleeping. Once you turn on the engine and start to practice, it happens without you having to do a practice to notice it.

1.21 On Controlling Your Thoughts

The Foundational Breath Technique is the first technique you will learn in The Intuition Method. Once you learn it, you have crossed the line to the place where your subconscious feeds your conscious mind and your conscious mind can reach directly to the subconscious. The Foundational Breath Technique is the easiest way to consciously connect with your Intuition.

When you can open the door to your subconscious based on what you learn here, it will begin to open more easily. It's like you had a closed, rusted door that finally opened. Then, each time you open it, it gets a little easier. Finally, you add some oil, and you can easily open it without thinking about it. What this also means is that you have to learn to control your inner thoughts and your inner state. Why? Suppose access to creating your world is open to you easily. In that case, you'd better be creating good things, because you can manifest or you can Manipath.

Manipath means to create bad things. If you have ever watched a video or heard something that led you to have fearful thoughts or feelings, the thought, vibration, and feeling you are resonating with is going to create something from this state of being. That is the opposite of what you want. Even when the news seems grim, you can learn to choose to call on a positive state because this state is from what and where you are creating your future. It's much easier said than done if or when you are going through a very difficult time, but that's the challenge in this work that you will find worth it. You may need to cry it out first and then choose a different emotional state to work with, but don't hold the difficult emotional state longer than you have to. You are in control of your feelings. It just takes practice and training.

This is a simple way to look at manifestation. When you use it with an understanding of how the present moment works, it will be easy for you to understand how to use it and how important it is.

Life can move fast. Having conscious access to your subconscious is going to cause you to manifest faster.

Here is how it works.

Sometimes, the secret answer is hidden in front of our faces.

Man I fest

Man: Man or woman- (a human)

I: or you

Fest: be in a state of festivity or joyous happiness.

Creation can always be a consciously chosen positive experience, so choose FESTive, and then you will be in the right emotional vibration for positive creation which is manifestation.

Can you manifest in a negative state?

Of course, you can, but it's not called Manifesting, and most people do it regularly. As I mentioned, it is called Manipathing. It's the opposite of manifesting what you want, "Man-i-pathos." Pathos, as in "not good," or the times when you call a negative situation a screw-up, bad luck, or bad timing. What would you expect when you are taught that things in life just happen, and for almost all of your life, every screen you look at has zombies, war, violence, fear, and unnecessary sexuality? This keeps you at lower survival levels of thought. All of the scary imagery affects you in the sneaky ways that slip into the subconscious, your manifesting zone.

A Challenge:

Spend 30 days watching and listening only to positive programming and have only positive conversations. BOOM! What do you think will happen? Take your journal and draw a line down the center of the page. Put a day number on each page from 1 to 30. Write down your positive thoughts of the day in one column and negative thoughts in the other. By the end of 30 days, see if they can all be positive, and with that, notice how your life is different. You will be altering your subconscious programs.

Let's do an exercise:

Step 1 is to *think in the positive.* Say what you want and not what you don't want. After reading the next couple of paragraphs, put down the book and follow the instructions.

Find a memory from a happy, positive time. Recall something that made you feel good. You accomplished something, you felt proud, or you felt loved or supported. You won a game or met someone amazing, you got the job or finished the project. Even if things didn't work out long term, think and feel the feeling you had when it first happened, and you felt good. These feelings are the frequencies you want to resonate with. These are the frequencies you can use to manifest more of the same positive experiences.

Keep one of these situations in your mind and ready at any given moment to replace a negative thought. To do that, think about the experience and feel how it felt. Let that feeling become your present moment. You are powerful enough to switch your thoughts and then choose to switch your feelings. You can get up and jump with your hands in the air, shouting something you would shout if you just won, “YES YES YES!” When you do this, your state of mind and being is already changing. You can see that by doing certain actions, you can sneak in and change your mood and state. You may need to move your body differently, too. Lift your shoulder up and back. Chest up. Shout “Yes! I am Invincible! I can do anything! I can achieve anything!” Go all in and see how you feel. This is a practice that will change your state whenever you need it.

If you have a negative thought that starts with “I hate…” or “I don’t want..,” it doesn’t work properly for the way your mind processes information. It doesn’t move these issues further away. It brings them closer. Your brain doesn’t recognize a negative statement. The negative words, like “not” or “don’t,” are invisible to the subconscious. It’s a subconscious blind spot. The subconscious sees only what is there, not what is not there. If you speak or think in negative wording using “don’t, won’t, can’t” types of words, instead, your subconscious mind sees the words that it’s followed up with. Example: Close your eyes for a few seconds, and **don’t** think of a pink elephant. I said don’t think of it, but you had to think of it for a split second to know what not to think of. Instead of saying what you don’t want, say what you do want. If you don’t want a pink elephant in your mind and life, instead, think of only what you do want. Maybe it’s a blue tiger.

Your subconscious is listening and paying careful attention to fulfill its mission to act however you program it for you for good or bad, so make it good. It's like being in a swimming pool or the beach. Ever stayed at a beachfront hotel that has its property marked off in the ocean? Does the water maintain the boundaries, or is it just the top of the water with a rope separating the sections of the beach for appearance? The ropes do not contain the water. It flows from one section to the other.

Have you ever been in the ocean and realized you are nowhere near your towel on the beach? The water carried you 100 feet away, and you didn't know it. The water has a flow, and it's going to move even if you create a floating boundary. That's your mind, too. The sections of your mind flow into each other and move your life without you realizing it. Knowing that you have to choose happy thoughts, feelings, and the happy emotions connected to them as much as possible, negative vibrations and thoughts are not available to flow into the part of your mind and consciousness that creates your life. If you think you can't choose your state, it's because you haven't been trained in how to do it. It's not that you can't be sad or upset or angry or jealous. All of these are normal, but you also have to choose to be able to put them aside at some point so you can do the good work for yourself that you are worthy of to build the life you dream about.

1.22 Intuition: The First Sense. Meet Your Guidance

Intuition is your first sense. It's your inner knowing. You don't need an external event to know the information.

You don't need to smell smoke to tell you there is a fire. You don't need to hear a thunderstorm or feel the strong wind to tell you to get inside. Your inner knowing is the first sense because it connects you with the outer world without having to have a direct physical experience. It will remind you to go home because you forgot to lock the bottom lock on the door. Then, when you get home, a huge storm hits the area you just left. Perfect timing. Yes. Totally planned by your inner guide for you.

You can remember times when you felt like you should go home, but you were waiting in a long line for an hour and you didn't want to give up your spot, but you had a strong feeling you should go. Because you were almost to the front, you ignored that urge to leave. Many of those urges that you ignored had hidden intuitive gems in them that were missed.

Intuition gives you an extra buffer zone. It puts a force field around you and nudges you into the right place at the right time (RPRT). After using it and trusting it for a while, it gets to the point where you may never know what it rescued you from because it told you what to do, and you did it, so you will never know what danger you avoided when you casually left a store you were in. It guides you often without telling you.

One time, at the farmers market, I saw a woman whom I had met almost a year earlier. She popped into my mind just a month earlier. I didn't call her because it had been too long, and I thought it would be out of place. Suddenly, there she was. I'm generally very polite, but at that moment, I was talking to someone, and I cut the conversation. Almost without a beat, I said, "I have to go." The woman I met the year earlier was with someone I knew. I joined them at their table.

We became very close, and she became a great friend and teacher. I resisted going to the farmers market that day. It was a thirty-minute drive. I was feeling lazy. She wasn't going to go either. We both decided to go, even though we were not feeling like it. However, two people who knew how to use intuition and manifestation could consciously create a plan and subconsciously meet over coconut water at the market. Intuition will guide you exactly where you need to be to win, even if you don't know what that win is yet.

LUCK

We tend to think of situations that work out perfectly in the right place at the right time as having good luck.

Being lucky is actually having a strong relationship with your Intuition. You are being directed behind the scenes by a part of your awareness or mind to steer you to be in the right place at the right time for the "Luck" to occur.

It has to happen without you consciously knowing until you learn how it works. Until you know your intuition's process, you call it good fortune or luck. Once you learn, then you call it empowered, which then makes it available to happen much more often.

1.23 Lucky People Are Intuitive People, And You Are One Of Them. Now, Let's Make It Stronger.

The secret to having good luck is listening or paying attention to your Intuition.

You only call it luck because you didn't know your intuition was quietly feeding you information and guiding you in the direction towards that result that will benefit you the greatest on your path.

Intuition brings you the exact moments and opportunities that you call "luck." It's easy to believe the world runs by chance and random occurrence, but it doesn't, not ever.

This happened to me. Did it ever happen to you?

I was at the airport, and I was tired. I was walking towards my flight, and I was a little bit relaxed in my thoughts and did not pay attention.

It was an early flight. Somehow, I ended up right in front of a coffee shop. My flight was on the other side of the terminal. What happened? I subconsciously followed the smell of coffee. I could have acted surprised that I ended up in a coffee shop, but I knew my nose smelled it from far away and followed it.

I saw a cartoon where a chef would cook a delicious meal and leave the window open so the breeze would carry its scent. The scent floated like smoke out the window until it found a rabbit, who began to follow it to its origin. The rabbit didn't know there was a chef who purposely did this to lead him to the kitchen, where he would be added to the dinner. This is how the subconscious leads you. It uses a tactic to get you where you need to be, even if you don't know it. If your energy and feelings are positive, that's where you end up. If it's negative or fearful, that too is where you end up, and like in this story, someone outside of you can direct you if you aren't being mindful and paying attention.

Choose your brainwaves, or they will be chosen for you.

Have you ever had a lucky time, where you can now look back and see how you had a strange occurrence that led you to that situation? Was it a thought or a circumstance, or maybe you forgot your keys and had to go back for them? That was the moment that changed everything. Write about a time this happened to you in your journal. If you don't yet have a journal, check out The Manifestation Journals on Amazon by Dr. William Kalatsky. They have messages hidden in the art that only your subconscious can see. They will stimulate and train your subconscious to manifest abundance, love, health, and clarity to connect with your intuition.

1.24 Let's Drive This One Home. Last Word On Luck.

Luck Exists Due to Intuition.

What you call luck is actually Intuition sneaking in and gently placing its message, telling you exactly where to be and what to do. You consciously weren't paying attention while it was happening. The "Intuition part of your mind", on the other side of the veil, didn't want your thoughts to question, analyze, or get in the way, so it gave you something to do that made sense for you to do that would lead to the results for your greater good. It set up a schedule for you to reach a goal and was smooth enough to do it without alerting you. Sometimes it's a multi-step process. A led to B. You had no idea that B would lead to C, which led to D. And D was the life you were manifesting for yourself. Keep this understanding in your state of mind. It doesn't have to be linear. Luck will surprise you, and it can come in parts.

Did you ever hear someone scream "DUCK?" I had a friend who, if I shouted "Duck," stood there and said, "Why?" A moment later, they were hit in the back of the head with a frisbee. After a couple frisbees to the head, they won't ask why they should duck anymore. What do you think would happen to someone like this when a much less urgent message comes through? I can tell you because I have seen it in myself before I learned how Intuition worked. It would go totally unnoticed. Your Intuition won't tell you out loud because you won't listen, but it will get you to be in the right place at the right time, because it knows your need to ask why you should duck when someone you trust shouts it at you.

Imagine how empowered you will be and feel when you discover that you are getting perfect instructions given to you throughout your life to be in the right place at the right time (RPRT). Your intuitive guardian angel is with you all the time, and it wants to connect with you directly. On top of that, your guardian is also you, but it's the 'you' that you don't know without the proper training to meet it.

Nothing is random.

You and another part of your mind make it all happen.

1.25 The Value Of Attention

When you pay attention, you direct your energy and focus in one specific direction. You aren't doing anything else. Your attention's value is all pointed in one place. This is why it is called **paying** attention. Consider your attention a valuable currency, like time on earth. Paying attention means giving your time and focus at once. It means you are giving your two most valuable parts of you, so make it worth it. TV shows try to get your high-value attention to sell you things through commercials, ideas, and product placement. Instead of watching TV, you could learn to play the piano. TV fights for your attention with TV programming to keep your attention. That's how valuable it is from an ENERGETIC AND CONSCIOUSNESS standpoint.

TV works in 3 ways to get your mind's attention. It uses frequencies that pull brainwaves in different ways into different states. It flashes lights on the screen. It also uses story to cause aroused emotional states while you are in a state of light hypnosis. Because you don't know you are hypnotized, the state is even more powerful. It also uses a beautiful and slick move, pulling the wool over your eyes and calling something a 'commercial.' The word commercial implies to you that it's the part of TV watching that sells you something. This gets you to let down your guard, and you miss the fact that the whole show is a commercial for products and new beliefs. You may not want to buy a hair product during a commercial, but you may notice that the star of the show drives a cool car and you admire the actor in the role he is playing, so you now crave that car. There are likely more ways the TV and movies use and control your precious attention. Find something worthwhile to watch that will uplift you, find some friends in your area or online in our Facebook group, and stay busy doing other things. Without the media, you wouldn't have many of the beliefs you have about the world. The media leads you to think and act in very specific ways. If you wear a certain watch, did you buy it because it was in a movie? This is something to think about.

Attention also has value in terms of time and energy, which also has financial value.

As mentioned earlier, there are different kinds of attention. One part of your attention is going to be used to **master your intuition and psychic skills.**

1.26 Active vs. Passive Attention

Active attention is the kind of attention you use when you are studying, problem-solving, or writing a paper. It is very conscious, and it takes energy and focus. Active attention is something you are very familiar with. You are using active attention right now as you take in this information.

Passive attention is more subtle. It is where you keep your awareness open so you notice something while doing something else that is active. As you are reading this book, you are focusing intently and absorbing the information with curiosity and, possibly, excitement. As you do this, if you want to, you can notice your breath coming into your body. You already know you are breathing, but do you notice it while you are paying attention to the words on the page or screen? If you were having trouble breathing, you would notice, because being in pain or discomfort calls your active attention. If something like that happened, then this text might become passive in your attention, as you forget that you are reading these words, and these words fall into the background because your breathing is more important. Let's take a deep, healthy, fulfilling breath, so you leave that previous sentence about breath behind us. And… At the same time, as you let go of any limited beliefs about who you are and what you are capable of, let it all out.

I was in a conversation, and a leaf floated by the corner of my eye. My active attention was on the conversation. I noticed the leaf and was aware of it in the background while the conversation continued. That was my passive attention noticing it. It's a gentle kind of noticing that doesn't take away from what I am actively doing.

This next example is common and used to be very common for me. I would eat something, and my head and my mind would feel fuzzy. Going on with my day, but feeling fuzzy in my mind is a passive form of attention. When the fuzzy and foggy feelings in my head overwhelmed me and became a primary focus for me, I made the connection between eating the food and feeling fuzzy. Then, it became active attention. I brought up something from my subconscious to my conscious mind. I found the subtle connection, and now, while eating, I will notice what happens to my body or mind from food. I also know not to eat something that I know will dull my mind. Some people with food sensitivities can go from passive attention to active attention immediately if they get stomach cramps as they eat or right after. If this happens to someone, their ability to notice and their awareness gets active very fast. This is similar to the difference between intuition having a quiet message for you that goes unnoticed compared to it screaming at you for something very important.

These are all states of noticing the subtle and finding the pattern.

Have you spent any time noticing your breathing as you read? The things that make you take a big relaxing breath are the messages that tend to resonate with you immediately. They are the messages that you were waiting for and are receptive to. The ones that make you hold your breath are the ones that don't sit well with you at the moment. It's the same way as watching a scary movie scene and holding your breath.

Reminder: This book is written in a way where you receive pieces of information, so as you read your mind finds a way to put the pieces together to make it fit for you as the information floats around in your awareness. This creates the epiphanies and AHA moments for you when they land. When you make these discoveries, I look forward to hearing from you. If you have questions or thoughts about what you've discovered, my email is listed many times throughout the book and on the intuitionmethod.com website.

Have you ever had this happen? Someone you know flows through your mind for a moment. You didn't really notice. Then the phone rings and it's them. Then you remember they just passed through your mind. This is **passive attention in hindsight,** also known as an intuitive moment.

You did notice the thought of your friend in your mind, but why did it just flash in and out with no meaning. It was forgotten until the phone rang and it was them. Nothing is random. There is always a formula. Passive attention is a skill that is needed before the instructions on The Foundational Breath Technique.

1.27 How To Use Or Pay Passive Intuitive Attention

You already know how to use active attention for conscious tasks. Now, you will learn to use Passive attention to recognize the messages being passed from your intuition and subconscious to be carried up to the doorway to your conscious mind, where the messages are placed. You have to learn to notice them before they fade away.

Imagine you are reading a book on a hammock next to a lake. A drop of water hits the quiet lake. It echoes; you noticed it, but you weren't focused on noticing it. You noticed it because you were in a relaxed state while reading or thinking, maybe even taking a break from working. If you were shadow boxing or dancing or playing loud music, you might have missed the sound of the water droplet, but in stillness, you heard it.

Think about your state of mind and state of your being when you heard the imaginary droplet. How did you feel? How did your body feel? How did your emotions feel? How did your stillness feel? Don't just think about it; write it down in your journal. Writing activates part of your brain, and it lets you retrieve information later when it is almost forgotten.

Passive Attention is not your intuition, but it's the part of you that is paying attention on the side while you are consciously paying attention to something else. This is what you will bring forward in your awareness, so you can use it together with your active attention.

Now you understand that passive attention is the state you are in when you are not actively paying attention but are still noticing. Your peripheral vision is part of your passive attention system, too. When you see something out of the corner of your eye while looking somewhere else and then you end up catching a ball that was coming towards you. That's passive attention crossing over and getting you to react with your active attention. Developing this with additional techniques leads to Passive Intuitive Attention. You get it by developing the Passive part of your mind. We are almost there.

1.28 Every Moment Is A Crystal Ball

When using passive attention, every moment becomes a metaphorical crystal ball. Every moment gives you a glimpse or clue as to what's coming next. Your subconscious sends messages to be processed, and if the timing is right and you are able to receive the message, it leads to EPIPHANY! With some practice, it happens very often, even to the point of annoying others with your excitement.

Epiphanies feel like a gift from an angel. They enlighten you and make you feel connected to higher consciousness, angels, God, or whatever word you might use for the creator of all and all the formulas of the universe. When you recognize the way the communications come in, the messages are still wonderful and wondrous, but they feel less like epiphanies as you connect more regularly and directly to your source. Instead, they become a conversation with yourself. The quiet self that is the 'you' behind the veil.

As mastery of your intuitive state grows, you realize you are the one manifesting the epiphanies. **You are THE ONE** in *contact with the higher awareness that is* part of you. You begin to understand that your higher awareness isn't separate from you and doesn't have to feed you the idea or answer in a secret way. When you fully know **it is you**, epiphanies will turn to self-empowerment and then turn to deep trust and gratitude to all the levels of your mind that are passing you the information. That gratitude will be from you for you!

Imagine you are trying to get a diplomat's attention without getting caught by their bodyguards. You whisper, or maybe you throw a pen in their direction. Maybe you make a bird sound to distract them. You do it this way so the guards don't catch you. You have to avoid the guards. That's how you get the attention of the subconscious.

1.29 Do You Think Or Know You Are Intuitive?

Intuition Journal

On a 1 to 10 scale, where would you place yourself with your Intuition today? Write it in your journal. This will be a marker for you to compare to after you have completed the exercises.

Write down an experience or message you recall where you recognized intuition played a part or you knew something that you didn't seem to have a way to know. You may have had one or more since you started reading this book because you've been priming your mind and letting it know it is meant to open for you. Suppose you are a regular meditator or have strong intuitive traits already. In that case, you will have more opportunities to notice recent intuitive experiences.

Wait! Have you been keeping an intuition journal? I hope so. This book has a lot of explanations and deep dives into consciousness, and it has exercises, too. One of the exercises is to journal as you go through the book, or you will miss out. Ever watch the end of a movie first? You missed out on all the things the character learned along the way, and that's where the growth is. This is like forgetting all of these intuitive and manifestive moments. You will definitely forget them if you aren't journaling. If you don't have a formal journal or the special one I made with subliminal messages to activate your mind, get yourself some paper and put a date on it. Write down when you recognize that you had an intuition or empathic, psychic, or manifesting experience. The more details that you write, the better. This will help you later to reference how the experiences and the path are all connected. Include any coincidences, déjà vu, luck, and things you desired to happen that appeared in a way that you didn't expect.

Because you are now keeping a written chronicle, more epiphanies and new awareness will come. Writing it down leads to the ability to find clues in the messages. Writing it down reinforces the new program you are adding to your mind's software. The program is scooping up something light and intangible and making it more solid for you. By writing it down, you feel the thud of its weight, and you are solidly aware that you have received the message. When you reread older journal entries, you will see the pattern forming. It will be like looking back on a map of a long hike you took and seeing all of the things you achieved. Without the journal, you will miss the broader view. The broader view from 10,000 feet shows you that so many things have been happening where you didn't see the pattern, and these are now part of your guided intuition and higher self-experiences.

Write down the random thoughts that pop into your head, too. The ones that show up and then quickly disappear. The same ones you disregard because they make no sense. The thoughts that are very good that you think you will remember to write down later, but forget in minutes until something reminds you.

These will be part of your training in noticing using Passive Attention. You will be surprised how many of these random thoughts show up. They only seem random and meaningless now because they have not materialized in your life yet. The timeline works differently with Layer One Mind.

1.30 Exercise: Feel Your Own Energy Field

- Let's begin to work with subtle energy fields and feelings

- The reason to feel your own energy field is because it is very simple to do. Because it's so simple, you can quickly **shift your perspective on the reality of energy.** It will make it easier to understand the Mind's Field of energy on a physical level.

- It teaches you to notice a very obvious but still subtle energy that is always there, but you don't pay attention to.

- It awakens a part of your awareness that has been waiting for you to wake up. New neurology awakens, unfolds and begins connecting when you find something that has been waiting to be discovered within you. Like learning to ride a bike, the additional reward is a new pathway for your neurons. This leads to you having a more powerful antenna and transmitter. It's like your brain is getting bigger inside.

- Feeling your own energy from your body begins to make you aware of the sensitive and subtle awareness that you can recognize and then refine, and then refine again until feeling energy and different aspects of energy is obvious. When you practice enough, you can't not notice it. This leads to Intuition, Empathic abilities, psychic abilities, manifestation, and other kinds of awareness.

Why is awareness so important? If you aren't aware, then you think everything you are manifesting to make your life better is luck and randomness. If you become aware of the structure, the pattern and the formula, you can reproduce it when you want to- and change what you don't want.

1.31 Exercise: Feel Energy With Your Hands (You may want to read this into a recording device and play it back to yourself.)

First, let's get into a feeling state of mind.

Close your eyes. Take a breath in. Hold it for a count of 4 and let it out. Do it one more time. A nice relaxing breath in for a count of 4. And when you are ready, let it out.

Take your time with this. Give each a few seconds or more. Imagine what something soft feels like. Imagine touching a freshly fluffed pillow with your hands. Now imagine what a hair dryer blowing on your palm feels like. Now imagine what putting your hand into a warm bath feels like. Now, imagine what pouring sand through your fingers feels like.

Run through the experiences again. It's good practice for your mind to be able to shift your imagination and feelings from one kind of feeling to another because energy and the energy of intuition and manifestation can shift slightly for different reasons, too.

Imagine what something soft feels like. Imagine touching a freshly fluffed pillow with your hands. Now imagine what a hair dryer blowing on your palm feels like. Now imagine what putting your hand into a warm bath feels like. Now, imagine what pouring sand through your fingers feels like.

You are now more in a state of "feeling." You can access this state anytime you want to by doing this exercise.

Feeling energy with your hands is simple.

After reading this text and doing the exercise, you will feel energy in minutes and maybe sooner.

Exercise: Feel Energy

Now that you've had a couple of relaxing breaths, please sit comfortably.

Hold your hands about an inch apart. Keep them relaxed, and don't touch them together.

Give that about 15 seconds to see if you feel anything. You want to have something to compare to once you start.

Now rub your hands together as if you are very cold, palm to palm very quickly for 30 seconds.

After you do this, separate your hands by an inch. Notice what you feel in your hands. Notice if you feel anything between your hands.

You will be writing in your journal after the exercise, but don't write yet.

Now, move your hands slowly apart to about 10 inches. When you get about 10 inches apart, bounce them together lightly, moving them about an inch closer to 9 inches apart and then back.

Notice if or what you feel in between your hands as you do this. I don't want to give it away yet until you go through the exercise.

Next, slowly move your hands closer. Very slowly until they are an inch apart. Then, slowly pull them apart again. By now, you might be feeling something. Start to spread your hands to 10 inches apart and bring them back together a little quicker. It may feel like there is pressure between your hands by now.

Does it feel like electrical energy or pressure, or are you pushing against something similar to a magnetic field?

Write down what you noticed in your own words. When you are finished writing, continue with the exercise.

How far apart can you separate your hands and still feel it? Does it get lighter at a greater distance? How far before you don't feel it anymore?

One last thing.

- Point the pointer finger of your right hand at the open palm of your left hand from an inch away.
- Don't touch them together.
- Close your eyes and move your finger around your hand from an inch away.

Are you aware of the energy line you are drawing with your finger?

Now you are aware that your own energy field, like your skin, is always with you. You probably haven't noticed your own energy field before unless it was in an exercise like this. If you have noticed it, you may not think about it or practice this very often. This energy field relates to health, intuitive ability, emotions, lifestyle, and more. So it's something you want to make sure is nice and healthy!

Practice this when you have time. As you can see, it's very simple, and when you practice it, you will become more sensitive and notice new things about your energy field, as well as other people's, too. When you do something enough times, you will notice new things that come up, but you haven't been sensitive enough to recognize them until you suddenly do. When you first drove a car, the road may have felt smooth, but as you became an expert driver, you were also able to feel tiny stones that you drove over. When you become proficient in a system, you notice more details that you couldn't notice without a lot of repetition.

You've now awakened a sense that you've always had, but no one ever taught you to develop. How is it related to intuition? It's awakening your awareness to the subtle states of mind and energies that are real and always with you, but you haven't decided to include them in your 3D physical reality. The more you do this, the more you are reminding your subconscious that you are conscious of the energy world or aware of levels of consciousness. Your subconscious takes the cue, feels acknowledged, and opens to you further. You will also notice when you do this, your mind and concentration moves into a unique state. You will recognize a shift in your mind with almost every exercise and practice.

1.32 Now That You Feel The Energy, Your Brain Has Begun To Notice New Things. Let's Keep Going.

Intuition, psychic skills, empathic abilities, and manifestation activate for someone in science fiction movies, but we want that fantasy to be real for us, too. In the movies everyone has different abilities or gifts, and some have them that are stronger than others. All of these skills are in the basket or container of Natural Strangeness, the name I use for unusual occurrences that are strange until they become more normal or repeatable for you.

If you have seen the movie XMEN, Professor Xavier is the leader. He is psychic and can take over someone's mind with his mind. He can read thoughts or place thoughts. He can shift your emotions. These are all traits of an empath. They are exaggerated to the point that he is a powerful superhero. You don't need your ability to be at that level. You need your abilities to be at the highest level you want them to be to make your life better and more awesome. You use it to make your own magic or to influence others to make better choices, too.

One person said to me that they were very intuitive, but they shut it off because its power scares them. Intuition will never be scary.

Psychic abilities can be scary because if you don't know it's you doing it, you might think there is a ghost in the room or an interdimensional being (which there might be anyway) or some other strange unexplained coincidence.

Why is intuition not scary? There aren't emotions tied to intuition that can scare you. Intuition cannot be shut off. You have messages coming all the time. You may not pick up the messages, especially the very quiet ones, but they are always there.

When someone says they shut off their intuition, they are probably naturally intuitive and are creating an excuse for why they aren't MORE intuitive when they want to be. This person didn't know there was a way to actively get better at it at the time that it was told to me. The Intuition Method hadn't yet been developed as a book or course. Intuition showed up for this person in spurts, and they enjoyed it so much when it happened. When it didn't happen on demand, or when they tried to call on it for a guessing game of some kind, they said they shut it off. Once it's developed, intuition has messages for you whenever you decide to open the gate, instead of only when you are having a "lucky" random moment. It still may not participate in a random card drawing unless there is a good reason. It's going to give you what you need, but not always what you want at that moment.

Think about how gentle it is when your subconscious feeds you an intuitive message. **It's like touching a strand of a spider web.** It almost feels like nothing is there. But like a spider web, if you push through it while moving quickly, you won't feel it. If you move against it slowly and gently, you will feel some light pressure against your fingers, so you know it is there.

Your subconscious breathes for you while you sleep. It's so gentle you aren't consciously aware of it. If you don't even notice your breath in a constant inhale and exhale cycle while you sleep, imagine how much more gentle an intuitive non-physical thought bubble floating up to the surface of your conscious mind is. The techniques you are about to learn will make it simple and fun for you to notice this deeper level of feeling and knowing so you *recognize what is happening when it happens.*

Write down what this means to you in terms of how you can use it and what you may have already noticed.

1.33 Seeing Energy or the Aura. Early steps.

What is the value of seeing the aura, and how does it relate to intuition, manifestation, and your other subtle abilities? Seeing is actually feeling. Your eyes are sense organs that feel vibrations and translate them to the visual field.

Seeing is believing. When you see it, it makes it real for you. It is more than a feeling. It's like love. You know it's real because you feel it, but when you can see the heart chakra or energy center glowing on the other person while you feel it, it makes it even more real and more beautiful.

You are going to take an early step now to plant the seed, and in module two, you will go further.

Exercise: Find the cursor

Get your computer or tablet and pull up a Word document full of text. If you don't have one, copy and paste text from a website onto the page if needed because you need a blinking cursor on the page. Place the cursor somewhere on the page without looking where it goes and see how long it takes you to find it.

Now, put the cursor somewhere on the page without looking at it by moving it around with the arrow keys or the mouse. Then relax your eyes and let your eyes gently stare at the page. Don't try to find the cursor. Just rest your eyes on the whole page. Your peripheral vision will activate, and after a few moments, your wider vision will notice a blinking cursor. Your eyes are meant to do that for safety or to spot something you need. You can also use it for more consciousness-related opportunities as you train the ability for a specific purpose.

Practice it a few times. When you are writing, practice it then, too. You are activating a part of your eyes and a part of your brain that you will be using later in the book and course to see auras.

1.34 "Listening" To Intuition

Wait, what did you say??

People experience intuition in many ways. We use the phrase "Listen to your intuition." This phrase makes it sound like intuition is auditory, as if you are hearing a voice.

This can be true. There is an inner voice. However, most people get an intuitive message and feel it first in the gut or somewhere in their being. Then, it translates or shifts from a feeling to knowing, and then imagery and insight follow from there. It may be different for different people. Depending on the kind of intuitive message, it may stay as a mystery until it's revealed as to why you had the urge to, for example, buy a ribbon at the supermarket, which later leads to a friend who is wrapping a gift and has nothing to tie it with. Then you shout out proudly like a superhero, with your hand to the sky, "Not to worry," and pull the ribbon out of your pocket. They are surprised, amazed, and forever grateful. This moment will not be forgotten. I've enjoyed many moments like this.

Here is an example of something recent that my subconscious told me.

I was on my way to a meditation retreat. I was hurrying to get out the door, and a quick message of "get band-aids" went through my mind. I ignored it because I was at the front door, and then I realized that it was one of those highlighted messages that didn't fit into what I was doing at that moment. I went and got 2. The feeling told me to get more. I grabbed 3 more. I put them in my bag and forgot I had them.

The retreat was at a nice resort, but the room service was slow. I had a crystal with me that I wanted to break in half so I could give the other half away. I broke the crystal and sliced my thumb. I immediately had an almost deja vú. I remembered the band-aids in my bag. I listened to my intuition, not knowing why but knowing they were in my bag. I also felt so clearly that if I didn't bring the band-aids, I would have forgotten that I had an intuitive message to bring band-aids. This would have led to an experience of déjà vu. This story tells two things. The first is I have crystals. The second is that there is a relationship between intuition and deja vú. One more is that there is a tone to intuition that stands out very obviously when your mind is peaceful and you learn its language.

It wasn't always this clear to me, but with the Foundational Breath Technique opening the door, it can quickly become this. Breathe, open channels, and the rest will begin happening on autopilot.

Some intuitive messages come in as a download or flash or "Direct Knowing," as if information popped in or was sitting there just waiting to reveal itself. It's as if it's something you already knew, but you didn't know it was there. It's like you dug it up from your mind. It seems so obvious that it had to always be there. And it was always there in the Layer One Consciousness. You just had to attract it to you. Another way to see it is that you had to figure out how to pull out the file that you wanted. It was always there and available once you tuned to the right frequency. Manifesting answers is very similar to manifesting physical objects.

So yes, listen to your intuition. Listen and follow the prompts and instructions it gives you, which may come as a feeling, a flash of insight, or something else. In my experience, the rarest form of intuitive messages comes in through the ears. I have found that when I have an auditory intuition where I hear a voice speaking, it is usually a higher self-message. It startles me, because it sounds like someone is whispering closely and loudly in my ear. I've turned around quickly to see who was behind me. No one I could see was there, and then I realized that it was that part of me talking to me.

1.35 Where We Are In The History of Human Consciousness.

When I was 11 years old, I was very thirsty to learn about consciousness, but I didn't yet have enough life experience or reference points to understand different kinds of awareness besides basic emotional states that we all know; Happy, sad, fearful, excited, mad, jealous, loving. ESP wasn't being taught in a learnable way, and the internet was not yet available when I was 11. The teachings and the mythology at the time said, "You had it, or you didn't." It was mostly considered pure fantasy. It was also said that if it existed at all, it may have been during a time in the world when there were more spiritually powerful or holy people.

Then, I met the mentalist performer, Marc Salem, in the Catskills. He did a stage show and pulled thoughts right out of people's minds. He said any 10-year-old can do it with 20 years of experience. That was a good boost for me, the 15-year-old. I knew with practice, I could do it, too. I saw him perform again 10 years later in NYC. I was chosen to come up on stage, where he pulled thoughts out of my mind and affirmed what I already knew. Still, this time, he wasn't pulling thoughts from my mind but opening his mind to my frequency so thoughts could pass like a breeze from my field to his. I probably had some of his thoughts floating through my mind, too, and I didn't notice it at the time because I didn't know how to pay attention to them.

The Amazing Kreskin, another famous mentalist, confirmed in his book that he too would suddenly know things without knowing how and that all mentalists who were experienced had the same unexplainable knowings happen.

As a teenage seeker, I had to find someone to train with, pay a bundle of money, and then not know if the information was good and true until the abilities showed up. That could take years- if the person was even a real teacher and expert.

There is a martial arts technique you may have heard of called "Dim Mak." They talked about this technique in the great comedic movie about Remote Viewing, "The Men Who Stare at Goats." It was said that a trained martial artist could kill you with one touch to the right point using a specific energy and intention. The problem with studying this technique was that it takes years or a lifetime of preparation and training. There is another problem; can you guess what it is? You can never prove that it works because to show that it works, you would need to try it on someone. If you knew that trying it on someone would kill them, then you wouldn't test it out.

If your high-conscious, loving teacher suspected you were someone whose traits would let you test it on someone they would never teach you. So, in theory, there is a lineage of people who might be able to use it to kill someone, but no one has ever tested it, except for in an emergency. The rest is legend. DIM Mak is one of the storylines in The Men Who Stare At Goats. Part of the story is that the people in this military psychic program are staring at the goats to attempt to use their conscious intention to stop the goat's heart. Sure, people hunt and kill for food, but in this case, to develop the skill to affect the goat's body in such a dramatic way, you have to achieve a high and very sensitive state of conscious awareness. In this refined state, you do not want to harm any living creature. This is a huge conundrum. When you know you are connected to everyone through all dimensions, time, and space, you won't do harm unless it's the least of all the evils. This is part of why the movie is so good. I recommend it. I also recommend the book, Psychic Warrior by David Morehouse. His story explains why so many of the military psychics left the military after achieving high states of consciousness.

Studying for ESP is like training with uncertainty for the first month or so if you are just meditating without the tools you need for your intuition to awaken. Meditation will start a part of the engine, but for it to enhance your intuition quickly, you need to know how to step on the brake, which might seem counterintuitive if you don't know the next step. The next step is to shift to drive, and then slowly take your foot off the brake and step on the gas. There is a process, and you have to steer the practice. When you open a dam, water flows in all directions, but you can also channel that force and use it in a specific way to create energy. With the Intuition Method, you are learning step-by-step bio-awareness into consciousness, so you can learn what you need almost immediately as you do the exercises and study the concepts. Although I use the word bio-hack in this book, I don't like it. It makes me feel like a saw or ax is cutting or hacking into the body or mind or brain, and there are much more graceful words that the mind will open up for and invite in before a "bio-hack." I like bio-shift or bio-enhance. They feel good in my mind when I say them. The subconscious listens to every word you say, and thankfully there is always a guard at the gate to protect it and you.

If you did find a great teacher for meditation, their goal was to teach their meditation system, which is great in itself, but the ESP types of abilities that start to develop automatically when getting the mind still were left out of the conversation because it distracted from the meditation itself. You had to quietly learn to notice on your own. This kind of meditation teaching is kind of like finding a tree and shaving off the bark to get to the beautiful wood underneath, throwing away the bark without realizing it has special properties that can help start better fires or be used in a cream to help with the pain. Sometimes, what we aren't taught to see has great value. You indeed want to go deeper in meditation to become more compassionate and caring and to get into the deeper or more subtle layers of consciousness, but there are valuable things to learn along the way.

During meditation, when a stray thought pops into your head, most teachers won't tell you to follow the thought to explore it and see what it's connected to. You are taught to keep meditating. It's important to keep meditating and get your daily practice in, but to add more real-world application, it's valuable to follow a thought that seems to come out of nowhere if it seems important. Your intuition sends messages like bubbles to the surface of your mind. They are easily noticed while you are meditating. The more you practice meditation, the more the deeper levels or smaller bubbles of intuitive messages and abilities floating up to the surface can be noticed. The smaller the intuitive bubble, the more specific and valuable the message. So keep a recorder or your journal handy to record the message, and then go back to your meditation and follow up on the thought later.

You also are not generally taught that your meditation practices open up that part of your mind and awareness that lets you know other people's thoughts, feelings, or experiences. Once you are working with the Layer One of your Mind, you are connected to everything. Then, it's a matter of getting comfortable in that space and dimension and finding your natural gifts.

One sign of how ready the world is for intuition, empathic abilities, manifestation, and other extra-sensory abilities today is how many people are practicing some form of meditation. For many, it's about peace, health, money, and abundance, but it will also give you freedom from having your thoughts controlled by others. When enough people can be without the mind's trauma filters, false fear filters and past programs that direct you to see in a way that isn't accurate and true, you get what's known as the 100th Monkey Principle. It's a tipping point and a pop in mankind's evolution of consciousness.

1.36 The Hundredth Monkey Principle

Have you heard of the ***"100th Monkey Principle"? It's also known as the "Maharishi effect."***

On a group of islands in the Pacific, monkeys were having trouble reaching coconuts in a tree. One monkey discovered climbing a tree and then using a stick to hit the coconut was the solution. Other monkeys saw this and did the same. Once one hundred monkeys on the island used the stick to get at the coconuts, the monkeys on the nearby islands suddenly knew to do it, too. The frequency, the brainwaves, and the collective consciousness field grew large enough. It became a new dominant frequency when it tipped the scales and reached a critical mass. The nervous system and mind are transmitters. The more antennas that are transmitting the same frequency, the more powerful it becomes. (Can you see why TV is so powerful in making so many people believe something at the same time?- Everyone starts to transmit the same brainwaves and consciousness on the topic that is being programmed into you.) This is one of the levels of awareness you achieve when enough people wake up their inborn abilities and practice them until it's an obvious part of you.

I've taught patients, clients, and friends the basics of using the breath to become aware of intuition. It's a first, easy step to waking up. I've taught cloud melting, energy healing, meditation, quieting the mind, and paying passive attention. I've taught classes to large groups on seeing Auras with 100 percent success for everyone in the class. The thirst for this knowledge is unquenchable once you get a taste of it.

You are part of this proof that more people are learning to gain access and use their intuition and extra-sensory abilities to awaken skills as an empath and gain access to powerful and empowering higher levels of knowing and awareness.

With information so available, the time is right for you to use your inner guide and guiding compass to gauge what is right or wrong. If you don't know how to choose what is right for you, it will be chosen for you, and you will be convinced by the ones who programmed you that their choice is correct. The more you become familiar with your inner guidance, the more you take back your power. Get one hundred others to do it in your circle of friends and friends of friends to help everyone in your environment get more free using the same principle or formula. It doesn't have to happen overnight, but it can. You can see it happening already. Something got you to meditate, and there was a time you didn't. Something or someone got you interested in this book, too. If everyone gets lifted and you are at a higher level, you get lifted even higher. It's a win for everyone, so invite a friend to meditate and do one (or all) of the exercises in this book. I can't think of a better person to invite others than you.

*Let **Compass**ion be your **compass.***

It's no coincidence that the Compass that guides you and gives you direction when lost at sea or in unknown territory is the first part of the word Compassion. Your heart and your feelings are your greatest guide.

We are meant to use compassion as our moral guide and compass if we are going to make good choices for ourselves and others.

1.37 Taking The Earplugs Out

Just like your cell phone is always on, always streaming data, you are now aware that your intuition is always on, too. In actuality, you now know that you can't shut it off. That option doesn't exist. You can choose to not pay attention, and you often do choose this by keeping your mind busy with distractions, like loud music or hours of video games, or even powerful emotions like lust, greed, and pleasure as an escape from hurt or from looking inward. You might have been using an addictive behavior like mindless eating, too. All of these can be moments where you gain power if you decide to choose your state. You don't have to do it all the time just like you don't have to meditate all of the time, but it's worth it to schedule in a time where you *choose* to sit down, quiet your mind, and meditate. Fortunately, you can also do some of the fun exercises in this book to give you more reasons to do it, too.

Your Intuitive and ESP abilities are always on, and you can make them stronger. When you step into that role, life will never be the same. Call it Life 2.0 with new abilities, perspective and awareness. Until now, you have been using sensory earplugs, so you haven't noticed most of the messages, even if you wanted to or thought you were. Very soon, you will take the earplugs out and take the blinders off, so you can experiment and practice with them at any time.

Energy Drainers: Uncertainty drains energy like nothing else. *Not knowing what to do or what you want to do. To correct this, choose one or the other. You will have direction. You can switch directions later if needed. To help with uncertainty, speak with a friend or expert as a sounding board. You usually know what to do, but somehow, uncertainty is like a hypnotic spell, where you can't easily make a choice on your own.*

1.38 Where Is The Mind Located? How Is It Fed?

I was taking a meditation class given by a meditation guide from a Buddhist tradition in NY. The teacher shared a teaching with me. I stayed after class to talk about it with her. "If nutritious food is good for the body, what is the nutrition for the mind?" She waited to give everyone a chance to answer. She was open to someone having a different answer than she was taught. What do you think the answer is?

Some things to consider here are that scientists don't know where the mind is located. It is a field. I think of it as a Mind Field or part of the field of consciousness. The way a magnet has a magnetic field around it, too.

The mind and the brainwaves get jumpy when you hear loud noises, flashing police lights, and other alarming distractions. Scientists can track brainwaves and see that when you look at peaceful images, brainwaves are extremely different from those of scary images.

If you haven't thought about an answer to the question yet, write it down or say it out loud and see if you got it right. What is Nutrition for the mind?

"Stillness."

I was blown away. It left me speechless. Stillness is how the mind gets strong and healthy.

If you meditate already, think about this for a few minutes. The mind gets stronger in stillness. In stillness, it is able to reconnect to its source like recharging a phone in a wall socket. The other day, I was trying to grab a piece of paper that had fallen into a fish tank. I moved my hand through the water to grab the paper, and the paper moved around my hand along with the water. I slowed my hand until the paper met my hand, and then I slowly closed my fingers. I met the stillness of the water at the same rate it was moving. I was able to connect with what I needed because I matched the stillness of the flow. So, slowing and quieting the mind works the same way. There is a world to create in the energy of stillness. Every bit of space is packed with potential energy that is literally waiting to be used for creation. Watch Nassim Harriman, a Quantum Physicist, talk about this on YouTube.

1.39 Make Up Your Mind To Be A Private Screening Room.

Would you watch a movie when there is noise all around you? You can definitely watch it, but you will have to focus and strain to hear it. It's much easier to watch in a quiet room. How many scenes will you miss when someone keeps calling your name or you are busy responding to texts or thinking about work? Let's turn your mind into a private screening room. This is what some simple mind finessing can do for you. These quieting and stillness exercises are all forms of different kinds of **meditation**.

Gaining or developing a quiet mind is not the purpose of meditation, but one of the many side effects or what I call "side benefits" of meditation. When meditating regularly, things happen along the way that are very beneficial. The healthy "side benefits" tend to be the reason people start to meditate. In this course, you will be learning meditations for intuition and ESP, while still getting all of the side benefits, as well.

If all of the great things you have heard that can come from meditation are not enough of a reason to meditate, we will be covering the other reasons that you may not know. With these techniques, you will create the mental space, the quiet, and the environment to enhance your intuition, empathic abilities, and psychic abilities, but the fundamental reason for meditation is something greater.

Becoming an Olympic runner isn't important when first learning to walk, but without learning to walk, you won't become one of the world's fastest runners. The real reason for meditation is coming later, and if you want to be a master of your life, stay tuned and take your practice seriously enough to believe it's going to change your inner and outer life because it will.

First, meditate for stillness and to advance your abilities, and then continue to more advanced levels, while also learning the true purpose of meditation. (Spoiler Alert. It's more than you have imagined.) Meditation gives so many physical and emotional rewards, and you are getting them even without knowing it. It's similar to the way food breaks down in your body into nutrition. You aren't paying attention, and you don't have to pay attention, but it's happening.

1.40 Meditation

What do you know about meditation? What does it do for you? What do you think it can do for you? Answer these questions in your journal. Do you meditate? How often? For how long?

Do you try to do it and stop after 1 minute or 5 minutes? What holds you back from doing it longer? Are you willing to do it more often if there is an easier way?

What if you knew the benefits and results come quickly, but like a planted seed, it's working and growing and building its foundation underground in your subconscious before you can see the results of its sprouting above the surface? You are about to do a meditation exercise to make you aware of intuition, and you will get all the other side effects benefits, too.

1.41 Why Meditate?

"One Meditates for one reason or for many reasons.

To be Calm is not why you meditate.

Calmness is a side effect of meditation."

-Dr. William Kalatsky

Take a moment and write all of your reasons for meditation.

1.42 Meditation Introduction

Without getting too detailed and scientific about meditation just yet, a simple explanation is:

Meditation is a gentle way to move your system or mind to a quiet, organized, energized, and recharged state. In computer terms, you are defragging, reorganizing, and then upgrading to the next software version.

1.43 The Byproduct Of Meditation: Upgrade

You may meditate to find a calm state to feel good or to still your mind for intuition, empathic abilities, and additional sensory awareness, but these are actually the side effects or side benefits of meditation.

Meditating is proven to change the shape of your brain. In doing it, you are refining your brain's neural plasticity and biotechnology. Feeling good or calm or getting healthier is the marketing bait and a very beneficial way to get you to do it. Intuition and control of your consciousness is also a side effect of refining and rewiring the circuits of the brain and mind.

Think about this. Humans and animals have sex as an instinct because it feels good, but feeling good is the bait that nature uses for us to procreate and keep the species growing and evolving. It's the same with most things. If you watch a good movie, it was sold to you as entertainment, but it's actually a way to place new products in front of you or to create a new movie star, so the actor you are being programmed to think is better than other humans can be featured wearing certain clothes or driving a certain car or having certain opinions you can agree with and defend.

They give you reasons to idolize the movie star (or musician,) so you want to be like them. So, the real reason for the movie is to get you in the seat and harness your attention while slyly slipping in products or thoughts to sell you. Of course, the story is entertaining. That's the point. If you just watched a movie with products and no story, you wouldn't watch a movie for 2 hours. We like to do what feels good for us, and sometimes we do it even if it has a negative effect on us because it feels good at the moment.

Upgrading your neurology in your brain, a living supercomputer, aligns your antenna. Your antenna is made of your neurology, and that includes your brain, the tail coming off your brain, known as the spinal cord, and all of your nerves coming off of the spinal cord that go to every part of your body. It includes all of your DNA in your body. Your nervous system is an antenna for controlling consciousness. Essentially, all of your physical body is an antenna for consciousness. The more you strengthen it, learn to shape it, and refine it, the more your connection and ability to maneuver within the states of higher consciousness and awareness.

All of the side benefits of meditation, such as inner peace, better decision-making, increased intelligence scores, better sleep, blood pressure control, reduced tempers, and quieting the chatter of the mind, are the reasons that get humans to do it. This is the entertainment for the story. It gets you hooked for a healthy reason. The benefits are already built in. Oh, but there is an even better reason to meditate. You build a better brain. Over time, Meditation will build your brain for mastery of consciousness, and then you have it all.

Your highly evolved brain doesn't need the upgrade. Humans don't need to procreate either, but all of humanity's inborn programming is linked to higher consciousness, which knows that the earth and universe require more people to keep evolving their consciousness. Your mind gives you a gentle bribe by giving you all of the sweet benefits of meditating, and as you do it, you get healthier and along with it, a greater understanding of the 3D reality you are in because you are processing information better. You are clearer. You get this clarity and depth of perspective in exchange for calming and quieting your mind. If you continue doing it regularly, you get all of the gifts that come with it.

Your subconscious and higher self are giving you a way to refine your brain and become the higher conscious being that you are meant to be.

1.44 How to Unblock Your Subconscious Access?

How many times has it happened to you that you couldn't remember something? You put your keys down, and they are nowhere to be seen. You look everywhere for them and nothing. Then you give up looking, and there they are, right in front of you in a place that you already looked. Sometimes, you don't find them, and when you forget about it completely, the location pops into your mind.

That's not intuition, but it is the conscious mind getting in the way of the answer from floating up to the surface. The moment you removed the conscious wall that you put there and got out of the way, it floated right up into your mind. This happens to all of us.

This is how the subconscious works. If you put pressure on it, it doesn't let you in. At first, you can't access it directly. You have to just get out of your own way. What if you stopped directly trying minutes earlier? Would the keys have appeared? There is a way to get out of the way.

The first step is the Foundational Breath Technique.

1.45 Last Message Before Take Off.

Your subconscious has some very important messages waiting for you, just like your phone has an important voicemail waiting for you. You already know that your phone doesn't hold the voicemail. The messages are stored on a server somewhere "in the cloud," like your mind stores messages in the mind's field. You need your PIN number to access the messages.

New messages are added to the queue of your subconscious messaging system all the time. Your mind is waiting for the right time to release them. Your subconscious does not use time the way you do in the normal 3D world. It can give you a message right now for something that will happen in 3 weeks, or in a minute, or from the past, or across the world.

Your PIN code gets you on the phone. You have a PIN code to open your subconscious awareness, too. Your awareness gate is partially opened based on what your life has been like. Your locked PIN code is in this order,

1. Relax
2. Be still
3. Pay attention
4. Notice
5. Breathe

6. Click, and it's open. The message unlocks, is released, and is translated into your mind.
7. How much it unlocks is based on how deep you go.
8. How you do this is, after some preparation, to notice your breath in a specific way with a specific intention. This lets you access a different level of your mind. Let's do it now.

1.46 The Foundational Breath Technique

First, get in the right state of mind and feeling. Read this and then follow the instructions.

- Imagine what something soft feels like.
- Imagine touching a freshly fluffed pillow with your hands.
- Now imagine what a hair dryer blowing on your palm feels like.
- Now imagine what putting your hand into a warm bath feels like.
- Now imagine what pouring sand through your fingers feels like.

Run through the experiences again. It's a practice for your mind to be able to shift your imagination and feelings from one kind of feeling to another because energy and the energy of intuition can change slightly for different reasons, too.

Now, the technique.

- Using your breath for intuition discovery is the foundation. Your breath is always available, just like your subconscious mind and intuition. Learning to be aware of it while you go about your day is important. You are going to learn how to use it now.
- Stand up, close your eyes, and put your attention on your breath. Gently notice it going in and out. Keep attention on

it. Gently switch to your passive attention and automatically feel it passively. This means noticing it without putting your attention on it. If you want to, you can feel your feet against the floor and then notice your breath as you do that. Or feel the weight of your shoulders as they hang, and passively be aware of how a natural, normal breath comes in and goes out. Read this text and as you do, notice your breath as you read. Breathe the way it would be if you weren't doing this exercise. Do not take deep breaths. Your breath should be like any time you are relaxed and breathing. Now, notice something about your breath. Feel the way it lifts and rises in your chest, the way your muscles stretch as you breathe into your ribs, or how it feels on the gentle way out. Does it go out slowly, or does it feel like you have to push it out? Follow the inhale and exhale for 10 seconds just feeling it, noticing it.

- Noticing means while you are breathing, become aware of how you feel as you breathe instead of only noticing your breath. Your breath's flow is a path that has been going on through your body for as many years as you are alive. You can trust it. The path is well-worn and leads directly to the doorway of your subconscious. Intuition's messages are handed off by your subconscious here. They are sent up to your conscious self, where you receive them. Now you know they are there, so you can pick them up. Your subconscious wants you to get the message, just like a ship sending out a SOS, the universal signal for help at sea. The ship will keep sending the SOS, waiting for the message to get picked up by a rescuer. Your subconscious wants you to notice the message at your conscious mind's doorstep before it gets blown away in the storm of your thoughts.
- This doorway happens to be the place where you can send messages to your subconscious, too.

- Write down any thoughts you have on the topic so far in your journal.
- The breath is the one trait that is controlled by the subconscious, yet you have some control over it until your subconscious takes over. You can hold your breath as long as you want to, but when you pass out, your subconscious takes over and starts breathing for you again. How it communicates with you is the same way it gives you access to your programming system.

1.47 Foundational Breath Technique Items Needed

Items needed to begin the exercise.

- Cell phone
- Organic fruit that you enjoy
- Organic vitamins that you take
- Chewing gum or any commercial candy with artificial sweeteners or lots of sugar.
- Clean, neutral, or alkaline water that ideally is filtered. Acidic waters like Dasani are not ideal, but you can use them as part of the experiment.

Exercise: The technique

You may want to read this into your phone recorder and play it back as you do it.

- Close your eyes.
- Take a normal, relaxed breath and follow it with your passive attention on the way in and the way out.
- Breathe a few times. Don't inhale deeply. Just a normal inhale and exhale.

- Once you see what that feels like, notice the weight of your chest as it goes up and down. Notice how tight or relaxed it feels as the breath comes in.
- Ease is what we want in life. If breathing isn't full of ease, there is some disharmony in one's being. Find the most relaxed and effortless breath you can.
- Now, pick up your cell phone. While relaxing, hold it against your chest and breathe the same way, in and out. Now do it one more time. Did you notice a difference in your breath with your cell phone next to your chest? Now, put your phone down and do two additional breath cycles without the phone. What do you notice? Don't second-guess yourself. Write it down in your journal.
- Now, pick up your phone and do it again, holding your phone against your chest.
- Very good. By now, you noticed something.
- Now, pick up your clean water organic supplement or organic fruit, hold it against your chest, and breathe in and out again. Do it three times.
- Now, put down the water or the fruit, and pick up the cell phone.
- Breathe a few times again.

Good.

That's it for the moment. The exercise is complete for now.

What you have done here is create a strong contrast. It's indeed subtle, but it's also very noticeable. You started with not holding anything because it's your control set. You have a baseline feeling to start with. Then you go to the cell phone because it will create a big contrast to anything else you are using.

With the phone, you likely felt your breathing more restricted and felt your chest heavier. It took more effort to raise up with your breath. To me, it feels like I put on a lead apron, like when I would go to the dentist or like a weighted blanket. It feels like my breathing is heavier, tighter, or restricted.

When you switch to something healthy for you, your breath feels so much lighter and easier to inhale.

A cell phone or piece of junk food with food coloring, aspartame, or genetically modified ingredients will serve the same purpose as the phone here. They will all reduce your ease while breathing, but it's easiest to start with the phone because it emits strong energy.

After you practice for a while, you will know immediately if a food is bad for you just by touching it and noticing how you breathe. You also can now be aware that when something is good for you, your breathing gets lighter and has more ease.

This is step 1 of the basics of the Foundational Breath Technique. It's like learning the letter A in the alphabet. New letters will add themselves as you practice until you can form a full word. Practice it for 2 minutes 3 times a day, so the difference becomes so recognizable that you notice it when it happens during the day without trying. It will be passive attention at first and then soon become active attention. It can and will become as noticeable as a small pebble in your shoe. By practicing, you will be creating pathways in your mind for your breath to become a launch pad to make your intuition conscious, using your breath as a bridge between conscious and subconscious.

1.48 Foundational Breath Technique More

Creating Parameters.

1. Make a statement that you know the answer to and see how it feels.

For example "My mother loves me," or think of something positive from your past you know is true.

2. Now, think of something or someone that wasn't right for you. It could be someone who took advantage of you or a time-wasting project that didn't work out.
3. Use your breath as a parameter, and ask yes and no questions before you answer.

Use the Foundational Breath Technique to calibrate yourself so you can apply it to any circumstance and learn what your intuition is telling you.

This technique will be used as a foundation for the advanced work as you develop further from here. Like any foundation, it's meant to be built on. It has a solid purpose, even though it seems simple. You will see that just like learning to walk, now means you can use walking to go on a hike or get some food from the kitchen; breath leads to its own adventure.

Remember, it starts small, but it unfolds with usage. It goes from getting a feeling of whether something is good or bad for you to knowing much more broad and specific things. It pops open like an umbrella. First, you give it a little push, and it takes some effort, then it pops open, and it's fully expanded.

I would love to hear your experience. Please write it in your journal and share it with me as you have amazing new awareness and experiences.

Some have asked me if this is like muscle testing. The answer is yes and no. There are no new principles, but I noticed that when I was stressed or fearful, my breathing stopped. I noticed when I felt good, my breath felt good. Then, I tested it with things I knew were bad for me, and it became obvious that breath is a gauge. The beautiful thing about breath is you are always breathing, so it becomes a radar detector for you that is always on and doing its job.

1.49 Slowing Your Perception Of Time.

One of the BIG Secrets of Intuition I Learned from the SAA (Sneaky Advertising Agencies.), and I'm sure they didn't mean for me to learn it or teach it.

Advertising agencies in the 1980s did research on how the mind processes information and discovered they could control your mind by inserting an image in a movie promo or trailer before the movie.

A movie in the movie theater plays a certain amount of picture frames in a film strip in one second. Typically 24 frames per second makes you see what appears to be a moving image on screen. Really, it's 24 different images moving very fast, so it looks like it's moving. That's actually how you use vision to process in the real world, too. Movement happens as single moments are streamed together to appear as if it's not a moment at all, but a moving scene of moments.

The ad agency discovered that by sneakily placing one image that said, "Buy This Brand of Soda" out of the 24 images that made up the one second that passed, no one could consciously see the message because it was played so fast in that second. They knew it worked not only because they must have tested it in a focus group, but because this brand of soda's sales went up by 80 percent after it was played in the theater. The audience's subconscious mind saw the statement that the conscious mind couldn't see. It received it as a direct command. When the ad agency was somehow caught for subconsciously manipulating people, they were fined some money and told not to do it again. I'm all for subliminal messaging if it's used to uplift people and make them feel good.

As a matter of fact, the manifestation journals I created are full of positive subliminal messages, so you can change the programming in your subconscious to get what you want in your life with less effort while you are journaling. It's a special bonus to help you make it easy and to lift you higher with every page you write or as you read it over again.

I also wrote a kid's book called Piranha Yama and The Art of Non-Biting (Amazon), and it's got positive messages hidden in the art to make kids feel good, secure and cared about. I use statements like YOU ARE LOVED or KEEP PRACTICING, for example. At the end of the book they are told that they can find the hidden messages by reading it again and studying the art.

This is a story that sticks with me about subliminal messages affecting me. I was driving from NY and headed south with an old friend. When I passed through the Lincoln Tunnel, I suddenly had a craving for fresh bread. The craving was so strong that I would have stopped for bread if I wasn't gluten-free. I could even smell the bread. I mentioned it to my friend, who didn't respond. Later in the drive, because I was so surprised that I was craving bread, I mentioned it again and said how strongly I wanted bread at that moment. She asked me if I was serious. When I said yes, she said she thought I was kidding because we had just passed a large billboard for freshly baked bread. I was driving and focused on all the confusing signs coming out of the Lincoln Tunnel, so I didn't see it with my conscious mind. This is the power of how our subconscious can be affected by what we don't know we are seeing.

So, movies play a fast-moving stream of 24 pictures ALL in one second. Your eyes see this as if it's a moving image or a motion picture. You can't see 24 individual pictures at that speed, so it looks like movement. How many times can you blink in one second? Try it! Did you get more than 3 blinks? Now imagine 24 blinks or frames in one second! Do you think you would notice if a frame with a message was slipped in that said -Eat Junk Food-?

This link is to a flip book. intuitionmethod.com/flipbook. Take a look. It's a YouTube video, so play it at normal speed and then play it at the fastest speed and the slowest speed.

This is how you perceive visual reality. Your brain stitches together pictures to make them appear in motion. At certain times, like during an adrenaline rush, reality appears to move slower. Your mind's software slows down the frames and can see much more per second, so you can see the perfect angle to jump away from an out of control car and get out of harm's way. But when messages are hidden like this at a higher speed than normal awareness, and you are not in a threatening situation, your conscious mind doesn't see it, but your subconscious does. You respond as if it's a command. They hacked into your mind, and now you can bio-hack your mind, too, and use it for your own benefit.

Intuition similarly speaks to you. These exercises will let you slow down, quiet your thoughts, and develop the ability to pay more attention to these unnoticed moments. Basically, you will be able to slow the speed of the frames so you can watch your thoughts and perceptions in Slow Motion. At first you will do it without being aware of it, then once you become aware, you will do it by choice. Understanding the reverse engineering of this technology allows you one way to understand and access your subconscious and intuition. Slow the mind and be able to notice the messages placed with the frames.

Here is another way to see it.

Find a large fan on a ceiling. Put it on a speed that makes it look like a blur. Now, look at the fan's blur of the blades rotating. In your mind, cut the fan in half or look at only one-half of the fan. In the direction the fan is spinning, look only at the top half of the side you are observing. You may want to put a book in front of the fan so you only see half of it. When you are ready, quickly jump with your eyes from the bottom to the top of the blades in the direction the blades are spinning. If you are looking at 12.00 o'clock, quickly dart your eyes over to 6.00. Go straight through the center point of the fan, as if following a string from one side to the other. If you do it right, you will see one of the blades become solid and separate instead of as a blur. This happens because you have caught up with its speed for a moment. You caught the still image frame, the fan blade by itself, by matching its speed. You can do that to match the fast speed of the mind with quiet meditative exercises, so you find not just the intuitive messages but the secrets that are waiting for you in the space in between your thoughts.

One analogy that makes it interesting is flowing your teeth. You have small spaces in between your teeth. When you floss, you search the space in between and you find things that you didn't know were planted there. The mind has things living in between the space of the thoughts, too. When you get still and quiet, you are able to slow your perception of time and see these messages.

Now you know where the messages are waiting for you. Let's improve your access with Stillness and Meditation Techniques.

1.50 Meditation, Stillness, Focus Techniques For Intuition

- The Foundational Breath Technique is the easiest way to begin to learn intuition's language.
- The easiest way to quiet the mind and tune in to the level of consciousness where the magic happens is Meditation. The stillness that is held in the Layer One of the Mind is before time and space. This space is pristine. It is nothing and everything. It is pure energy and information and

nothingness. When you are there, you can notice any movement, any sounds, any bubble of thought or insight. For the kind of work we are doing here, at this stage in your training, meditation does NOT include activities like hiking and running. Some people say this is their form of meditation, and I know it can be a source of great peace and joy, but it's not the meditation for this training. Remember, stress reduction and peace are side benefits of meditation. It takes a specific kind of practice to get the brainwaves to a consistent place of stillness where you can maintain it and repeat it for this purpose in the beginning. Once you are a natural at connecting to your intuition, you can do any kind of meditation that you want to. You will also be sensitive enough to know which one is best for you or at least know which one is not best.

- There are 3 main types of meditation, and one I call Intentional Meditation.
- Vedic, Mindfulness, and Visualization, Intentional Meditation.
- There is an overlap between them. Each includes many teachings. Vedic is widely known as Mantra (Repetitive sound, word, or phrase) based. When you hear yogis chanting, this is usually a Vedic style.
- Mindfulness is breath, heart or visualization based. It's often guided.
- Visualization is something you do all the time when you aren't meditating. Some guided meditation systems teach you how to use visualization for specific things that you want to achieve, like the Silva Method of Mind Control.
- I have a series of Guided Intentional Meditations for you to use your intent for what you want to create once you get to the deeper levels of the mind and clarity of emotions.
- There are fairly standard instructions for each kind of meditation, but like anything, practice will lead to

inspiration. Inspiration will lead to new insights that may get you to switch up your meditation in some ways for a specific purpose that you figured out yourself.

- For now, let's begin with just 300 seconds of each. That's 5 minutes. 300 seconds may sound easier for those who decide that 5 minutes is too long. You may not realize how short 300 seconds is and want to go a little bit longer. If you do, I applaud you for your commitment. Don't do more than 600 seconds or 10 minutes, though, if it's your first time unless it feels easy. If it does feel easy and you wonder why you haven't done this before, go for 20 minutes. We are going to cover 4 kinds of meditation. One includes standing up with movement in case you aren't comfortable sitting. This will be helpful if you don't like seated meditations with your eyes closed. That will change once you know the value that meditation brings to you will be so much greater than that part of your ego manipulating you to say it's too difficult to sit with eyes closed.
- 5 min mindful attention to breath
- 5 min mantra or word repetition
- 5 min super slow movement
- Guided intentional meditation
- 5 min energy up the spine through pineal gland- 3rd eye meditation.

1.51 Guided Meditation And hypnosis

Guided meditation and hypnosis aren't too far away from each other in some ways. Before you start meditating, let's start with a meditation bio-hack or bio-shift. You are going to give your subconscious a message. You can do this for each type of meditation except for the standing movement meditation.

Close your eyes and relax. Take a couple of deep breaths in and out. Now, say to yourself in your mind to your subconscious. "For each second I meditate right now, subconscious mind, please process it as 5 seconds of meditation." You are giving instructions to speed up your process. It's not the time yet to ask for each second to be a minute or an hour, so just do this for now, and when you have more experience, you can switch it to a longer amount of time and phrase it differently. Let's begin. Take a few moments to sit with this feeling and get to a deeper layer of mind.

Read this to yourself and record it so you can play it back. Set your timer for five minutes.

Mindful Attention to breath

- Your breath is always flowing. You can exhale it all and keep it out for a small amount of time, but it will force its way back in. You can inhale and hold it in for a short time, too, until it forces you to let it out to exchange it for a fresh inhale. Breathing is almost imperceptible while awake or asleep. It is directly connected to your subconscious and your intuition. It is your first access point.
- Following your breath is very simple. You gently put your attention on your breath. Sit up straight in a chair or on the floor, whatever is most comfortable. Hands are placed comfortably on your lap. Feel your breath going in, feel it going out. Breathe comfortably. You aren't trying to breathe deeply. Just normal breathing that you would be doing if you weren't thinking about it. Feel your stomach rising and falling with your breath, or if you choose, feel the air going in and out of your nostrils. Feel it going in and feel it going out. You can even count with each breath from number 1 to 4 and then start over at 1. If you want to, you can say to yourself 1 in, and 1 out. Then 2 in and 2 out. Go to the

number 4 and then start over at 1. Your mind will naturally wander off. It always does. Notice when it wanders and bring it back to your breath. This builds the muscle to learn to put your attention on one thing, your breath. By wandering off in your thoughts and then remembering you are wandering and bringing your attention back to your breath, you work the mindful awareness muscle and develop the skill of focusing your mind. As you do this, you also learn that your mind is getting more quiet because you don't have as many stray thoughts showing up uninvited. You are letting them go in exchange for putting your attention in one place, on your breath.

- How do you know it is working? That was my question when I first started, and I didn't have a teacher to ask. It is working. The first time you sit is equivalent to digging a small hole. Next time, you are planting seeds. Then, covering them up. Then, you are watering and putting a fence around it so it is protected from animals that will eat it. All the while, it is growing below the surface, but you can't see it yet. It's building roots and strength underground in your subconscious. As you read on and practice, or if you take the online course or come to an immersion retreat, you will already be ahead by having a practice.
- Set a pleasant alarm tone for five minutes and see how it feels. Do it longer if you can manage. The more time you spend gently putting your attention on just one thing, the more powerful you become. The breath is one of the best ways because it's always there, like waves of the ocean coming in and going out without needing your help to do it.
- In this book and course, if you choose it, you can create milestones and goals for yourself so you can recognize the benefits. You are opening and widening the subconscious door for intuition, manifestation, and everything else you want. Consistency is the key to changing your life here now.

1.52 Mantra Meditation. Word Repetition.

- A mantra is a word or sound that is repeated over and over in the mind during your meditation. You repeat it until it begins to play itself over and over like a whispered echo in your mind. Some teach that you should choose a word that has meaning to you, like the word "Love" or "One," while others teach you to choose something with no meaning, like a sound, "bing" or "OHM," so you don't have any thoughts attached to it. Whatever you choose is ok as long as you are consistent.
- My Mantra is from Vedic meditation, also known as Transcendental Meditation. I was taught to not say it out loud. The only time I did was with the teacher who taught it to me. After more than 20 years of using it, when I do any form of meditation, it may still play itself in my mind, like a welcoming hum letting me know I'm in the right place. It's etched in my subconscious from doing it twice a day for 20 minutes at a time after so many years.
- Let's begin. Close your eyes
- Get comfortable in a seated position. Do not do this lying down. You will fall asleep and that's wasting time.
- Begin to say the word or phrase you chose. (For example, One, Om, I am powerful, peace on Earth, love, God.)
- With your eyes closed, you can roll them upwards into your forehead as a way to access your mental screen. It will make you feel like you are somewhere else. You may even see images as you do it, but do it without expectation. You can also just relax your eyes and let them fall wherever they go naturally with your eyes closed. Experiment and see which you like better. Do it each way for 2 weeks and compare. They each have a slightly different purpose and feel.
- When I first began meditating and began to understand its power and potential, I would meditate for 20 minutes, and

my alarm would go off. I would then think to myself, what if I do it for one more minute, and that's the minute I have a breakthrough or become enlightened. I would add a minute, then 5, then 25. If I didn't have something else I had to do immediately, it made sense to meditate longer and add more light into my life or enlighten myself further. Knowing what I know now, it was very worth the extra time I put in.

- Keep bringing your attention back to your mantra when your mind naturally wanders, and set your alarm for 5 minutes.
- Keep your journal nearby so you can take notes on your experience. It tends to be that Mindful breathing feels more grounding, while Mantra meditation feels more light and expansive. How do you feel when you compare the two?

1.53 Meditation: Moving And seated

- Suppose you regularly practice tai chi, chi gong or any of the forms of meditation. In that case, you are probably very intuitive and have awakened abilities already. Still, if you aren't paying attention or don't know what to look for, you may not recognize it. Intuitive or ESP-related experiences can be happening, but if you aren't shown what to pay attention to then you could miss it or just call it coincidence. In a sense, the same thing happens for everyone who doesn't recognize it, but if you are practicing a moving meditation, you are already doing something that leads you in the direction of the result you want. You already know how to hammer a nail. Now you need the tools so you can do it. You likely have synchronicities and intuitions often, but to you, it's a normal part of life, and you may not give it the attention it is worthy of because it's become so normal. Said another way, this means that you are not adding conscious awareness to it, which welcomes your subconscious and conscious mind to be the powerhouses of manifestation that they can be for you. They want to act as two all-star players who are great as individuals but are even greater when playing together. *Your abilities and skills are sitting there in a state of potential, waiting for you to discover them and use them.*

- I remember many years ago playing Little League. I was strong. In softball, I could hit that ball hard. I'd hit it over the fence every time, but in baseball, the size of the ball and the speed of the pitch always got the best of me. I didn't know how to connect the bat to the baseball, and I didn't know why that was. I watched the coach hitting baseballs around the field like it was part of his nature. I thought I didn't have it. Everyone else could do it except me. Then I found out that everyone has it in them, they just need the right instructions from the coach because there is a technique or formula to hitting a ball. There is a technique or formula for gaining access to your master control room to create your life. You have the natural skills to do it already, so let's make you aware of it and then make you better at it.
- Suppose you already practice a stillness exercise or technique like meditation. In that case, the reason you are ahead of the game is that these systems you are practicing have a different purpose than awakening intuition and psychic abilities, so they don't teach you to look for mind control, intuition, manifestation, or ESP-related occurrences, BUT they are happening anyway. If you aren't aware of them happening, you are sensitive enough for them to be available to you once you know the steps.
- If you practice Tai Chi, you know that your movements went from choppier and fragmented to smoother and with more flow. When you practice enough and train yourself to move slowly, so much slower than you realized you could, your brain and your mind begin to let you see time differently. You started to see the space in between the space you used to move right past. It's like listening to music where you can

hear the silence between the notes. This is where the intuition's messaging can be found and noticed most easily in the space between the moments. It's happening in the space between the fast-moving chunks of time, so by meditating in this way, you hit the slow-motion button and notice the messages frame by frame.

1.54 Exercise: Super Slow Movement

Read the instructions into your phone's recorder so you can follow along with your eyes closed when you play it back.

Using Super slow movement is an easy way to increase the connection to your intuition by opening the door to your subconscious in a physical way. Your subconscious knows everything about you, but it is very curious, too. It gently opens its eyes when you consciously choose to do something out of the ordinary. It thinks to itself, "Are you really opening this door? I will watch with one eye slightly open and stay quietly hopeful that you can get my interest."

Here are the instructions: Pay attention to your movement. Stand up. Have your arms hanging at your sides. Raise one arm that is hanging at the bottom of your waist up to the sky. Do this in whatever way feels most comfortable at whatever normal speed is to you. It should feel like something you do every day. The movement would be like you are flapping your wings from the bottom to the top one time, but you are only flapping one wing. Do this before you go further.

Now that you have done the movement, did you notice each moment and increment of space you moved through from the bottom to the top? Did you notice the whole movement you moved through as you lifted your arm? Did you notice the big broad movement you made, but missed each inch of space in between? Maybe you notice the inches but missed every half inch or centimeter of the movement?

This movement is about enjoying the journey and paying attention as if you are sightseeing on a road trip on the way to your destination. In a sense, this is where the 1 frame inserted into the 24 frames per second is located, so let's practice paying attention now.

Do it again, lifting your arm from your side to above your head in a comfortable way and count to 10 slowly as you move your arm from the bottom to the top. Match the movement to your slow count of 10. Do this before reading further.

Did you pay attention to make sure your arm was going to be at the top at the count of 10, but not earlier? Where was it at the count of 5?

Let's do it again, silently counting to 50 in your mind with your hand reaching the top at the number 50. If reading, put the book down and do it now.

You may have noticed your arm didn't move as smoothly as the last time because you are now making much smaller and slower movements to give yourself the time and space you need to get to a 50 count before getting to the top. If you are like most, your muscles and your brain aren't used to slow movement like this. It's like the second-hand on a normal second-hand styled watch compared to the smooth way the second-hand moves on a Rolex. They both cover the same amount of space in the same amount of time, but the regular watch goes tick, tick, tick, and Rolex rolls smoothly, right on through, because that's how it's built. You are made to move smoothly, too. With some repetition, you are instructing your brain while building new pathways for your new practice. As you practice, you will find more access to your subconscious messaging and abilities.

Pay attention to the small space where intuition happens. You may not know where that space is yet, but you will. Your brain will notice smaller movements in space and time until you notice the moments between those moments, and you begin to pick up the messages that are placed there for you by the YOU that is behind the veil. The messages are much more than just words and feelings. Discoveries are waiting for you, too.

Now, let's do it one more time with a 100 count.

Do the 100-count version 3 times a day. Put it in your calendar. It will take you 100 to 200 seconds. You will notice shifts in your perception where you can see spaces in between the moments during the exercise. It will be like hearing the quiet between the loud notes in a song. In music, it's said that the quiet in between the notes is what makes the song. That's what you are looking for with your levels of awareness; what is happening in the quiet in between.

Consider the hidden meaning of this: The word "interesting" implies that "resting" is the normal state and "inter" are the things that happen between our states of rest, or stillness. If we consider the word and life from that perspective, then everything we do is the stuff in between that we then bring home to process, and bring it back to a state of stillness for what's most important, which is the primary resting state of the mind where we create our life. What about a show at intermission? The purpose of going to the theater is for the show. That's the mission. The "inter" part is when you are on a break from the real reason you are there. When the time comes, you go back to your primary reason for being there, which is the show/mission.

You know what is next. Write about your experience in your journal. What did you notice? What did you become aware of?

This exercise will increase your awareness. It is a stillness exercise that bio-hacks or bio-shifts your perception so you can begin to notice the "Frame" slipped in where intuition inserts messages. It is like a meditation in that in moving your arm and counting at the same time, it takes full attention to match the movement with the counting to get to the top at the right speed.

You are training your brain to notice subtleties that have always been happening. Creating new neural pathways feels good. And what it does for you will be even better.

1.55 Guided Intentional Meditation.

This is the meditation you will ultimately be most focused on in this book for creating your reality. You can use any of the others to get into a deeper state of mind.

Before you do this meditation, find an intention of something that you want very much. Make it something achievable but something that you don't have an idea of the steps to make it happen, but that you know could happen. You want the end result, not the steps it takes to get there. It may be something on your vision board or something that just came to you today or right now.

Bring the intention into your being and find the feeling that you would have if the intention of what you want has already happened or is happening right now. It's the feeling where you have what you want right now and are living your life having that. Put yourself in exactly that situation and experience it, bask in it, feel it, and enjoy it. It's happening now. It's a 360-degree experience for you. It just happened and is still happening. Feel the radiance and glow of it. Feel the smile and how good you feel about it. Like a trained actor, be fully in the experience of it. Later, when we talk about the Present moment, you will be able to bring that awareness into this practice to make it easier.

Because frequency runs with the same frequency, the longer you stay in the space of the now-moment, feeling what it is you want, you draw it in faster. It's attracted to you faster. Hold the space. Breathe if you get distracted and go back to the intention and feeling. Make it real. Turn up the volume on how it feels. Imagine what it's like to see all of the people you know congratulating you on your success and achievement. Imagine a doctor telling you that it's a miracle because you are totally healed. Imagine the bank teller's face when you make that big fat deposit and they congratulate you for gaining that financial freedom. Whichever applies to you, make it real and make it specific in your own way. Set the intention and begin.

Do this for 5 minutes.

When the alarm goes off, gently come out and back to the physical world with your new emotional state and frequency that you just moved into. If you can't stay in the feeling or the moment for too long, that is ok. It takes practice. It's much easier when it's fully guided, too. You can always join me for Monday Night Meditations for Manifestation or check the meditation library. Check the Intuition Method website for more information about it.

Now, notice how you feel. Notice the changes in yourself by creating that state for yourself.

Write about it in your journal. Do this every day. The more you become coherent with the frequency of what you want at this moment, the faster you get it. Practice is all it takes. Each thing you want to create or manifest may take different levels of practice because each is attached to different emotions, memories, beliefs, and even competing thoughts and beliefs of worthiness. Each time you do it, it gets easier until it's your go-to plan for creation.

A great tip for this meditation is that while meditating with an intention to manifest what you want, say to yourself as you make it real, "This is so cool." Feel the awe in your mind as if the changes happened already and you are very pleased that it worked out the way you wanted it to.

See and hear yourself with the result you want and feel how you feel when you say proudly, "I did this when I set my intention for it. I just changed my life!" Feel that feeling.

See your friends cheering for you and congratulating you on getting just what you wanted.

One more tip. Imagine wanting to listen to a radio station on an old-style radio. You have to turn the dial until you get exactly to the station you want to get good reception and a clear frequency for the best clarity. If the station is channel 100 and you are on 99.99, you will hear the music, but it won't be perfect. The way you turn the knob on the radio gently until you get it perfect is the same way you work with your intention and emotions to make it the perfect state for the frequency you want. If you are tuning the radio and hit a speed bump, then you have to readjust the frequency to get to the right channel. If you aren't on the right channel, you don't get what you want. You get some static or disharmony. So, you will need to adjust your emotions and the imagery you are using as life brings you little bumps. It takes practice. Sometimes to be more effective and drown out the thoughts coming in, you can turn up the volume. Turn up the feelings and add to the imagery to make it more real and make it bigger than anything else that can come in.

1.56 Meditation Studies

This is a general summary of what studies show regarding as little as 4 to 8 weeks of meditation. I have not cited the studies here, but they are available if you want them. Studies show that brainwaves become more balanced and coherent, more active in the higher function regions of the brain and relating to areas of compassion, areas where psychic phenomena occur, and the areas where inspiration occurs.

People who meditate regularly, without knowing it, access brain function to deal with stress extremely efficiently. Even where the stressful situation hasn't changed, you, the meditator, have changed and perceive the situation as less stressful. You have built a new "muscle" in your nervous system. You have deleted programs and made space to add, install, and attract new programs that get you to see things in a more natural, positive light without the filter of stress or anxiety from your past.

Meditators have healthier blood pressure and aren't as tempted by cravings. You reduce and slow down the aging process and feel or perceive time differently. Meditators often hear a question and perceive it as if they have more time to respond to it in their mind. They are less reactive. Perception has changed. You are in the flow and you may not even notice. Meditation reduces the size of the amygdala, the anxiety-processing center in your brain. You no longer have the space and processing power needed to have as much anxiety. You now experience the situation more calmly and take care of what you need to in a more effortless way. Those are some good reasons to meditate and we haven't gotten to the best reason yet.

1.57 Third Eye Meditation. A Note Before The Meditation

When I say to "feel or imagine or sense" during the 3rd eye meditation, the subconscious mind doesn't know the difference. Feeling or imagining is real to the subconscious mind, so make it feel as real as you can.

As a child, when you went to a haunted house, you knew you were in a haunted house. It wasn't dangerous. Your parents were with you, but your body and emotions reacted as if it was real. You have a massively powerful ability to experience your thoughts as real and it gives you access to your subconscious. If you went to a haunted house today, you might still get scared, even though you know it's not dangerous and not really scary. Someone could even have a heart attack in a fake haunted house. The body reacts to what the mind believes. You are imagining it, before you feel it. The mind creates the stories, and the heart feels it and pulls in the energy with its frequency and desire. Have you heard the phrase, "Whatever your heart's desire?" That's what we are talking about here.

When you think of a scary thought, your body responds immediately to the feeling and speeds up your heart rate. You know this because it's happened so often. You can also choose to think happy and fulfilling thoughts and feel them, too, to make your body think it's real.

Here is an example. I was about 12 years old when my family watched the horror film Poltergeist together. I still haven't seen it to this day because I was terrified of horror movies. Scary movies would ruin my day, my week, and my year. I was already scared of the dark for very obvious reasons to anyone who is scared of being in a dark place by themselves. I also bit my fingernails. I have found a strong correlation between nail biting and fear of the dark. About 90 percent of the time, when I see someone who bites their fingernails, and I ask them if they had a fear of the dark as a child, the answer is, "Yes, how did you know?" This is for a different conversation, but I also figured out why this happened because it happened to me. These people tend to be very sensitive to energy and intuition. They can be great manifestors with practice.

Back to the scary movie

While my family watched Poltergeist, I was in the kitchen listening and very curious about what was happening in the movie. My mother came in, and I asked her. She told me that there was a window that opened during a scene, and a tree reached in and grabbed someone by the throat. When she said it, she reached for my neck at the same time to show me. I jumped back and screamed. I was hypnotized that quickly. My heart was pounding. My mother apologized and also laughed uncomfortably. She thought it was sad that I got so frightened, but she also thought it was cute. I believed the movie was so powerful because of the way it was marketed. I was hypnotized by the idea of it in just a few sentences of the story that I firmly visualized in my mind. I thought it was real, and I jumped out of my skin.

The body and mind also do many things that are less obvious than changing heart rate, so you don't even notice. However, you can still be affected by them or affect them.

So use your imagination as needed until you feel. If you feel very quickly, feel deeper and make it more real. Add more to the visuals to make the feeling more real. Use your imagination to see what it's like to imagine hearing something in the scene you are creating to expand your imagining abilities. How does it smell at that moment? How does it taste at that moment? Keep adding to it. Make it a 360-degree experience now. The more real it is to you, the more you will benefit from this meditation.

Write down your thoughts on imagination and senses and this meditation. How was it for you? Was it easy, or did you encounter resistance? Did you decide in the middle that you wanted something different? Refine your intention of what you want if you need to.

I have a meditation class I host online called Monday Night Meditations. It is a one-hour class that is 25 minutes teaching about a consciousness-related topic or energy healing and then choosing an intention. Then, I guide a 25 to 30-minute Meditation for Manifestation. I hope to see you there.

I got a message from someone saying they want to join the group meditation because meditating alone with their eyes closed scares them. They felt like their third eye will open a portal while their eyes are closed, and the fear of the unknown takes over. I understand where they were coming from because I meditate with a blackout eye mask very often, and if it's at night and I wear it, I can sometimes feel strange or nervous if I hear a noise while I'm in blackness. It's the old patterns of fear of the dark. Third Eye meditation can open creativity fast. It doesn't mean a portal is open, but it can get very creative, which can seem unusual and also enjoyable. Suppose you have a belief that something can be scary. In that case, it can be scary to your mind, which causes the body to act as if it's real, even if there is nothing really harmful nearby. So make sure you know you are safe so you can enjoy this meditation.

1.58 Third Eye Meditation

Then, let's begin the Third Eye meditation.

We are going to do 2 cycles of the technique as a sample and then discuss it. Then, we will do the full 5 minutes.

Sit down and get comfortable. Once you are comfortable, breathe in for an 8 count and then breathe out. Make sure it's comfortable to breathe in for the full 8 count or count a little quicker if you need to.

As you breathe in, imagine and feel a light or energy rising from your tailbone and up your spine as you count toward the number 8. When you get to the number 8, feel energy flow just over the top of your head like water going over the top of a hill and down the other side. Let the energy flow down the front of your forehead. When it gets to just below the center of your forehead or third eye area, let it turn inside your forehead as if there is an opening there and spill into your skull, passing through the center of your brain, passing back at the height of the top of your ears, as if a pipeline existed there to the back of your head, and then pour it down your neck and back down your spine to your tailbone.

Let it go down much faster than it came up. Now, do it again. Imagine and feel a light or energy rising from your tailbone and up your spine as you count towards the number 8. When you get to the number 8, feel energy flow just over the top of your head like water going over the top of a hill and down the other side. Let the energy flow down the front of your forehead. When it gets to just below the center of your forehead or third eye area, let it turn inside your forehead and spill into your skull, passing through the center of your brain as if a pipeline exists there to the back of your head and then down your neck and back down your spine to your tailbone.

It may feel the same as the way a roller coaster goes up slowly, and when it gets just over the top of the track, it speeds up and comes down fast. Then, it goes right back to the beginning of the tip of your tailbone. You will begin to feel pressure in your forehead and the mid-center of your brain above and behind your ears. This is your pineal gland noticing the movement. You are grabbing its attention. The Third eye, subconscious and intuition all work together and are contacted by using indirect methods. This meditation is doing something that a specific part of your mind notices, so it wakes up.

Think about the way you might have a shoelace untied and a cat decides to follow it, even though you didn't intend for this to happen. The cat notices the action. A cat that you call to come over may never come. However, now that you know a shoelace moving along the ground will attract it, you might use this method on purpose if you want the cat's attention. You have learned a formula to attract it. This is another way you get the attention of the Third Eye or the subconscious. You find the indirect method that works and then do it on purpose. It is no longer indirect to you. You are doing it directly because you figured out the strategy that works. To the subconscious, it is still indirect, but you know a secret formula. Did you ever have a partner that was upset, but if you said the right thing, they calmed down? Or maybe a child was upset, and you gave them a hug, and they felt better. The hug doesn't solve the problem, but it subconsciously meets the rule or the need in that case for letting go.

Set your timer for 5 minutes with a gentle chime. Use a sound that will let you reach your time goal but also something calming enough that you can continue without having to shut it off if you want to go longer. It often feels even deeper when you stay in the meditation longer than your timer because you know you hit the goal, and the rest is a bonus. If you feel like you want to go further faster, do it for 10 or 20 minutes. That's what I would do.

Write down your thoughts on this technique before you start, and when you are finished, take a moment and write down what you noticed. Compare your expectations with the results and write down your experiences.

Early Advanced Level Bonus

Hey, fellow explorers! Let's embark on a short mind adventure together—something that's not only fun but will boost your intuition fast. Get ready to create a pattern, starting right now, and it's going to be a powerful experience for your mind. Commit to this for 30 days straight, and trust me, you'll thank yourself later.

Now, here's the trick: we're sneaking in a more advanced intuition mind hack, and we're doing it during meditation. When your mind slips into that altered state, and you feel yourself dropping deeper, reach back in time in your imagination. Travel back in time in your mind to yesterday. Connect with yourself in yesterday's time, and give yourself an important message about what's coming your way tomorrow (which is today for you in your awake state so you already know what you would want the 'you' from yesterday to know.) You are connecting your consciousness through non-linear time and sending messages from the future to the past. Does it remind you of Deja Vú at all? It should. More on that later.

Here's the magic: as you make this a regular thing, your mind catches on and learns the pattern. Soon, your future self, your non-time-bound subconscious, will start doing this for you. You are creating a loop—you in the future reaching back to the you of yesterday. Time has completely different rules when working with the subconscious mind.

Consistency is the key. When you find yourself in that deep state, notice there's a spot in your mind's eye where there are no boundaries. Move around in that space; make yourself comfortable. This isn't easy to describe until you're there. It's a unique mental space that feels different, and you can stay there in that space while thinking about other things, solving problems, or moving your consciousness around—all while your body stays still.

This journey isn't only for intuition. It's a pathway to other skills like remote viewing and remote healing, which are advanced forms of intuition ability. So, get ready to dive in, stay consistent, and unlock more of the secrets of your mind!

1.59 The Best Time To Meditate To Improve Intuition

You just learned meditations and quieting exercises that you can easily practice every day, BUT outside of your regular meditation practice, when is the best time to meditate for intuition purposes?

The best time is when you feel inspired, have an epiphany, or have a feeling that moves you. When you watch a movie, and something resonates with you in some way that moves you to feel energized or lit up or emotional in a positive way, these are the best times to meditate for intuition and manifestation abilities. At this time, the bridge is connected and the door is open from the conscious to the subconscious.

There have been movie scenes where a hero has to enter an ancient structure at a certain time when the light comes in a specific astrological alignment to open a locked door. Imagine, for 30 seconds, a movie where the actor must do one more good deed to get to a secret treasure waiting for him or her that she doesn't even know is there. As the viewer, you cheer for the actors to make it because you see the big picture. You know the prize is waiting there., but the actors don't know it's there. They don't know that they are a few steps away from the results that are hiding just around the corner and out of sight. In the movie, you can see what they can't. Their angels and guides are directing them from behind closed doors, waiting to give them their rewards. You have feelings and desires for the actor that come from both your deeper and higher levels of consciousness. You know what the actor is thinking because you see everything on the screen. You cheer for them as they get closer and tell them to keep going! You connect with these movies because they are magnetic to your mind, they vibrate the part of you that wants these things, too. They connect with the frequency and symbols of your challenges, hopes and breakthroughs. These stories are all symbols and metaphors to access deeper levels of consciousness and manifestation. And they do a great job of it!

With your feeling centers open, due to the inspiration or feelings of awe from the movie, you will gain benefits fast. Now, when you watch a movie and have this feeling, pause the movie when you feel it. You can stop a song in the middle of that powerful bridge that lifts you up. Choose any of the meditations that are included in The Intuition Method or the one you already practice. Intend to connect your conscious mind to your subconscious mind while the door is open, while you feel that feeling, and then drop in and bathe in that healing awesome frequency for a while.

1.60 A Shortcut To Intuition And Understanding How To Create: Energy Work

A powerful shortcut to becoming aware of intuition and manifestation and understanding how to work with energy is to get energy work done or learn to do energy work. Reiki, Field of Consciousness work, Network Spinal Analysis, and Headaches Heal Method-(which can be used to heal migraines, but can also be used to expand consciousness and increase brain coherence and install new patterns).

At first, sensitive people may notice the energy moving through the body during a healing session, and if you are less sensitive, it can take longer. Suppose you already see an energy practitioner or healer. In that case, you are a step ahead because you have learned something without trying. You went to an energy healer for one reason, but while being there, you got something else out of it. You now are able to feel the subtleness of different kinds of energy. You either feel it during the session or know you feel different after. If you only notice how you feel afterward, begin to use your passive attention during the session so you can tune in. If you are already practicing some kind of energy work, make sure to have it done to you, too.

As you get energy work done, you become more sensitive, which leads to more awareness in the body/mind, which leads to more connection to everything around you, which leads to more awareness, which leads to recognizing your inner guide's messages, which can lead to learning to shift to male side or manifesting side to manifest like the pro you were born to be.

Now, I don't want you to confuse male energy with testosterone or force. Instead, consider it like the feeling of intuition and heart, but prjected outside of you. Of course, it's inside you because your consciousness is part of everything, but the manifestation is the outward projection of your consciousness to create festivity. I wanted to mention this here so you don't have a misperception of male energy in this situation.

1.61 Your Subconscious Never Sleeps.

So… Put It To Work While You Sleep.

Your subconscious never sleeps. It's always running your systems for you, breathing for you, pumping blood for you, digesting for you. The part of you reading this doesn't get to meet it at the curtain or gate that separates you very often without proper training, but you do get to meet it at least twice every day when you go to sleep and when you wake up.

It happens when your waking mind passes your consciousness to your sleeping mind and again when your subconscious mind comes back up and hands off what it's worked on and worked through to your conscious mind when you wake up. This is a very powerful time and a must use tool if you want to manifest quicker and faster.

If you are already meditating daily, this is much easier to remember and do because you can stay in the twilight state before you fall asleep easier and longer. You already know how to work in the deeper brainwave levels of your mind. It's like scuba diving and knowing how to maintain a specific depth in the water without sinking deeper and without rising to the surface. You will be doing this with your mind's consciousness level.

Instruction: When you go to sleep, you MUST have a thought, intention and feeling of what you want ready to go. Prepare this in advance. Shape it into the feeling of what you want to be, have, and live like, as if you already have it in that moment. If needed, find a similar feeling to something good you've had in your past. Then, feel it in the past and present. Even if it's not yet true, now is the time to imagine that it is. To imagine is to bring an '*image in*' your mind, so plug in the image to make it real. Feel it as if it's real. "I always have more money than I can spend, and this is how my life is because of it." How does it feel to have this kind of wealth? Notice the difference in the feeling if you had just achieved this wealth today and how excited you would be if you gained wealth or love today, compared to if you have had it for 6 years and it's completely normal for you now. Are you still buying expensive extra toys for yourself after 6 years of having massive wealth? Maybe you love to quietly help others or stay low-key, feeling secure in what you have. Whatever you choose, feel its energy. Make it big and enjoy it.

Double the feeling and make that frequency even bigger. This is to be your last thought and feeling as you fall asleep. Your meditation practice has trained you to keep it in your mind as you drop into your subconscious dream state and let go. It's like watching a coin fall into a magic wishing well. I believe that the Wishing Well has always been a metaphor for your subconscious, after all. The coin hits the water and passes below the surface to where the magic happens, the subconscious. Getting to know your subconscious through the exercises and making requests to your subconscious at the right time makes it feel comfortable opening for you.

During sleep, the feelings and images are given over to the subconscious to call it in for you with the matching energy. The physical reality begins coming together seemingly out of nowhere when you are awake. Can you see how you can use this to increase intuitive and manifestation abilities? Spend a week's worth of nights putting in that command. Make it what you ask for. Think about the last time you had great luck and feel the feeling you had. Hold it close and feel how it feels so you vibrate as if it's happening now.

In NYC, I got to see a spectacular production of Phantom of the Opera. Every actor was perfect. It's a huge production, as you know if you have seen it. The curtain opens, and the set is phenomenal. The performances were big and superb. After the show one of my friends who performed in the show gave me a backstage tour. I got to see all of the tech and mechanisms that made the show happen. He took me to where the set designers did their work and where the actors got ready. I didn't see all of the writers and producers and all of Santa's production elves working to make sure everything was prepared for the show that the audience would see. It takes massive amounts of effort to make it happen, but when it's done right, it just seems to happen on the side of the curtain that the audience gets to see. Everything that is happening backstage is equal to what your subconscious does for you while you sleep, but in sleep, like in meditation, you manifest your reality faster than creating a Broadway show. Use your sleep for a greater purpose. Prepare your plans and give them to your subconscious as you enter the sleep door.

1.62 Increase And Refine Physical Senses

On the receiving side, if I were to define the most essential benefit of intuition, it is being aware of subtle messages because they come in so many different ways. Intuition can happen when a breeze blows by, and you smell a scent, and then suddenly, you know something out of the blue. Being aware or paying attention to the subtle leads you to a continuous curiosity and fine-tuning of your perception. You are able to notice on a deeper and deeper levels until the finest hairs or filaments of your internal antenna relay a message to the part of your mind that translates it to or from your intuition mind. The more you notice, the more YOU WILL notice and discover. You are building a muscle. As you get stronger, you can lift heavier weights, and you can then get even stronger. It works the same way with intuition, energy healing skills and manifestation.

When you upgrade your physical senses, you get the result of better communication with the parts of you that control your gifts.

You've already felt energy with your hands. Have you practiced? Have you remembered as you are reading that you are giving off an energy field and that you are an energy field? Feel the energy from your hands again now to remind your mind that there is always something that is happening that you are not noticing but that you could be aware of if you put your attention to it. You just have to know the technique or formula. Remind yourself to take it seriously and train your brain to notice.

Exercise 1. Refining Taste Exercise

Can you detect a hint of sweetness when you indulge in something salty? It's a subtle nuance that, with practice, becomes more noticeable. The ability lies in refining your awareness to pinpoint these delicate flavors.

Here's the exercise: Grab one grain of salt and a 1/16th teaspoon of organic sugar. Mix them together and let it rest on your tongue. Close your eyes. Can you find the taste of salt on your tongue? How long did it take? Perhaps it required a few attempts. If you eat a lot of sweets or salt, you may find it easier or harder to notice one than the other. Now, consider this: Once you've detected it once, it becomes easier to notice the next time. You are unlocking a heightened awareness. You are creating new pathways in your brain.

Why does this matter? Well, as an object diminishes in size, it becomes more challenging to feel with your hands or, in this case, your taste buds. When something becomes infinitesimally small, it transcends the physical realm, transforms into the intangible and becomes energy. This exercise trains your mind to perceive sensations at an ultra-small level on your tongue, enhancing your ability to notice subtleties that might otherwise go unnoticed.

It seems like an unusual exercise, but the goal is to hone your mind's ability to notice very slight experiences. Now try a pinch or two of salt with 1 grain of sugar and see if it's easier now that you have done it before.

Exercise 2. Heighten Your Sense Of Touch.

Can you feel a hair under a sheet of paper? How about under 10 sheets? If you can't feel it under more than 4 sheets, close your eyes and run your fingers over the paper gently. Now, do it more gently. Now, do it with your eyes closed. Feeling gently with your eyes closed allows you to have less sensory stimulation from the outside in, so you can focus on your touch. The lighter you touch, the easier it is to feel once you stop 'trying' to feel and just feel instead.

Focusing on your awareness and intuition are the keys here. First find the hair under one sheet. Then a second sheet. Keep adding sheets until you don't feel the hair. When you stack multiple sheets of paper, the thickness should prevent you from feeling the hair, but you will find that your mind finds it anyway. You are finding the hair's energy field. You are firing off fewer neurons in your fingers when you run your hands gently over the area. You've become aware of something your physical sense can't perceive on its own. If you push on the papers with force, you won't feel the hair. You also won't know that you found it until you open your eyes and see that you are on it. Your fingers are becoming a direct extension of your consciousness and you will use this later for healing others. Getting positive results with this exercise will help you learn to trust in your subconscious mind's abilities.

Exercise 3: Water temperature.

Grab 2 pans, water and a thermometer. Turn on the stove and heat one to 75 degrees and the other to 70 degrees. Put your hand in the 75 degree water. Now, take your hand back out. Confirm the temperature with the thermometer for 70 degrees and then put your hand in. Can you feel the 5-degree difference? If you can, reheat the one pan of water to 75 degrees and one to 73 degrees.

Take them off the heat and see if you can feel the difference. How long does it take for you to notice a 1-degree difference? Once you can do it, do it again tomorrow and notice if it's easier or harder. This isn't training your hand to feel the heat. It's training your brain and mind to notice very subtle differences and find the contrast, so it becomes obvious. This means you can be aware of small and smaller increments of change until they should seem impossible to notice, yet somehow you can.

1.63 A Ground Rule.

As you practice what you have learned in Part 1 of this book, remember that you are learning techniques that are part of a bigger system. As you practice and it becomes effortless, it comes together as a completed package. You are beginning a new stage of your life with new perceptions and understanding of the abilities you possess. That being said.

Follow this ground rule: Only invite others to practice if they believe that intuition and manifestation are real. They may even ask you to teach them, too. Until you are 100 percent confident of your abilities, don't invite a skeptic to learn, or they can affect your mindset. Join our online group to find like-minded seekers and friends.

1.64 Before You Begin Reading Part 2 Of This Book.

We have grown up with the idea that bigger is better. Sometimes, it's true, but the concept distracts us from the truth that subtle and refined is also better, depending on what is needed. We miss too much when we notice the material life but not the ethereal or energetic life, which is what creates the material. Every creation is a thought in consciousness, in the spirit and energy before it is made solid in the 3D reality we live in. If you want to build a table, first you have an idea which is energy, and then you think of what it looks like and what you need to build it in your mind, and then you gather the tools.

Regarding the ***Foundational Breath Technique***. Once you become comfortable with the Foundational Breath Technique, you will know not only when something is good for you and true for you, but you will learn the feeling of tension and pressure in your body when your breath changes. Soon after, your body will respond and you will find that you won't have to pay attention to your breath. It just becomes a knowing and a feeling or sense of lightness, heaviness, peace or tension. ***Then you just know without knowing how you know.*** You learned the steps needed, but the steps aren't used anymore. It becomes a natural state for you, like feeling a sudden cool breeze or noticing a sudden smile on your face.

This crosses the line from an intuitive trait to a psychic trait once you know without needing any practice or effort. Your breath becomes a warning system and a divining rod for what is good for you, and it motivates you because it gives you reassurance that you are making a good decision. Use it for simpler things at first, and it will start to happen noticeably without you asking. Intuition is a big-picture view. You have to consider and remember life is not happening to you but for you. If intuition tells you to take a left and you think you are suddenly lost and out of gas, trust that when the tow truck comes, and you get to the gas station, it's perfect timing for something, and your subconscious knows what it is. If you relax into it, you may even get an image of it. And if you ***use the PRE-Sent moment technique***, you will consciously create what's coming next. We will get to that soon.

I remember how much work it was to learn to type on a keyboard. Today, I don't think about what it was like when I first learned. I remember I was always searching for letters, and my fingers didn't do what they were supposed to. I finally took an online class. At some point, my mind knew enough, and it took over for me. We all know typing is not considered intuition or psychic because it's a physical skill that anyone can train to do.

It works exactly the same with intuition, empathic abilities and manifestation! At first, exercises, and then expertise. But, it's not being publicly taught enough, and for now, not too many people are seriously training in the one thing that will make life seem like magic. This means when you become really good at these innate skills that are waiting to blossom in you, people will think you are naturally lucky or you have an angel on your shoulder.

In my opinion, intuition, energy skills, manifestation and others should be more common than typing on a computer because not everyone has a computer, but everyone has a mind, consciousness and programs built into their DNA from their first day on earth and before. There is a massive shift in awareness in the world for the better as more people keep getting tuned in.

After you practice feeling the hair under the paper exercise and refining your taste buds with the sugar/salt exercise, you will know how to tune in to and focus on the more subtle states where your subconscious/intuition takes over for you in a physical way.

Knowing how to ***feel your own energy (aura) with your hands*** lets you know there is more to feel than just the physical. You practice, and you will normalize feeling energy fields, just like you can feel nonphysical emotions using your own feeling centers that are also feeling something that is not physical. These fields and feelings all give you intuitive or non-physical information that can bridge information from many different levels of awareness through time and space (or non-time and non-space.) You will then learn to feel energy from things other than your body.

Once meditation is a part of your routine, you have pathways in your brain that will take you deeper and higher. You have only just begun to **refine your senses.** You are carving a block of wood to discover what shape is inside of you and what your best traits in this energy space will be. Practice the techniques you've learned for at least 1 more week for the best results before beginning parts 2 and 3. Write down any thoughts about the refinement of physical sensations and any other interesting thoughts in your journal.

1.65 Exercise: Activating The hands. Knowing Without Seeing.

Objects vibrate. They also partially take on the vibrational rate or frequency of what they touch for some time, and the memory of everything that happens on earth will always be stored in the earth's magnetic field like a giant magnetic memory bank. Can you pick up an object and know where it's been? If this can be done, how would it happen? If time is no longer linear, once you are working through the subconscious to layer one or quantum mind, can you pick up the frequency? Would it matter if it was now or in the past? Did you know that modern science has discovered that it can bounce energy off of walls and hear conversations that were said in the past? In the near future, you will be able to open a gift, and with some software and speakers, you will be able to hear what the person said while wrapping your present. This means the energy is stored. The frequency exists right now and is always here.

In a slightly related story, years ago, I used to be a guest on a radio show where I would speak about holistic health. I was listening to the station as I drove over to be a guest that night and a celebrity of consciousness was the guest who was on right before me! Russel Targ, one of the fathers of Remote Viewing, also known as the

Psychic Remote Viewing used by the military. Dr. Targ was a physicist for the military when he got involved in this program. I hit the gas so I could get there early and meet him. I sat down next to him in the studio like a fanboy, and on a commercial break, I asked him how to remote view. He reached into his pocket and said, "I will show you. I have something in my hand. Close your eyes and start to draw whatever comes to mind." I started drawing the shape of a square standing on one of its points like a diamond. He said, "Good, keep going." I drew something that I don't remember, and he stopped me and said to go back to my original drawing and draw what came to mind. I drew a half circle off of the square.

He said, "That's it. You got it." I didn't know what he meant. He opened his hand and had a small red plastic square. He pulled out a circle halfway from inside of it. It was a magnifying lens that slid inside of itself. He kept it with him because his physical eye vision was so weak that he needed it to read. How strange that his 3rd eye vision would be so powerful compared to the physical eyes in his eye sockets, though this might be how he was led to figure this inner vision out.

If you can see through space, in this case, the space taken up by a hand covering an object, doesn't it make sense that you can see through time, being that time and space are directly connected? In the 3D world, you can't move through space without moving through time simultaneously. They are always connected through their program or formula. There is no way that you can move your body without time being a factor. You also can't move through time without existing in physical space. If laying still and letting time pass, you still exist in space. You are breathing in space. You are thinking within your body in space. You are taking up space. This means if you have one data point, you can use it and make your consciousness or connection to your stream of consciousness your sniffer or your detective to find the other. In this case, I didn't know what was in Dr. Targ's hand. The information was in the field of consciousness. If he didn't tell me what it was, I would have never known I was correct. A skeptic would say it was luck, which, by my knowledge of what luck is, makes sense, too.

Ask someone you know for an object that they know the history of. Use the intention that you want to know something about it and then relax and stop thinking about it. Go into the feeling state as if you are in the shower. Feel the water hitting you in your mind. This will get you out of your thoughts faster. It's one of the indirect ways to leave your thinking mind behind.

Let go of what you want to know and drop into a mild, deeper state. Breathe, meditate. Forget what you want to know. Hum a song in your head so you get your active mind out of the way and let information drift in the back of your mind without expecting an answer. Don't think. Just relax and be. Get out of the way the same way you can't find your keys, and then you let it go, and they are suddenly there. You programmed what you want; now let your mind's stillness attract and make room for the information.

Write down or draw what comes to you because the insight will come fast and very gently. It will be the thought or feeling or image that doesn't feel like a thought of your own. It may seem like an imprint in your mind. It may seem like you stared at a bright light and then looked at a wall and you now see a reverse imprint of the shape of the light burnt into your mind for a few seconds. It may be something different for you. You can have it work in a way that is different than someone else. It will feel very natural like it's meant to be there, but you didn't put it there yourself. It's very easy to miss if you aren't in a state of inner stillness. Don't fall asleep. Keep your mind on the humming or on the feeling of the shower so you are out of the way, and the thought bubble, image, or feeling can slide in. Write down your impressions or experience even if it makes no sense. Don't try to define it. The person with the object will show you the object, and you will see if you are correct. Write what you got. It could be the shape, or the smell or what it reminds you of, not what you think it is. A star shape doesn't mean a star. It means a star shape. Ask the person who gave it to you if any of your writings make sense or to tell you which part of the sketch is on target so you can go back to the right space of mind and use it as a starting point for more information. You will start to recognize when the right state and space of mind opens for you.

Can you do this with humans and read them? The obvious answer is yes and it's easier than with objects. I call it Frequency Matching. It's powerful, but also can be very unhealthy. Why powerful? When you can get your mind and excitement out of the way, you can bring your stillness to a place where you can bridge the other person's frequency. This means you will suddenly get insights about them. It's an intuitive trait. It's a very feeling trait on one level and a very knowing trait on another. But, there is danger waiting for you. Why? When someone tells you a story about their life that was very difficult for them, you feel empathy and sadness for them. You will also feel happy they made it through. This is dangerous because now you aren't getting the information 2nd hand. When you 'frequency match,' you experience the tone of everything firsthand and it can stay with you. You can pick up feelings, emotions, memories of their trauma and even illness without knowing why you are experiencing these strange and unsettling feelings. It's probably similar to someone who gets an organ transplant and now has traits of the original organ owner.

When I first started, I discovered I could do this. It was good for business. You could be very insightful as a doctor when you tune into someone's frequency at that level. I remember I had one patient who was a Mailman. I will call him Joe. Joe was super healthy in his diet and routine. I worked on him one day and suddenly, without expecting it, I felt a flash of yellow and felt a little off. I said, “Joe, yellow food coloring?” He said, “What do you mean?” I said, “I don’t know. I just had yellow food coloring pop up in my head.” He said, “I don’t eat that kind of thing.” He left the office after the session. I knew what I felt and saw. The situation felt unresolved to me. He came back ten minutes later laughing and said, “I just remembered that I had one of those little yellow banana cakes from the deli today. I never eat that kind of thing.” We both enjoyed it and it also became a story we both told to others. Other patients started asking me more often about what chemicals they ate or ingested that day until I said that I didn't do it anymore because the expectation of it was making me exhausted.

I mention this because some of you will do it by mistake, so it’s good to be aware of it if you don’t feel good or don’t feel like yourself after practicing an exercise or after working on someone.

It’s a lot like being a strong empath. You pick up the other person's emotions. This is very similar.

When people ask me how I protect myself from other's energy when I work on them, the answer is that I don’t go into their energy, so I don’t have to protect myself. I’m working with the field and they are the ones inside making changes. If there was a person’s energy that felt like it was too much, I wouldn’t work on them, even doing distant work. Some people are not a match for me and my work but maybe a match for someone else. Keep a good energy healer in your phone book, in case you need them to clear patterns of energy from this or just for good healing work in general.

1.66 A Consciousness Joke :)

Just for fun.

And to get you to access the creative, free-flowing part of your mind.

What might a person be called who connects with or works with source energy?

Write your answer below. It's likely the first thing that comes to your mind.

Go to ***intuitionmethod.com*** and send me a message to let me know if you got the answer.

1.67 Now That You Have the Foundation.

What's Coming in Part 2 and Part 3?

- The principles that bring it together.
- The difference between creating and manifesting.
- The Present Moment is for the manifestation
- Manifestation that you can do more easily than you think.
- Uploads and Downloads
- Increase your energy and feel instant appreciation.
- Feel others' energy.
- Increase your Empathic abilities. You are already an empath. Now, learn to control it.
- The Body as Antenna for Empathic Achievers: *Feel others emotions on purpose.*
- Learn the cues to know when your subconscious and intuition are open and easiest to access. (Luck, Cravings, Coincidence, and Déjà vu)
- Donate your emotions to others so you can lift them up.
- See auras
- Change your state and shift your mind's awareness to feel different kinds of energy, from physical to emotional, to mind to spirit.
- Law of Attraction bio-shifts that work!
- Déjà vu explained
- Coincidence and luck are siblings.

- Intuition and Manifestation are 2 sides of the same coin in Layer One of your mind.
- Layer One Mind
- How to use the Coincidence formula
- Change hindsight to foresight and access the glimpses of the future that you usually miss.
- Visual energy (non-medical) diagnosis, aka medical intuitive.
- Intuitive picture reading. Learn about people from a photo. Blending empathic with energy reading.
- For energy healers: Why do some feel energy from you and others don't. The Inert Metal Analogy
- Melting clouds or cloudbusting.
- Feeling radar from police cars and high-powered fields when you pass the EZ pass toll.
- Have an understanding of slowing down the perception of time, so you are already noticing the messages in between the moments.
- What to do when you feel in Awe.
- Connect with your Higher Self as often as you would like with the Hi Yourself technique that I discovered by spending time with a yoga master.
- What stops your intuition from working?
- What does it mean to become enlightened?
- Why bodyworkers and energy healers become so intuitive.
- How to turn your kiss into a transmitter to your partner.
- The 3rd I technique.
- Manifesting while you sleep.
- Increase your creativity exponentially.
- Use your TV to gain Empathic awareness.
- Tuning fork diagnosis. (Non-Medical)
- Direct Knowing, where you just "know." It's not as much fun as experimenting and learning how to become intuitive

because it "just happens," and you aren't consciously putting in the effort at this point.
- The Present Moment Technique. The Most powerful of them all.

1.68 Write Down Your Notes And Thoughts.

Please take time to write notes, questions and awarenesses.

What is your favorite exercise from this book so far? What are you taking away so far? What is unclear that you would like more clarity on?

As your connection to your subconscious and intuition opens further, write it down. Writing is better than recording because you can see it with a quick glimpse instead of having to listen to an audio recording to find the gems that are hidden in it. Your mind sees words on paper and shows you things you didn't catch the first time it was written.

The realizations you have will be keys and stepping stones to other new realizations or downloads. That's how intuition works. It will give you a clue and a personal roadmap to any one of the possibilities in your awesome future.

Like a Dream, Intuition's messages are fleeting, but they want to be remembered, so practice and remember who you are.

Write it all in your notes. Take this seriously now so you can have more awe and awesomeness in your life.

1.69 Part 1: Complete.

Congratulate Yourself! This was a lot of mindful work while giving you the basics to start at the same time. I promise it gets easier. The module was written in a way to stimulate the deeper parts of your awareness. As you move on to Part 2 and Part 3, come back to Part 1 and start over when you have time. Part 1 has layers to it, just like your mind. Once you go through the book, each module will take you deeper, and each lesson will take on a different meaning as you progress to more sensitive levels of awareness. If you do the exercises and read the book twice, I assure you, it will be as if you are reading a different book with exercises the second time. The epiphanies will come because you are now going to experience it at another level.

Practice, Practice, Practice.

Once you are comfortable with what you have learned, teach someone! When you teach, you will become aware of what questions you have, and you can post them in our private group for me or someone else to answer. The more people who get in touch with their inner voice, natural born abilities, empathic abilities, manifestation abilities, and ESP, the more people who know what foods are good and which make you slowly sick, which additives are bad and poison you over time, which supplements will get your immune system working better and clean up your body, which people want to help and which mean you harm; once enough people know this, it's contagious in the best of ways. It goes viral but with a positive message to spread. Going Viral typically means the spread of a virus, but in this case it is usually memes or videos. The information being shared is entertaining, a waste of time, embarrassing and silly. I can't think of any positive messages related to going viral at the moment. Consciousness and health have to go "viral". It shouldn't seem abnormal to read ingredients before buying food or taking prescribed medication for safe ingredients. It should be normal for people to want to sit with their eyes closed for a few minutes and meditate if they know the benefits like enhancing benefits that await them. We need a better word than going "viral."

It appears that it's used knowing how the subconscious can be tricked using language and slipping in hidden frames. You see, even if it's in front of your face, a word or phrase with a double meaning will have the meaning that was missed slip into the subconscious to program you.

When you learn and teach these skills, you create a world with people who use consciousness for their growth-oriented life and not just to live in and be caught up in the current directed by the herd. Then many more lives get better, and the world gets healthier. The 100th monkey principle begins when enough people are doing this, so share and teach others.

Additional reading:

- Super Normal by Dr. Dean Radin
- China's Super-Secret Psychics by Paul Dong.
- Piranha Yama and The Art of Non-Biting by Dr. William Kalatsky. (Written as Dr. Bill Kalatsky)

Read books that will give your mind a reason to be open to intuition and deeper states. It's another way to have the subconscious mind relax its guard as it realizes that this information is nourishing.

If you have any questions, please email me at:

William@IntuitionMethod.com

Please practice for at least 1 week before continuing to Part 2.

Part 2

2.1 Flash Of The Future.

Did You know it would happen, or did you make it happen?

I've had flashes of the future so often that they seemed normal. The phone ringing phenomenon, dreaming of lottery numbers, knowing someone was going to follow me with precise details of what would happen, and I knew the exact words to say in advance to be able to walk away without an altercation. I regularly dream of upcoming situations. Sometimes, I'm dreaming that I'm teaching a class or workshop and I get to see what worked best or what didn't work, so I can change it in my next 3D physical REAL workshop that I do.

Many people have had flashes of the future at some point. The more present you are, the more you will notice because when you are present, you will notice something "extra" that pops into your mind that doesn't belong there at that moment. Whatever pops in that isn't "supposed" to be, there is easily noticed. If you stood outside in a windstorm, you would find it much harder to notice when a sheet of paper zooms by in the wind when there is so much flying by with it. When you have a day with hardly a breeze, it's much easier to notice when that paper blows past you as it slowly slides across the ground. When you have a day where the wind is still, the paper is very easy to notice sitting there on the ground. It's easier to find the contrast. This is the difference between how easy it is to notice with a busy mind compared to a quiet mind.

I'm about to ask you a question that I want you to ask yourself. First, ask your conscious self. Then, ask your hidden self. I want you to open a conversation with the hidden self. Before you ask the question to the hidden self, you can say, "My Self that is hidden behind the veil. Yes. I'm talking to you, the part of me that is hidden. I know you are there. Am I seeing a glimpse of the future or creating it?" At first, you will only know it was a glimpse of the future when you arrive at that experience that showed itself to you earlier, so you won't be able to confirm this until it is consistent. So first, ask yourself consciously and then ask your hidden self using the questions written below. They stay quiet and listen for or feel the answers.

1. If you did foresee the future but didn't know that your quick feeling or insight was foresight, how do you learn to recognize the feeling or the vibe of that moment? This is for when it happens again, so you know you are in a "foreseeing" state of mind?
2. Suppose it's you or your subconscious hidden-self manifesting it. How do you learn to feel the feeling or vibe you were in at that moment so you can drop into that same state and manifest it whenever you want to?
3. We aren't up to the manifesting methods yet, but we are getting there. For now, asking the questions and writing down the answers in your journal will prime your mind for answers and the pathways needed to be the expert you are already born to be.

Ask these same questions to yourself and then ask them again to the you behind the veil. Sit with each question and wait for a response. It could be in words, feelings, or something else. It can also be nothing for now.

Because we are working with both sides of the veil, separating the hidden self from the conscious self that you consider the 'you' reading this, it's helpful for your subconscious to begin hearing its name being called in class and reminding it that it's invited to participate in this course with you. Please write any notes and thoughts in your journal.

Side note: I am using the term "present moment" here in the traditional sense. Later, we will get to the present moment technique and it will take on a whole new meaning.

2.2 Exercise: NLP For Intuition

This is a technique that I learned many years ago when I studied NLP. It changes the way you hold a belief or a certainty about something that might not be helpful to hold onto anymore. You can use it to change habits, instill confidence, or even to make it easier to choose healthier foods.

This is how it's done: Take a minute and get comfortable.

Read this out loud if needed and record it as audio so you can play it back.

Close your eyes. Imagine there is a mental screen opened in front of you. Think of something you fully believe in. It could be God, a skill you trust, a friend, or the ocean. You can see or feel different things on that screen. Notice where on the screen you see it. Point to it. Now think about intuition. Where do you see or feel "Intuition" on the screen of your mind when thinking about you being intuitive or having intuition? Point to the area as if there is a 360-degree movie screen in front of you and around you. Like the movie 'Truman Show', all around him was a dome in the sky that was actually a screen. Point to "Intuition" on the screen. Your mind puts things in certain places of importance, just like you might put your keys in an important place so you remember it.

Now, think of something you know you are great at. Choose something easy and natural for you. It might be cooking, making friends, reading, breathing, fitness, or anything you enjoy that comes easily to you. Point to where it is located on the screen in your mind.

Is it the same place or a different place as the first two that you thought of?

Now think of "Intuition" again. Reach with your hand to where you see "Intuition" and move it, like a chess piece, to the location of the choice that was natural and enjoyable for you. Use your mind and imagine that you superglue it in place. Make sure that it's stuck in the new spot and can't be moved, no matter how hard you try to move it. Try to move it and if you can, glue it back to that spot even stronger. Bang it in with heavy-duty nails. Look away from that spot in your mind and then look back. If it's still there, you've got it. Take a deep breath and relax.

Now, think about your beliefs about your intuition. How do you feel? Do you notice more certainty? Do you feel a similar certainty to the other option that you are naturally good at or enjoy with ease? You will find that you feel a much better and more flowing connection to your Intuition now. Check the image again tomorrow and make sure it's still in the same place. If it moved at all, do it again. When you find something else that you are really good at, see where you notice it on the screen. Is it near Intuition? If it's not, consider how you feel about this skill that is easy for you and see what it's like to move intuition into the same spot to compare how it feels.

Do the same process with manifestation, empathic abilities, or any other skill set that you want your mind to process more easily.

2.3 Exercise Part 1: EFT For intuition

The first time I used EFT, I was in a difficult relationship. I knew I was leaving, but I felt really bad about it. I learned about EFT and bought a book about it. Then, I tapped on the feelings of hurt, loss, and heartache. The negative feelings were mostly gone very quickly. Each time they lessened, I tapped again. When we finally broke up,

I felt like it was just a normal day. My former girlfriend at that time said, “Why aren’t you upset?” I said, “Because I already cleared it.” But I did feel very guilty that I wasn’t upset. When I later spoke to someone who was an EFT expert, he said, “You should have tapped out the guilt, too.” It didn’t cross my mind at the time because I didn’t know all of its possible uses.

EFT, or Emotional Freedom Technique, does much more than freeing trapped or difficult emotions. It’s almost as if the name was chosen not to attract too much attention because, for many people, it helps clear emotions, phobias, physical symptoms and, in the case we are using it for, subconscious beliefs. It can clear blockages that you may not be aware you have, or you may be aware you have them and need some help releasing them.

The EFT tapping points are listed here. You will be making the statements that you want to clear as you tap on them.

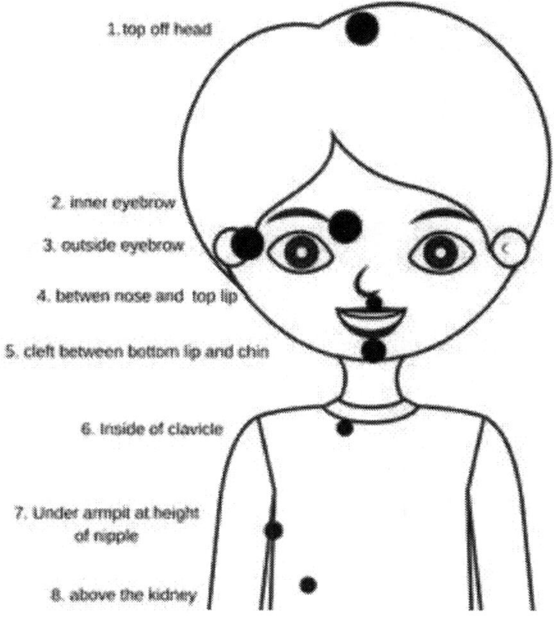

Tapping Points for EFT

Tap them as you read along.

- First, tap the side of the palm on the Karate chop point. Tap continuously as you repeat these sentences out loud.
- Even though I don't know how to access my intuition, I deeply and completely love, honor and accept myself.
- Even though my intuition isn't as strong as I would like it to be, I deeply and completely love, honor and accept myself.
- Even though I don't know how to make my inner knowing more powerful and available to me, I deeply and completely love, honor, and accept myself.
- Then tap the top of the head 5 times or more while saying…My intuition
- Then tap the top of the inner eyebrow bone 5 times or more while saying... I don't trust it
- Then tap the outside of the eye and the eye socket 5 times or more…I can't hear it.
- Then tap below the eye in the center of the bone 5 times or more… I'm not sure.
- Then tap the space between the bottom of your nose and your lip 5 times or more… This intuition, my intuition
- Then tap the space between your bottom lip and your chin 5 times or more… I don't know how to recognize it.
- Then tap the space at the top inner side of your first rib where it meets your clavicle 5 times or more…. I'm not aware of it.

- Then tap under your armpit at the height of the nipple 5 times or more…I can't learn this.
- Then tap on the ribs above the kidney, drawing a line strain down from the nipple 5 times or more… My intuition.
- Go back to the top of your head and start again. You may feel like you want to tap certain areas longer. If you do, do it. Something is clearing there. After a second round is done, take a breath and relax.

Do you feel lighter and clearer? Any time you clear a pattern or programming layer, you also clear things attached to it and new levels can come to your surface awareness. Run it again and see how much deeper you clear. After doing it a few times over a few days, change the words if you want to. Your subconscious will tell you what words to use. You don't have to consciously agree with the words here. You are clearing the parts of you that may be related to these sentences and the words that are hiding from you in your subconscious and holding you back. If you don't want to use these sentences because you are sure these issues are there, I am going to assure you that there are parts of these that ego is hiding to sabotage, so do it a few times and see how you feel afterwards.

2.4 Manifestation Exercise. Positive Self Talk: Conversations With Yourself.

As you get better at connecting with your intuition and subconscious, it's extremely important to take time to close your eyes and have positive conversations with yourself. In these talks, work out what you need to get what you want.

Structure it like you have two voices in your head. One voice asks questions, and the other voice answers, or if the answer doesn't come right away, the other voice says, "I'm not sure. Let's let our subconscious mind figure that one out for us while we aren't paying attention or while we sleep."

This activates your subconscious and higher self to send you the answers. Notice how you aren't talking directly to your subconscious but around it? Like whispering loud enough so someone else can hear you, but they don't know you are doing it on purpose. You can do this every day until it becomes a normal response when you want a certain result. Then, keep your passive attention turned on because your subconscious will provide the answer using intuition's messaging system. Not knowing something won't stress you out as much; it might even become fun because you trust your intuition to give you the message you already have in your mind's Layer One.

You can do this during your meditation even more effectively because you are already in a deeper state of mind and brainwaves.

2.5 Reminder for Advanced Level Intuitives And Empaths

Being at an advanced level with your intuition gives you awareness that makes you seem to have a lot more "lucky moments" than those who haven't learned and trained to use their intuition. Please feel welcome to share the information with others so they can access their gifts too, but choose who you share it with because some people will say you are imagining it, and even those who believe you may not want to learn, so don't let them deflate your inspiration.

Every person will decide it's real, and they want to develop it when they are ready. Trust me. When they want the next step to enhance their life or just to have answers, and they see you living that way, they will ask you for help. Enjoy and respect their journey. We are learning this now while they are learning something they need more than this. When they are ready to learn, you will get the joy of knowing you will be on the same page and in the same private club.

2.6 Exercise: Empath Development And Mind Reads. Body As Antenna Technique

Until now, everything you have learned has helped you develop sensitivities for Intuitive and empathic abilities, which tie directly into creation and manifestation. This exercise will specifically train your empathic skills on demand instead of just noticing it or being a victim of it.

- It's like the Foundational Breath Technique in that after practicing, you can choose to tune into someone else's emotions or tune out.
- It is an exercise.
- It takes practice.
- You need at least one partner to do this exercise, and 2 is much better.
- Do it 3 times each.

Your empathic skills will open quickly and will surprise you, too. This will help you recognize and know when you are feeling others' feelings instead of wondering why your mood changed suddenly.

You will know what others are feeling and, at times, what they are thinking using **The Body as an Antenna Technique** by putting your body and breath in the same position and rhythm as another person. You are aligning your *antenna* with theirs, and you will quickly have their internal experience.

When this exercise is done correctly, you will get detailed insight into even what they are remembering. Take some time with this and take turns with your partners so each person gets to have the experience, and you can learn from what they do and see. Practice this, and later in module 3, you will learn to donate emotions.

It's very important to write in your journal here because you need to chart progress and note the changes as you practice.

Person 1. Recall a situation that had very clear emotions for you. You passed a test, you fell in love, you broke up. Take the time to really feel it. In remembering it, let your body get into the position that it wants to. Feel the ease or tension in your jaw, in your face, in your muscles.

Person 2. Look at person 1 and get into the same position they are in. Notice how they are breathing. Fast or slow? Match their speed of breath. How deep do they breathe? Match it. Chin forward or back? Match it as exact as possible. What else do you see that isn't the same? Make it the same. How are the shoulders? Are they leaning slightly forward or back?

Person 3. You are the observer. Compare person 1 to person 2 and tell person 2 how to change their position in any way to make it match person 1. Breath, leaning, tapping of the fingers? Find whatever is different and make it the same. Is a foot turned in or out more or less?

Person 2. Maintain that matching position and then say how you feel and what you feel. What comes to mind? Emotions? Thoughts? Images? Tell the others and let person 1 tell you what memory and experience they were recalling. It should be very close to their experience.

Then, switch to the next person until everyone gets to do it.

You now understand how you are a resonant being, an antenna. Just by taking on the same posture, position, breath, tilt, and tension, you can know someone else's experience.

2.7 Curiosity Gives Your Mind Something To Solve. Say It Out Loud.

The power of "I Wonder."

Asking an inner question out loud when you are wondering something, especially if it comes up during a healing session, meditation or certain other times, invites your subconscious to search for the answer.

Posing a question out loud to another person allows you to hear it out loud and also get an idea of what someone else might answer. Your subconscious gets to consider it in a new way and moves to solve it for you.

My friend, Lubaina, is a healer who practices a form of energetic bodywork, tuning fork sound therapy and astrology. During a session I had with her, she told me about the current planetary alignments. I asked her if knowing the planetary alignments so well, "*I wonder if* you can feel the tension or blockages in my system (body/energy) in relation to energy and the gravitational pull of the stars and planets?"

That question started the gears turning and led to an Epiphany moment for her. Soon after, she began to tune into the feel of the planet's energy in relation to where people had energy stuck and where it flowed. Suddenly, she was given a gift of tuning forks that matched the frequency of the planets in our Solar System.

She now feels the astrological energy and how it causes tension or peace in a person's energy system. She said that my asking the question created the space for self-inquiry to open her up to this concept.

The subconscious mind loves to be asked about **Wondering questions**. Maybe because “I wonder” are words that start a question while having "wonder” or “wonderful” means having a sparkly awesome experience. The mind loves words with two meanings because it gets to explore in 2 directions and bring them back to one.

2.8 Being Conscious Of When Intuition And Empathness Are Happening: Examples.

There are many times that you have an intuition or empathic message, and you miss it because you are not keeping your passive attention open to the Natural Strangeness experiences of Deja vú, luck, coincidence and the present moment. These are some common examples that happen often, so you can use them to calibrate your sensitivity. When you create sensitivity in different levels of your mind and in the physical body, you become more intuitive. You gain more awareness. They give you what seems like magic to others who don’t practice paying attention. This leads to intuition and a greater ability to manifest.

Another example is when you see someone’s face and know something about them that seems apparent to you, but others don’t know how you know. Here you are noticing a subtlety that quickly translates to an energy and imagery or feeling about them. Subtle awareness of something without being sure what it is, is a skill of intuitives and empaths.

There may be some things where in the past you couldn't explain how you knew, but now you are getting a handle on it. What is physical gets more subtle and smaller until it goes from physical to just energy. You can notice the energetics without knowing what you are noticing. it becomes a feeling or insight.

Example: When you stomp on your car's brake before the car in front of you stomps on its brake. This moment before you hit the brakes is intuitive, but at this point, you unconsciously glimpse the future. You didn't know why you did it until you did it. Your work here is to make it conscious so you are able to find and recognize the message that just told you to hit the brakes and then have the ability to do it consciously. Once you know how to get the message, then you can apply it to other situations that are less of an emergency.

Energy Exercises: Man-made and Artificial.

There are energy-emitting devices all around us. It's become so normal most of the time we don't notice. When you do notice, most don't connect the discomfort, agitation or mood swings to the radar, radiation, WIFI or electricity. Now you will.

Exercise

This is one of the simplest exercises because you can choose to do it instead of it just happening on its own. It is happening anyway.

- Notice your breathing when going through an EZ pass toll on the highway. It happens every time.
- Pay attention to see what it's like. If you have practiced the Foundational Breath Technique, it will be easy.
- This is one of the easiest ways to practice feeling energy, too. You are being hit by radiation as you pass through the toll.
- Notice how, as you pass through, your breathing stops for a few moments. You hold your breath without realizing it.
- Then, once you are about 50 feet away, you take a deep breath in again.

- Notice if you get a pain or cramp in your body as you pass the EZ pass toll. After a few times, notice what you feel as you get closer instead of just the direct hit of the radiation. Write about this in your journal. It's a big one that is worth writing about.
- Relax and drop into a peaceful state anytime you see a police car on the side of the highway. See how your body feels. Noticing a headache, heart flutter or fuzzy head? You are now aware that it can be caused by police radar. You are reacting to radiation.

Test it with your phone.

- Turn off your phone and see how you feel.
- Now turn it back on, close your eyes and notice how you feel. Take some time with this. Do it a couple times if you need to.
- Put it down and have a friend text you at a certain time so you know when the text is coming. Close your eyes and notice how you feel when it happens.
- Turn off your Wi-Fi in your home for a few hours. Unplug it completely from the wall. Stay inside while it's off.
- Hours later, turn it on and stand near it. See if your ears ring, any muscles twitch, or maybe your head feels pressure or your heart feels different. Pay attention so you know what is you and what is not you. This can help you take control of your health.
- When any of these things happen, write about it in your journal. I know I am repeating this. Having a history of the experiences shows you the progress of how often it happened. Writing it down lets you track your history and find patterns to help you evolve further.

You have to remember that your conscious mind, YOU, thinks your subconscious isn't you. The YOU reading this knows it's there because you've learned about it, but YOU also don't think that you have another being living in you that is managing more of your life on the inside than you are managing on the outside. By writing down your experiences, you are telling your subconscious mind that it is recognized. Like a good pet or human, it wants to be acknowledged and will speak up more often and in more ways. So, acknowledge it as much as possible.

2.9 Gratitude Leads To Manifestation.

This sounds theoretical, but it is literal. We are going to start the manifestation lessons now, but we will start with some emotional priming to feel more gratitude and good feelings because otherwise, you are creating but not manifesting.

What is the difference between creating and manifesting?

Well, before we go there, let's back up and talk about the relationship between intuition and manifestation.

Intuition and manifestation both happen on the same layer of the mind. I call it Layer One Mind because it's the base layer of mind for humans.

To make an analogy to explain this, let's use electricity. Electricity could be considered layer one. Your internet would be layer 2. It needs electricity to run. If you lose power in your home, there is no electricity, so no internet. You can do many things on the Internet. So shopping on the web could be layer 3 experience or layer 4. By itself, electricity just doesn't do what it does until humans learn to harness it.

Some great teachers call *Layer One Mind* the Quantum, the Void, The Super Mind. These names are Interchangeable. To me, Layer

One Mind makes me feel more connected to creation. It gives me a landscape to work in.

Intuition is the receiver. It is the feminine aspect. It's Internal. It's the feeling and knowing. Women and people with feminine energy are natural at this. They are the feelers. They naturally will feel others hurt or others love. The sensitives.

Manifestation is the outward projection. The male energy. It is the male aspect. The word starts with Man. It is creation, but not in a forceful way. It is the energetics of hunting without the physical aspects of aggression. It is building and creating. It all has to be done from a high level of clarity and festivity. Something that you will celebrate.

This is the nature of manifesting. It's what you will celebrate and be FESTive about. ManiFEST.

Here's an example; the union of man and woman can allow each to be the best at what they do and then they are a perfect complimentary team. The woman is the wisdom of the village and shares her inner knowledge. The man builds. Together, it's a complete system. Yin and Yang. They check and balance each other.

Still, today, we work at this for different reasons. Both sides want inner knowing and both sides want to manifest their lives. The good news is: If **you are good** at one, you can **be naturally good** at the other with some training, practice and commitment.

Intuition and manifestation reside on the same spectrum. Layer One of the mind. They both float there, passing each other by, slightly repelling each other like 2 magnetic poles keeping each other away. Why are you initially better at one than the other? Why do you have to develop each? One is easier for you based on your life experience, and then you still need to learn how to use it. The other is more foreign and less familiar, but you have the DNA coding and programming to know how to use it, too. If you had both at once, without training and knowledge of how they work, it would alter the human condition. If you had both skills simultaneously without learning the steps, you would be many steps higher on the ladder of life than other humans on the planet. It takes training because it takes the refinement and sensitivity of consciousness to get it right. You must honor the abilities, and to honor them, you must know how special they are. As you learn, you value these subtle beautiful energies and don't take them for granted.

It's like being born with a massive trust fund and never knowing the value of money, because you were always able to have what you wanted at any time. You wouldn't be able to understand many people's struggle with not having enough money, unless you had a reason to know or are an empath.

If you had this magic door that was always open for you without any emotional development, you would miss many life lessons that you needed to learn to make you more caring and compassionate. Now that you have been through enough, you are learning to do something that has value for you because you know you need it, and you want to make your life better in some way. In doing this, you make it more true for yourself and others that getting all you want is possible. You become an example.

A male and female energy-based relationship completes the structure of a yin-yang partnership. There are always 2 perspectives involved. It's like checks and balances. If one person was born fully activated with both, imagine what a child would do when he wished a dinosaur ate the city or that he was 100 feet tall. A world dictator would be bad with these traits, too. There has to be training, honor and reverence. If there are negative emotions involved, many of these abilities will not develop. Inner peace, or at least inner quiet, has to come first.

Women are naturally more intuitive, and men more naturally manifest (or manipath). This is programmed in nature. Today, it's all shifting as there is an awakening. More people are doing both.

Overcoming programming.

Do you think that society programmed us for positive outcomes?

You are always creating, but you are not always manifesting.

When you think of yourself, most people think of the self as the one in the body, the same one who is answering this question. There is another self that people don't know personally. It's an invisible part of you. It is the self that is directly connected to god. You talk to yourself, the self that you associate with, in your mind when you ask yourself what you want to eat. That very conscious self is always making phone calls that connect to another part of yourself that is hidden behind the veil. It's the part of yourself that connects to god. It's your manifestor self and part of your creator.

You have to choose how you feel and think when you talk to the hidden self so the right message gets to the other side of the veil between consciousness levels for your request to happen the way you want it. You see God's creation and miracles every day, but you don't see God, or higher consciousness or whatever you believe the mechanisms are that run the universe and its laws. The self that feeds you intuition's messages is the self that is directly connected to God or source. To get better communication with that deeper level of you, instead of just saying "Thank God," also say, "Thank you, self." You will gain more of the attention of the self that is behind the veil and your connection to manifesting.

Everything around you is part of your creation. It is projected through a consciousness filter that comes from your deeper levels of mind, from your subconscious. The state of things in your world often comes by default as part of mass consciousness, which is controlled by the media unless you are purposefully choosing yours.

Manifesting is a choice. You must choose to be festive. You must choose to hold the emotion and space of festivity to manifest. The word hidden in there is the key. FEST. This is the state needed to bring the joyous experiences barreling into your life like a freight train coming at you that makes you jump up excitedly and say, "I can't believe this happened to me. Thank you!" It's not luck. It's your frequency. Choose the right frequency.

This may make you wonder about those who seem to get everything without knowing about manifesting. They are the ones who are in the frequency all the time. It became a flow state for them because it has worked so many times that it's become expected. It's what they resonate with. When you feel good, good things happen. When you are constantly winning, you keep winning unless something causes a change in your emotional state, like a scary moment or a trauma. We see this in pro athletes who always win until they can't win anymore. Then, one day, they get the right coach, and they are winning again. They never lost their skill. They lost their frequency.

Choosing Emotions: Setting the State and Intention

When you learn to consciously create, you must learn to choose your emotions. To choose your emotions, you don't just say, "I'm happy now," and you become happy. You have to trigger and hold the emotional state. If you are in the lower emotions, you will create a lower life quality. We know this based on the hormones released due to chronic stress that cause your body to breakdown and age faster. But there is the other aspect that comes first. The aspect of energetic or consciousness creation. If you choose positive or higher emotions like happiness, love, and gratitude, you release hormones that help your health. It takes practice to choose, but with practice it gets easier.

To choose these happier states when your life is in a groove you want to change, you must *choose* to change your state or mood and then do it the same way you access your subconscious. You do it in a roundabout, indirect way. I like to think of it as sneaking in through the side door so the guards at the gate don't see you. You find the state and hold it. Make it real in the present moment. Feeling gratitude is one of the best ways.

Let's do an exercise.

Exercise: Conscious Rockstar & 1 Trillion Fans

Feel massive appreciation, gratitude and love.

Feeling appreciated boosts your energy and wakes up the positive, feel good, healing, anti-aging hormones, as well as activates or lights up your DNA. Having and giving gratitude does the same. **Feel Massively Appreciated** with this exercise to upgrade **your nervous system** and **release happy, healing, anti-aging hormones.** Decide what you are thankful for here because this is powerful for creation.

Here, you get the "Rockstar" feeling without the dangerous side effects of being a rockstar. You gain all of the benefits and none of the danger.

Stand up and close your eyes. Make sure you know the room you are in so you don't trip over anything. Put your arms out to the side like you are feeling the wind. Imagine that around you are billions, trillions of molecules, atoms, protons, electrons. Imagine that they are all living creatures. The whole room is buzzing with life on this microscopic level. Take a step forward. You brush by a billion of these tiny little creatures with every movement. Every time you brush by them as you move, they cheer like they have been touched by their favorite rockstar or hero.

Imagine that as you walk through the room, you are brushing the billions of these tiny creatures with your arms, legs, stomach, face, and hands. You can hear them and feel them cheering. You share your energy with them, which is what they want and need most, and that's all you need to do to create this joy, excitement, and privilege for them. They wait for exactly this to happen everyday. Everywhere you go, this is happening. These tiny energy beings are alive and just hoping and praying that you brush them with your body as you pass them. It's what they live for! Your energy takes their existence to the next level. You just elevated them. Hear them cheer and feel their excitement as you move through the room. Feel it? It's so amazing, isn't it? You are giving them the greatest gift ever and they are so thankful they cheer for you like the rockstar that you are. Feel the love they have for you and they are bathing you in.

Do this twice to get the experience. Then, make this a part of your morning practice. It should take only 30 seconds. Do it when you want a boost. It's much like blessing your food before eating, which elevates the energy in your food. You are elevating the energy every place you go and blessing yourself by creating energy of love and gratitude all around you with this exercise.

Write about your experience, then share this with someone else who can use it.

2.10 Cloud Melting.

Have you heard of cloudbusting or cloud melting? And if it can be done, why would you want to learn to do it?

My opinion is A. It’s cool. B. It shows you that you are connected to things outside of yourself in unexpected ways. C. You can control energy and consciousness outside of your body. D. It increases your ability to be in a passive attention state while being active.

When you learned to feel your energy from your hands, you discovered a new kind of awareness and ability to pay attention with a different part of the mind to something that was always there but you didn’t give awareness to. With cloud melting, you are letting go and being mindfully active as you do this activity, but also extending your mind or energy field outward so it can later be used to gain information or affect others.

Sometimes to do something, you can just put your attention on it in a passive way, like putting a hand on someone’s shoulder who is sad to calm them and change their state. You are using intention to transmit your caring.

You can’t force a cloud to melt, but you can connect with it while staying relaxed in a state of passive attention as you “disappear” it. The cloud is a good example of the mind. It’s there, but it’s also ethereal or, like mist, mystical. When something (like a cloud) is already a subtle, ethereal body that you can easily see, you can also easily meet it with your subtle body, meaning your consciousness.

This is how it’s done.

Go outside on a day when the sky is clear and find a small cloud. The smaller the better at first, so you can get comfortable with it. Look at the cloud in a relaxed way. Feel a connection to it. In your mind, imagine yourself pulling the cloud into pieces like it's made of cotton. You can use your hands if you want to or just your mind. It will work either way. You will notice the cloud starting to shift. Often, once you start the process, you will notice it gets smaller, though, at times, it starts to expand. You can stop doing it, and it will keep disappearing. Keep pulling it apart. Keep going even when it's only a small speck that is left. Finish the job. The last few pieces that linger can take the longest. Now it's gone. Do it again to a different cloud. Don't overdo it too much on day one because it will get tiring. Like seeing auras, you are using a part of the mind that you aren't used to using on purpose very much, so you will get tired. Practice, then take a break and then practice some more.

A friend of mine didn't believe it. I don't blame him. It's not easy to believe unless you are into this kind of work and practicing it to prove it to yourself. He said to me that clouds are supposed to melt. So I told him to choose a cloud. When I made it disappear, and all the others around it were still there, he still said clouds disappear. He wanted me to try it on a tree. Trees don't naturally disappear, so it's not a great way to feel successful when learning a new skill or ability. Trees probably wouldn't like it too much either, just like humans wouldn't want it to happen to themselves either.

Once you understand you can disappear clouds, also known as water vapor, consider anyone you know with fibroids, tumors or cysts. Imagine them and use the same technique every day for 5 minutes a day for a week or longer and then see how they are doing. If you have any health concerns like this, try it on yourself, too. It's not a treatment or a medical intervention. It is all energy being held in place on the level of Layer One Mind and belief systems. You can repaint the canvas and change the image that is on it. In your mind, melt the problem and let healthy tissue be there instead. As you do this more often for yourself and others, your mind and abilities will get stronger. You will have more power, and you will be certain of it. It is empowering.

2.11 Exercises To Increase And Refine Physical Senses

I know you did this exercise already, but have you practiced? Even if you have, let's do it again. It was a more intermediate-level exercise that I put in part 1 to prime your mind and get you started early. If you do it just once, you won't grow the neural pathway, the grooves in your brain, so you can literally get into the groove and the pathway is carved out for you. Each time you do it, you evolve your brain further until you can tell the difference between very subtle differences, and this is how you notice energy, intuition, auras, and manifestation states of being. You are learning what each different state feels like, so you know when you are in it. Then you develop into someone who doesn't have to work to get into a zone for these states because they become natural to you. The mastery is in repetition. The importance of "less is more" here means that the less the intensity of a feeling on your taste buds or in your hands, the more you develop the skill of feeling it and growing your ability. Take a few minutes to do it again, and you will find it easier this time than last time.

Intuition is being aware of your mind's subtle communication style and the way it gives you messages. Being aware of the subtle, leads you to fine-tune your perception. When you upgrade your senses, you gain the byproduct of learning the language of your mind, Intuition and Empathic abilities.

Exercise 1: Refining Taste

Can you taste a sprinkle of sugar when you eat something salty? You may notice it, and with practice taste it every time, but it's subtle. So, it takes practice.

Exercise 2: Heighten your sense of touch.

Can you feel a hair under a sheet of paper? How about under 10 sheets? Now, do it with your eyes closed. This is a way to fire off less sensory nerves in the fingers. The lighter you touch, with minimal practice, the easier it is to feel.

Exercise 3: Water Temperature change.

Grab a pan, water and a thermometer. Heat it on the stove to 75 degrees. Get another pan and heat the water in it to 73 degrees. Put your hand in one and then the other. Can you feel the 2-degree difference? If you can, get another pan of water and heat it at the same time as this one. Heat one to 75 degrees and one to 74 degrees. If it's easy, try it at 84 and 85 degrees.

How long does it take for you to notice a 1-degree difference? Once you can do it, do it again tomorrow and notice if it's easier or harder. This isn't training your hand to feel the heat. It's training your brain and mind to notice very subtle differences and bookmark them. This means you can be aware of smaller and smaller increments of change until they should seem impossible to notice, yet somehow you do.

2.12 Exercise: Feeling Energy from Others Using Hands

For this exercise, you need another person and your Passive Attention skills.

You will be feeling the other person's energy in different areas and learning what it means.

Have the other person lay down comfortably on their stomach and explain what you will be doing.

Place your hands a quarter of an inch above their spine. Let it hover above them slowly while you are using passive, gentle attention. As your hand is hovering there, don't try to feel something. Just notice if you do. You can sing a song in your mind and make that your active attention if you need a way to make what your hand is feeling more the lesser of active. Now, move your hand down the length of the spine while hovering above it. See or feel where you notice a feeling or energy coming off the person's body.

Do you feel heat, tingling, cold, a blank spot or even sudden irritation while over an area? Do the feelings shift or change as your hand moves to different areas? Does the person move or does their breathing change while over a specific area? Take notice. Everything means something. As I like to say, every moment is a crystal ball if you pay attention and see it from the right angle.

Now, move your hand from half an inch to one inch above their body. Slowly, move your hand upwards towards their head and then slowly down towards their waist. Do you still feel it? The feeling might be stronger or it might be less noticeable. The energy comes off of the body more strongly in some areas and at different distances for a number of reasons. It's like the way a microwave heats up a spot on your pizza while the rest of the pizza is still cold.

Now, move two inches off the body and do the same. After you feel all the way up and down the body and notice what you notice, then do it again, but this time 6 inches off of the body. Keep your journal nearby. Write down what you notice, so as you practice and compare you have a reference to how much easier it happens as you do it.

How far away can your hands feel the energy? Why might it feel stronger at 3 inches than at 1 inch?

Think about a magnifying lens that can start a fire. There is a point where the light is directed into a stronger energy beam and comes together to start the fire. It may not be the closest to the ground, but the most light or energy is concentrated at that distance, even if it's further away. This new practice is probably already leading you to wonder what to do with this new skill and awareness that you are developing. Why learn this, besides to awaken your brain and mind to something that you always could do? How many other energetic skills do you have that you were never told you have or never noticed consciously? They all lead to more powerful and usable abilities depending on your nature. If you are a healer, you now know areas of disharmony and inflammation. There may be pain there, or it could just be an area to keep an eye on.

If you want to learn to read energy at a deeper level, by practicing this it will develop into smaller chunks of information until you get insights or downloads about the person that comes as a surprise.

I was on a flight to Phoenix, Arizona, to visit my family. I sat there, and suddenly, I started to sneeze and sneeze and sneeze. The sneezes let me know there was something in the air that I wasn't aware of. Something that was there the whole time, but I wasn't sensitive enough to know it until part of my senses showed it to me. This is what you are doing here, awakening to what your senses can show you that you never noticed. It is powerful when you apply these abilities to your practical life. You will be seeing things that you have seen all of your life and suddenly they are different. Now, let's talk about the actual uses that you can do right now.

2.13 Exercise: Practical Use Of Feeling Energy

In Part 1, you felt energy first with your hands because you are used to using your hands to feel, but this was just a starting point. As you practice and pay attention, you will notice other parts of your body feel something, too. You can feel the heat with your hands, but when you pass by a radiator, you may feel heat with your leg.

You may have already noticed that your breath changes while you are feeling with your hands. If you haven't, ask someone if you can scan them with your hands and be aware of your breath. Soon you will simply notice your breath changing without the need to use your hands first. Then, you will notice the feeling that comes before your breath changes. You are following the steps back until you get to

Layer One. You won't need to use your hands or your breath, you will just internally know.

Your heartbeat will change when you feel the energy, just like it changes when you have an emotional experience. With your passive attention skills and awareness, you will suddenly notice your heartbeat has changed, whereas, in the past, it would go unnoticed. It will become a new level of the Foundational Breath Technique because that is where the FBT leads. The FBT is the start of the process. As you notice this more, you will find you may use your hands as a fast wave or scan over someone like an antenna, but you are really feeling and knowing something in your whole self, body and energy field.

What is it good for? Knowing you are connected to everyone around you. Growing your awareness of the subtle so you are closer to being the metaphorical Jedi. Finding areas of disharmonious energy in other's bodies so you can help them heal. Knowing where someone's body is locked up so you know how to help them before disease develops. Finding areas of harmony in someone, so you can connect with that feeling to help that frequency spread in them and to resonate with it yourself, both to feel better and remember the tone so you can use it for others. This lets you access a new energetic state when needed. It's worth learning as much as possible about the states of awareness where the physical world is created before it becomes physical.

There are many things to learn from developing the skills to feel different kinds of energy.

Write down your thoughts. What else can you learn?

2.14 On Being An Empath: Feeling And Donating Emotions.

As an empath, you feel others' feelings. An untrained empath may not know they are feeling the feelings of others. It can make you wonder and question why you go through such strong mood changes for "seemingly" no reason. It's like you are a boat with cheap oars and a non working rudder being carried by the waves of the ocean without a way to steer.

A conscious or trained empath is aware when they are picking up others emotions and can also donate feelings to others. If you are an empath, you do it already but mostly aren't paying attention to when it's happening. It's the same way you aren't paying attention when you are taking on others feelings. Being an Empath is a great responsibility that has great rewards. Everyone is a natural born empath to one level or another.

To use your skills as useful tools, you must pay attention to your own states of emotions so you notice how, why and when they change. You also have to be aware of others' states because when you donate emotions and energy to someone, and they suddenly get lifted from feeling down, you want to be aware of their state change. You must notice the state you were in when you made the donation so you know how to reproduce it.

2.15 Your Cravings Are A Key To Intuition

Required: A moment when you have a CRAVING and your *passive attention skills.*

Cravings are an internal feeling that seems like it's not your feeling. It feels like you are being pushed to do something that you don't want to do. There was a time when I was craving something sweet and creamy, and I was committed to fasting for 22 hours that day.

The craving didn't make sense. It was gnawing at me. It was like another voice inside me that was speaking to me saying, "No big deal. Just eat something. Eat anything." I was committed to the fast, but I wondered about this powerful voice and urge. CLEARLY, it was my voice or one of my voices, but it wasn't the voice that I wanted telling me what to do. I sat down and closed my eyes. I followed the voice. As I followed it, it went deeper and deeper from my conscious mind. The craving faded away. I followed it further. It was like we were on an elevator going down until it brought me levels closer to my subconscious. I could feel the connection of where it came from. That's when I knew that cravings weren't just something that wanted to pressure me or trick me into doing something I didn't want to do. It was something that I could use to access my subconscious.

By now you recall that the subconscious is the part of the mind that hands off the messages to your intuition to deliver it to the part of you that consciously is reading this. The subconscious is also the place where you can create or manifest the reality you want.

Think about it like this. When you have a craving, it's not just an uncontrolled feeling that you want to eat something. It is actually a runway that is all lit up, and it takes you directly to the part of your mind that can give you what you really want; more powerful abilities of intuition, empathic skills, manifestation and expanded awareness. In a nutshell, real power to navigate and create your life.

A craving is a tool to alert you to when your subconscious messaging system left a door open to your conscious mind. It's so strong you feel compelled to do what it tells you. It's able to get you to give in to the craving, even though you don't want to, because it's coming from the same place that hypnosis works within. Your subconscious is teasing you and coaxing you in the best way it knows how to follow the craving, but you taught it to do that, so you are in control. But now that you know this, you can turn the tables and use its power for a force of good.

Now that you can hitch a ride on the back of that craving as it sinks back down to the depths of your mind, you can access a deeper level of your mind more easily. The message system causing these cravings due to your old and now unneeded patterns, protective mechanisms and wounds are stored in a nearby system (frequency) to your intuition. Once at that level of mind, you have some control.

What do you do from here?

First, notice the craving and what it wants you to do. Give yourself a congratulations for noticing the craving as something useful to you, instead of something to argue with. Then, be happy and be thankful. This craving that you are aware of is an open door for you. It is a massive opportunity to increase your power right there at that moment. Instead of feeding the craving, close your eyes, drop in and meditate for a few minutes while this door to the subconscious is open. You have the power to choose to do this. The craving can wait a few minutes to be fed after you do this amazing work.

Feel the feeling of the craving and follow it down. Use this solved mystery that is now a part of your Layer One mind access. You now have another formula for accessing the deeper parts of your mind, intuition and more.

Write your thoughts on this process in your journal. Fold the page so that next time you have a craving, you can write how you processed it. It might have to happen once or twice to remember this formula, just like some of the other formulas we will cover, like coincidence and Déjà vu.

It's so commonplace that it's easy to forget at first. Then soon, it becomes very easy to remember. When you do the exercise, you completely restructure the pattern.

Then you realize, cravings are your friend and your teacher.

2.16 Exercise: Your Cravings Are A Key To Intuition

This exercise is more of a practice. It attunes your awareness to your intuition by using your cravings as an alert when your subconscious messaging system is WIDE open.

This exercise uses your passive and active attention. You must be present with yourself to recognize what is happening.

When you have a craving for a snack, drink, or any substance that you think isn't ideal for you (or is ideal), your subconscious is speaking to you.

Use this time as a tool. Take a few minutes and ask yourself if you are bigger and stronger than this craving. Who is in charge here anyway? The craving is the starting horn at a horse race. YOUR CRAVING IS A WAY IN! Sometimes, you crave learning something. That's your subconscious telling you that there is something there for you. Use one of the meditation techniques and sit with the craving for a few minutes. The craving will pass as you follow its path to the system that is sending it. This will give you more access to your subconscious and intuition. This leads to more recognition of the constant information that is always coming through…and that helps make intuition a normal happening for you. You are building a big toolbox to allow you to access your inner knowledge and abilities in many ways. The Foundational Breath Technique is the most conscious technique because you can choose to use it at any time. Cravings are a bonus. When they show up, it's like getting a cheat code that lets you skip ahead faster in a video game or in The Matrix.

2.17 If It's Always On, Won't It Distract Me?

The question you might be having is… If messages are always coming through, doesn't it get to be too much when you have to function on a normal day?

Look at it this way. You have watched TV or listened to the radio at some point. You are always aware you can change the channel or station. You can pay attention to the show or the music or ignore it. Access to your subconscious and to your intuition and all of its messages is like turning a radio dial or changing TV stations. The access is always there, but you choose which channel you will be on. You can also have the channel muted or dim the screen if you want to.

You can use the Foundational Breath Technique to change the channel or station to get to the intuition channel. Then once you access the openness, you can hold and maintain the space and enjoy a day in the park in that awareness. Notice what nature is telling you.

I was lying in Central Park in New York City in this state of mind when a tree I was looking at suddenly flipped upside down in my mind. I saw the image of the tree's branches as the air pathways inside the lungs in my body. It awed me that the trees breathe for the planet and look just like the inside of the lungs. The openness allows for a new perspective and will increase creativity infinitely.

Here is one more way to look at your intuitive mind in this context. You have the keys to the car, and you aren't driving it all the time, but you have access when you want it and when you need it. Just maintain the vehicle so it works when you need it.

2.18 Foundational Breath Is The Foundation.

DO NOT SKIP THIS! Practice it again.

Have you practiced 3 times a day? It's good practice to do it 30 seconds at a time. Pick up a food and check with your Foundational Breath. Reach for a portion of food and check your breath before you touch it. The technique quickly becomes a part of you. Your breath is the intuition shortcut. It makes it a physical experience. This physicality translates to other senses and knowledge. Do it and feel how simple it is to use it for right or wrong information.

The technique is a building block, like letters of the alphabet are building blocks. Soon, you will use the letters to build words and then sentences. In an extremely short time, you will "know" without having to do the exercise.

By training yourself in this way, it's exactly like learning to drive a car. First, it's a step-by-step, very conscious process. You sit down and shut the door. When you learned to drive, you went through a checklist in your mind. You put on your seat belt, adjust your mirrors, step on the brake, look behind you before pulling out, and shift gears. Now, you do all of this without even thinking about it. It's become subconscious or unconscious.

This is the way your breath becomes the foundation for intuition. With 1 week of consistent practice 3 times a day, you will know immediately what's good for you or what you want to avoid, including foods, events, and relationships. You will feel it and know it without pausing to check your breath. Your intuition will have a simple way to let you know every time, now that you know how to use it and understand it.

As long as you stay out of your head and base emotions, it is a skill that is always with you.

2.19 Exercise: Feeling Energy From Wi-Fi

Required for this exercise: A Microwave or Wi-Fi router.

To feel energy with your body, first feel it with your hands as in Part 1 of the book, "Feel your Own Energy Field."

Now, you are about to learn to feel with the body. Your body has been transmitting to you and now you will start to notice it.

Take 3 deep breaths and relax. Keeping your self relaxed, turn on the microwave or turn off and then on your wifi router. Stand a foot away or as far away as recommended in the manual.

While in your relaxed state, notice what you feel in your body.

What might you feel? Fuzzy head, clouded thinking, twinging pain in the neck or elsewhere, short twinge of a headache, heartbeat changes or skips a beat. Your breathing may get shallow, or you might notice you feel a little bit panicky or have unclear thoughts. You may notice jaw tension, clenching of your jaw or tooth pain. Some of these will become obvious when you use the microwave or wifi as you become more sensitive to the different kinds of energy. This is already happening. You are now learning to notice it.

This exercise will affirm to your conscious mind that your body feels energy from different kinds of sources. You know this because heat is energy, and you feel that, but energy from wifi is something you aren't trained to notice, yet it could be a cause of your headaches, cloudy thoughts, tiredness or your moods or more.

2.20 Exercise: Auras And White Dots Of Energy In The Sky

If you think you haven't seen an aura before, you probably have but didn't realize it because you weren't trained to notice it. The mind will delete things that don't make sense to your understanding of the world. This is likely why highly creative people tend to have more psychic experiences. The reason is that they believe it's all possible, so the mind doesn't make it invisible to them. You may have heard the now famous story of the Native Americans who didn't see the big ships that came to America landing on the shore because they didn't know something like this could exist. It's easy to imagine that by not knowing it's real, it passes you by.

To see the aura you are using a different part of the eye and the mind. A kind of soft peripheral vision sees auras. A purposely relaxed or "spaced out" gaze will allow you to see auras. You just need to know how to adjust your mind's lens and then have what you are seeing pointed out to you. You can also suspend your doubt and become aware of what is already there.

Do this first.

On a nice day, step outside and look up at the sky. Relax your eyes as if you are staring lazily at nothing specific. Choose a cloud and use a relaxed gaze to look at it. Don't stare, but let your eyes rest on it. You will see something in the air between you and the cloud while you gaze. You will see little white dots of energy shooting around. Once you see it, you can't miss it. This is not the aura, but this is the same gaze you will use for seeing auras.

Something to consider is that these white dots of energy shooting around have always been there, right in front of you. This might be the first time you've noticed them. This shift in the way you are looking at the sky gives you a completely new perspective. The dots have been in a different part of the visible spectrum until now. You still won't see them until you decide to look at them, and that's how it works with seeing an aura, too. Fortunately, you have already felt an aura by doing the energy-feeling exercises, so now you will use your eyes.

Once you learn and practice what is being taught here, the messages and insights you have always been getting but have not seen will be just as clear.

Find the dots of energy a few times during the day before moving on to how to see the Aura. Remember that the way you relax your eyes is the same for both.

2.21 Exercise: See the Aura

Required: Your hand and a dimly lit room with white or light-colored walls.

The Relaxed Stare.

Lift your hand up against a white or light-colored wall in a medium to dimly-lit room.

It should be light enough in the room to easily be able to see everything in the room, but not at all bright.

Hold your hand up towards the wall with your palm facing you. Stare at your hand, and then let your vision go past your hand to see the wall. You want to see your hand in your vision but look at the wall behind it. Don't look at your hand.

With your relaxed vision, look for the shadow cloud or layer of light or even a dim aura around your fingers. It may look like you are seeing double. Let your eyes relax while gently looking around. Now, begin to notice the area around the tips of your fingers. Don't look at the tips of your fingers; just look at the wall behind them. Then, use your relaxed gaze or peripheral vision to see the tips of your fingers while staring at the wall. You will see an outline of light. You are seeing your Aura and beginning to train your eyes' awareness so your ability grows. Don't second-guess yourself. If anything, congratulate yourself, even if you think you are imagining it. It will become normal to see auras soon.

2.22 Exercise: Auras: Partner.

Requirements: A partner to work with.

Ask your partner to hold their hand out and repeat the instructions from the last exercise using their hand.

Then, have them stand about a foot away from the wall. Stare at the wall behind them the way you stared at the wall when you looked at your hand. Although they are in the way, just gaze at the wall behind them. With the edges of your vision, notice their shoulders while you look at the wall. Don't look directly at their shoulders. Notice the outline of light, or what might look like a shadow that comes off their shoulders about a ¼ inch. You may think you are seeing double at first. You are not. You activated your aura vision.

Have your partner take both hands and touch the tips of their pointer fingers together above their head with the wall as the background. When you see a slight glow or shadow around the touching fingers or the whole hand, have them slowly move the fingers an inch apart. Keep staring at the wall, but notice what is in between the fingers as you do.

This is the part that will prove to you that you aren't seeing double. What you see in between the fingers is the aura or a part of the energy field. As you see, there is now nothing behind it, so it can't be double vision.

Some have asked about their eyes playing tricks on them or maybe they are seeing double vision by having the eyes out of focus. Do you see the aura, like a dim light, gray shadow or possibly an electrical arc between the separated fingertips? There is no double vision there with the fingers separated. People perceive auras differently at first, so any of the choices I use to describe it are possible.

No matter how you perceive seeing auras or if you readily accept what you see or not, continue to do it because your ability will get stronger and as it does, you won't question whether it's real. It might lead to many other questions.

What do you think of this experience and new ability? Write it in your journal. How long until you saw it? What did you notice at first? Did it get clearer? When will you practice again? Do you have a goal in mind?

You've always had this ability, and now you are being shown how to use it. If you practice, you will have a world of new information open up to you. I believe this should be common knowledge to anyone, considering it's built into everyone's vision.

What if you could see the difference in the energy of whole foods and living foods or good clean water compared to chemically treated water? You might consider different food choices. What if you could see darkness or holes in someone's aura and learn to rebalance it or alert them to a potential problem so they can get a head start on healing it. Imagine how many of you could help by developing this skill.

Lastly, if auras are so well known and some cameras can take pictures of the human energy field, why isn't this part of biology taught in school?

Think about these questions and add some of your own. I'm sure you have some that are different from mine because your life journey will lead you to questions that lead to answers for you based on what you have been through.

2.23 Pay Attention To This. Intuition Insight.

When you put seemingly random thoughts or experiences together and make a connection between them, or if you have a new insight about something unrelated to either, give it some attention.

Example: I was living in NYC. I hadn't made ice cubes for most of the winter. One Friday, I saw the empty tray, and although I didn't feel like it, I decided to make some ice. After a moment of being busy with something else, I decided not to bother. It's winter in NY. It's freezing. I'm not craving ice cubes with anything. Then something in my mind grabbed me and said it would take just a minute; why not do it? So I did it. It was like a speed bump on the road of my thoughts that I could have driven around, but I decided to slow down and drive over it. The choice was there, and I didn't notice the sensitivity of the message to make the ice, but my subconscious and intuition led me to do it anyway. That night, I went to an event. On the way, I fell and badly sprained both my wrists. I stayed at the event, wrapped my wrists in towels and put ice on them. When I got home, I opened the freezer to put some frozen bags of fruit on the swelling and saw the ice cubes. This is a moment of Unknown Insight. It is a moment of intuition, but it doesn't have a strong charge or feeling to get your attention, so it's not clear that it is intuition. As you become more aware through intention and practice, these insights get louder and more clear. It is intuition like anything else, but so specific that it takes fine-tuning to notice the vibe of how the moment feels.

I can remember the strange way it felt when I had the idea to make ice. It didn't seem to make sense, and it didn't feel like I had a reason, but I did it anyway. My subconscious knew I had frozen bags of fruit, too, so it likely didn't grab my awareness as strongly.

2.24 What Is Uploading? Creating And Manifesting.

You are always downloading information. What is uploading?

Let's talk about uploading, creating or manifesting your reality. Taking in your awareness of everything around you is your download, and it's happening all the time. When you get a good new insight or something out of the ordinary, many say they just downloaded something, but all new information is downloaded.

Your reality is what you upload, have uploaded and you keep uploading all the time. You process it while you sleep or while you meditate. Change your reality by changing what you upload. This means changing your mind, your thoughts and your feelings. Find the feeling that feels good and keep it with you. Let it buzz you once every 30 minutes or an hour until it becomes a part of you as often as you set a timer on your watch every 30 minutes.

Manifestation System of mind.

How to manifest. There is an old joke about a man who reads the New Testament. He reads that Jesus said, "Faith can move mountains." This is perfect because he has a mountain obstructing his view of the beautiful lake on the other side of the mountain just outside his window. Before bed, he commits to moving the mountain with his full faith by the time he wakes up in the morning. In the morning, he excitedly goes to his window and there is the mountain, just where it was the night before. He nodded his head and said, "I knew it."

The point of the story is he didn't really believe it, did he? To manifest, we have to fully know it, feel it and believe it. It doesn't have to be true, but we need to believe it's true at that moment. It takes commitment to practice it until you can do it without any mental or emotional beliefs or feelings that are obstacles to what you want to create for yourself. You have beliefs since childhood that have deep roots. It's time to change them. It can be slowly or quickly. Start with something like opening your heart, improving your vision or better sleep. If you need some foundation to build on, choose one that isn't high stakes. Once you see changes, it will reinforce that you can make bigger changes.

Manifesting is a subcategory of creating.

Creating or uploading is always happening. As covered earlier, manifesting is a conscious effort to create the life you want and make it FESTive for you.

Here are the steps to practice with. Why practice? The concept is easy, but if you don't practice, it's not as easy.

Why? You aren't a trained actor easily able to drop into the state of mind and emotion and make it real. If you are a trained actor, you have a benefit here.

Disharmony: You may have beliefs that tell you what you want isn't possible at this time. If this happens, and it does in the beginning to many people, find something low-stakes that you aren't too invested in to practice with. Maybe it's that you will get a surprise, like a small amount of money tomorrow. Maybe someone gives you $20. Don't think of anything that will excite you too much, but something that you can practice with to make it emotionally feel real because you already know it's possible that this could happen, and you don't have a blockage about it.

Then…Make it real in the present "*Pre-Sent*" moment.

Pre-sent present moment. This is a good exercise from Tony Robbins to understand the Pre-Sent Moment.

If you don't have any injury or pain, try this.

Place your feet next to each other and face the wall. Lift your right arm in front of you and point your finger toward the wall. Begin to turn at the waist, twist your body to the right, and keep twisting as far as you can comfortably go. Reach that arm behind you and point your pointer finger as far as you can go as you twist further. Note how far you twisted on the wall behind you.

Now, slowly come back to the center.

Now, close your eyes and imagine that you twist as far as you did when pointing your finger, and then imagine you can twist another halfway around. Now, in your mind, imagine twisting a little more until you are twisted all the way around and pointing in front of you. It's a full 360-degree twist in your imagination. Then, come back to the center in the starting position.

Now, physically twist again and see how far you go. This is a shortcut of how creating your future works in the present moment. You just pre-sent what you wanted to the short-term future using your mind and your feelings.

Now try this.

Do it again, but this time, do it in the house of your dreams, with big fat amounts of money in your pockets, the relationship of your dreams, and perfect health and a fit body. Create all of that first in your mind and your feelings. Now, do the turn. Add whatever you need to the turning that will be with you as you manifest the ability to go further right now. Remember to feel how it feels to have just what you want as you do it.

Every gift you've ever received was worth an unlimited amount to you. The reason is that you can draw on that feeling of gratitude anytime to use it in your intentional meditation to attract what you want now.

When I was in chiropractic school, people would make fun of the placebo effect. Someone got adjusted, and their headache was gone, and someone would say there is no double-blind study, so it's the placebo effect. They were essentially saying that the person was tricked into believing the chiropractic adjustment got them better. Modern medicine or modern drug companies want to address a physical problem with a physical change. I love what is called "the placebo" because the placebo is based on the energy, consciousness and spirit reconnecting you to your source field and your highest power, connected to the intelligence of all to heal from your own energy and life force, which is highly refined compared to physical matter. This is greater healing than if only using a drug and a drug may help or cure, but healing is a different process. If the belief and energy haven't changed, likely, you aren't healed or made whole and sometimes you may need that drug for management forever. The placebo effect should be called using our consciousness to heal ourselves. It makes a lot of sense considering that a body that has no life force in it or is dead won't heal no matter what medication it is given, so all healing has to do with life force.

When you are manifesting, you have to be selfish.

Here, being selfish does not mean being stingy or mean. It means taking time for yourself. It means putting down the heavy bags of stress that you carry. It means letting go of the person you love and worry about and letting go of your problems for some time so you can do what you have to do now to create a better world for yourself. Then, you can pick up the heavy bags again with more resources and a completely new frequency. You will have a different perspective after a manifestation practice, and don't be surprised if the situation has gotten better already.

2.25 Pay Attention To Dream Intuition Messaging

When I was in chiropractic school, I had a friend in my apartment complex who called me. She was frantic and screaming. I could hear her door being slammed into as if a person was throwing their body against it. She was shouting, "I called the police, and I have a gun." She was screaming to me that she needed help. I lived just a quarter mile away. Someone was trying to break in. This was early afternoon. When I got there, the person was gone. She told me the backstory.

The building's laundry machine was outside her door and around the back of the deck on her floor in the building. She did laundry the night before and was going to pick it up before class. As she went to open her door to get the laundry, her dream flooded into her mind from the night before. She got scared and decided not to go. In the dream, a man was perched on the laundry machine in the small laundry room, waiting for her. When she opened the door, he grabbed her.

Remembering the dream, she decided not to get her laundry and minutes later, she had a knock at her door. She looked through the peephole because she wasn't expecting anyone. The peephole was covered up. She asked who it was. When there was no answer, she didn't open it. Seconds later, the person tried to break into her door.

Her subconscious spoke to her in her dream and saved her life. This is a very good example of why to practice remembering dreams. Program yourself by telling yourself to remember your dreams before you go to sleep and that they will come fresh into your mind when you wake up or soon after. Then, record them, even if it seems unimportant at the time. Dreams may not always be a part of the future, but they are always solving something, so it's good to remember them.

There is one system that teaches you to have a glass of water next to your bed. Before you fall asleep, drink half the glass of water and then say to yourself, "When I wake up, I will drink the rest of this water and immediately remember all my dreams from the night." When you do this, you create an anchor for your mind. You are also starting a process by drinking the water that isn't finished until the next day. You are creating a bridge for your mind to stay connected from before sleep to after sleep.

2.26 Enlightenment. To enlighten. To make it lighter.

When you sit outside at a restaurant and roll back the awning that protects you from the rain, there is now less dark or shade and more light coming in. The light was always there, but it couldn't get through. With moderate effort, the curtain is pulled back, and more light comes in.

As you get more light, you are literally "enlightened." This is the step-by-step process of adding more awareness by allowing in more light, the energy from the electromagnetic spectrum and part of what gives nutrition to the mind and body.

Yogananda, the Yogi who brought yoga to the west from India, tells the story of a man who was very ill. The man prayed every day, "Lord, fill me with your light." The man did this every day, hours a day for months. One day, the man had an explosion of light inside his mind and body. He was immediately healed. He spoke to God and pleaded, "Lord, I didn't ask to be healed. I asked to be filled with your light." A voice came from everywhere at once in his mind that said, "Where there is light, there can be no darkness."

For now, take a moment, read this next part slowly into your phone and then play it back with your eyes closed.

Close your eyes and drop into a meditative, quiet state. Before you go fully into it, imagine for a moment that you are sitting in a dark room, and an awning above you is being slowly rolled back. The light that was not reaching you because of the shade is now able to touch the edge of your shoulder. As the shade pulls further back, you feel more light spread on your body. You feel its warmth as it spreads over your face. You see it against the inside of your eyelids. You feel it penetrate your skin and now feel it inside your cells. Your blood is pumping everywhere in your body. Every organ is getting passed the light. Getting enlightened. Now feel it enter through your head, going deeper and merging with your mind, as if the sun itself is a great mind, sharing billions of years of information while lightening the parts of you that need to be energized, seen or burned away.

Light stores and transmits information. Intuition distills information from consciousness and translates it for your conscious mind to discover. Think about this for a moment, then meditate on it and move on. Please write about this experience in your journal. What did it feel like to let more light in or enlighten you? How did your eyes feel? How did your body and mind feel?

2.27 Exercise: Use Your TV to Break The Matrix

Required: A TV or Internet access to TV shows.

The truth is in front of you if you take away a physical sense.

By disconnecting or blocking some of the 5 senses and using only one, you will see or hear the programming in fewer dimensions and recognize that it doesn't look or sound right for some reason. Often, we know something is wrong, but we don't know what. We can still be convinced that we are not being lied to by the person who is lying to us. This exercise will reinforce the awareness when something is not right, so you will know it in real life, too.

First: Turn on the news. Any channel will work. Turn off the volume and watch only the news actors' faces. You will see that many look like bad actors doing a poor job of acting. You will see fake anger and fake pouts on some of their faces. With the volume turned on, you miss this because you are engaging many of your senses, and it creates a much more 3D illusion that what you are being told is real.

The truth is some of them may believe what they are saying is true, or it might actually be true, but you will know when it isn't.

NEXT: Turn up the volume on a kid's vampire-type series that is notorious for B-grade acting. You could even use a soap opera. Then leave the room. Make sure the volume is loud enough to hear easily. Keep listening without watching. When you don't see the actor's face, you again are separating the senses, and you can hear the lack of authenticity in the person's voice. This exercise trains you to become a human lie detector. You may not know why someone is saying something untrue, but you will know it's not true. Try it with different news channels and news-type morning talk shows where the hosts complain a lot. You will hear fake disgust and fake authenticity. They are giving you free lessons on how to read people. There is a lot to understand here. It's also possible that it will sound true. It doesn't mean it is, but it means they believe it is. Or it may be true or partially true. We know that with so many new stations telling the same story a different way, at least one of them is not correct. Practice and figure it out. Any time you refine your physical abilities to notice something new, you also train your passive attention.

I first noticed this because the TV was on at my parents' house, and I was in the kitchen. They were watching a show, and the voices of the actors sounded like very poor acting instead of trained actors. From a well-trained actor, you like a good movie because you believe they are experiencing what's in the script, but when an inexperienced or bad actor is in the scene, it pulls you right out of the movie and back into your living room's reality. Some might say that it's a good thing to break the hypnotic element of the program being watched. I've wondered, "Did the director stick a bad actor in that scene to remind us that this is all fake and not to let our minds stay hypnotized?" The subconscious will believe what you watch on the screen if you deeply feel it, so even if you know it's fake, your subconscious may still get programmed. Keep that in mind.

What will you notice in the voice? The pitch will be wrong. On the TV news, they may sound like someone who is guilty of something and use their "pleading, convincing voice" to make you think they are innocent. This is like when a cookie is missing and when you ask the child if he ate it. His eyebrows go up, and his voice pitch rises, and he says, "I didn't do it!" The high raised eyebrows are known to be a tell when trying to convince someone of something that isn't true. The high pitch, too.

Watch some politicians speak. Not during a prepared speech, but during an interview where they act like they are just on TV to have a conversation. They are actually saying something so you then can repeat it to others as if it's your own opinion. Most people do it without realizing it. This is another reason that the TV fights for your attention. It also overrides your intuition by getting you emotionally invested and excited about their topics. The negative emotions are much louder than your inner knowing. So, if you watch, watch it while observing without emotion. It will change the way you watch TV.

You will notice in many cases, news actors' breath has too many exhales, inhales and pauses. If you are watching the TV while listening to it, the sensory illusion makes you think this is normal. Close your eyes to listen or leave the room, and you will know that the breathing patterns often don't make any sense. It's almost like they don't know where to put a breath or a sigh compared to the idea that breath normally comes in a flow.

Fine-tune your physical senses so they trickle to your non-physical senses, and continue to learn to trust your awareness again. The more you fine-tune your physical senses, the more you will notice non-physical, out of the ordinary, so you will notice more natural strangeness, which leads to more awareness of your inner guidance system.

For example, when you intuitively know someone is lying, but you really, really, really want to believe them because you care about them and hope what they are saying is true. If they say they are being honest, and you choose to believe them, even though your inner guide screams danger, this creates a crack in your inner knowing system that will need to be repaired. Repairing it takes work, which takes time because you have to calibrate it and learn the feeling again.

It's a shame when your intuition tells you something, but you don't trust it because someone is telling you something is true, and you really want to believe it. It's also a shame when intuition is overridden by emotions, so you can't hear and feel the truth. Both lead to time wasted and emotional or physical pain.

To avoid this, stay out of your strong emotions of greed, anger, desire, lust, hope, and others that give off louder energy transmissions than your gentle inner guidance of intuition unless you know you are in a place that is safe for you to have these feelings.

2.28 Healers, Energy Fields, And Magnetic Fields

This message is for healers and for those who want to knowingly energetically connect with others.

If you hold a magnet next to a plastic little figurine, nothing noticeable will happen. Imagine the plastic figuring is going to a healer. The healer is a metal magnet. The plastic figurine just isn't going to feel the magnetism, however anyone made of metal will feel the energy pulling or pushing immediately. Plastic is not magnetic, no matter what you do or how you try. It does have an energy field, but the field may not be obvious when connecting to something magnetic. There is always an energy field. It is often invisible until proper matching energies come together.

A healer may connect to many people, but one person may not have the right receptivity or may have blockages that take time to get through. This can leave the healer feeling unsuccessful, and it will also make the client feel unsuccessful, so the healer might choose to not work on that person again or maybe he will give it one more try.

The healer may also sense that the client is challenging them because they don't believe in energy healing, and so the healer may either want to prove to them that they can get well, or the healer may not want to be around that energy.

Ultimately, there will be someone better attuned to the client. Both healer and client want to be successful as healer and healee. There will be someone out there who is a match to the 'magnetic' force that they are able to receive, so to speak. Plastic is not magnetic, though, so if you, as a healer are not getting through to the person, consider they are of a material that doesn't match with your magnetism.

After a few sessions with a different practitioner, the blockage that kept you from doing your amazing work with them may be removed and you may get another chance to make a difference in their life. This is why it's good to have a number of healers in your circle. It's helpful to be able to refer out and also to ask questions about what they did when the client has some nice changes.

Nevertheless, the energy field is always there. In the online course, I have a video of how the magnetic field is invisible but still affects metal shavings to show an example.

2.29 Déjà Vu. How To Use It.

Déjà vu: Intuition is giving you a cheat code for your future. Suddenly, it feels like you've been here before. This has already happened. It might even feel like this right now as you read this page.

This is the secret of Déjà vu. Déjà vu is a flash back to an intuitive message you already received but you didn't notice at the time. Déjà vu is the 2nd time you are getting the message. If you got the message the first time, there would be no Déjà vu.

When you have the experience of Deja vu, don't waste time. Drop in and feel how it feels. See if it travels you back in your mind's calendar to when you first received the message. Find the feeling of it, but get out of the way and let your passive attention notice it. You have to be gentle, like you are following a breeze, or you will miss it. Find the pattern of what it feels like. Déjà vu is part of the code or tools to become a master of intuition and then on to manifestation.

When you get the intuitive message at the time it is given to you, you will have less déjà vu because it has no need to show up. You got the message on time! But in time, déjà vu returns because as you become more sensitive, a new softer level of messages comes up to the surface. There are always deeper layers.

Déjà vu is key, like a cheat code in a video game. It's letting you know you are at an important moment or fork in the road. It may not feel important, but sometimes, the small moments lead to finding your life partner, getting a job, or buying that lottery ticket. It doesn't have to seem like a critical life path moment, but it is an option to change something that will change your future. It's exactly like intuition giving you little steps one way or the other until they lead to a bigger picture that you couldn't have known just from each small step you followed until you arrived.

Déjà vu is meant to be a clue to revelations. The more you quiet your mind, the more déjà vu you have. The more déjà vu you have, the more intuition you discover. The more intuition you have, the more you are guided on your life path. The more you are on your path, the more clear you are. The more clear you are, the more you manifest everything you want.

2.30 Exercise: EFT To Break Programming

Let's release the negative conditioning and programming and then check to see how much better you can feel. Let's use your breath as your gauge. Follow along, tap the different Meridien points and say the phrases out loud to help release some hidden programs. You are saying the things that you will be clearing. You may feel like you don't want to say these statements because they don't seem true, but you are telling them to let go of the parts of them that you may have

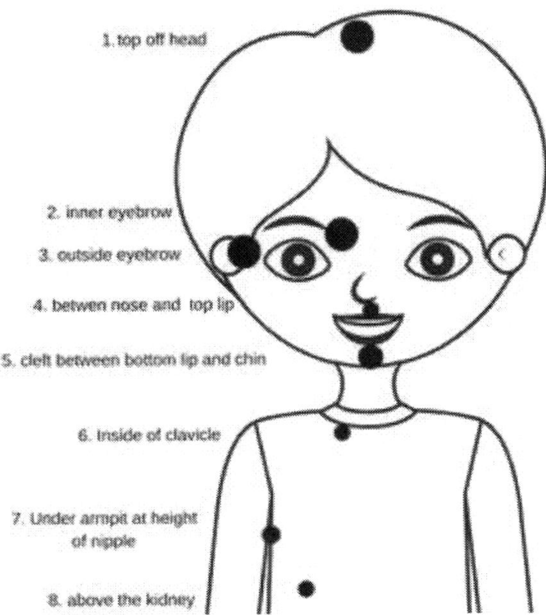

Tapping Points for EFT

that are hidden. EFT releases patterns and beliefs that are both known and unknown.

The EFT tapping points are listed here. Say the words out loud as you tap.

- First, tap the side of your hand on the blade of your palm known as the karate chop point. Tap 5 to 10 times on it for each sentence. Tap continuously as you repeat these sentences out loud.
- Even though I can't feel my breath as much as I would like, I deeply and completely love and accept myself.
- Even though I have programmed beliefs that I don't even know are there, I deeply and completely love and accept myself.

- Even though I am not sure I can be intuitive and manifest what I want, and even though I know I'm already getting information from my subconscious and creating my life to some extent, I deeply and completely love and accept myself.
- Then tap the top of the head while saying…My breath. I don't notice a big difference.
- Then tap the top of the inner eye brow bone while saying... I don't know if I trust it.
- Then tap the outside corner of the eye socket…how does this work?
- Then tap just below the eye in the center of the bone… This doesn't make sense.
- Then tap the space between the bottom of your nose and your lip… I can't manifest
- Then tap the space between your bottom lip and your chin… I'm not in charge of my intuition.
- Then tap the space at the top inner side of your first rib where it meets your clavicle…. I'm not aware of it.
- Then tap under your armpit at the height of the nipple…I can't learn this.
- Then tap on the ribs above the kidney, drawing a line strain down from the nipple… My intuition.

Go back to the top of your head and start again. You may feel like you want to tap certain areas longer. If you do, do it.

- Then tap the top of the head while saying…Self-trust
- Then tap the top of the inner eye brow bone while saying... Trusting in my guidance.

- Then tap the outside corner of the eye socket ...My intuition isn't strong.
- Then tap just below the eye in the center of the bone... I'm not sure I can manifest.
- Then tap the space between the bottom of your nose and your lip... I can't manifest.
- Then tap the space between your bottom lip and your chin...Life could be random.
- Then tap the space at the top inner side of your first rib where it meets your clavicle.... I don't trust.
- Then tap under your armpit at the height of the nipple...I don't know if I can do this.
- Then tap on the ribs above the kidney, drawing a line strain down from the nipple... I'm not sure about this.

Something is clearing for you. After a second round is done, take a breath and relax.

Do you feel lighter and clearer? Any time you clear a pattern or programming layer, you also clear things attached to it and new levels of awareness can come to your surface for you. Run it again and see how much deeper you clear. After doing it a few times over a few days, change the words if you want to. Your subconscious will tell you what words to use.

2.31 Developing Contrast To Find the Message.

If you have eaten some chocolate mousse and then afterwards eat a banana, the banana will not taste as sweet.

If you have had no sweet foods for a week and have the same banana, it will taste very sweet. Contrast helps you notice and become aware of slight, subtle differences.

If you are always busy and not often committed to quiet or stillness, it's more difficult to notice the quiet inner voice and feelings while you are in the noise. It can seem foreign to notice the stillness if you haven't become familiar with it yet. It's not that it's hard to notice, but it's that you don't have the receptors to notice it easily yet. Once you purposely observe the messages just a handful of times, you build up the noticing muscle. Like building any skill, it takes practice until it's got an energy pathway formed. Then, you can be busy and noisy and still be aware of the quiet and important messages that you are being sent. It is true that as you do these practices, you will enjoy quiet and stillness even more, but who wouldn't when you know you are going to get secret messages and guidance and make your life better almost effortlessly at the same time.

Let's get to the place where you can notice the tiny difference in contrast until it becomes obvious. Get quieter than the noise and quieter than the quiet voice of your intuition so it speaks as loudly or even louder than your thoughts. Continue doing the stillness meditation exercises so the difference becomes clear. You will know it when you have that AHA moment. You will be aware when your mind is at a quiet enough level and an intuition message bubbles up. Every day, you will get quieter inside until you hear what you didn't know you could.

2.32 Karmically Aware And Careful.

As you continue to learn to awaken your abilities, you automatically become a better person. The reason is that you are connecting to your inner guide that cares about you more than you care about you. What this means is that you begin to understand altruism at a new level because you are now giving it to yourself.

You are now feeling more of what others are feeling, and you are aware of it. You may even know why they are feeling it. This all occurs from a more broad perspective. It's usually a non-judgmental or neutral space. This state of mind is important. Your empathic abilities can, at times, be a challenge to use but not for what you might think. The reason is because you are open to the rubber-band effect or Karmic effect.

When you become sensitive, what you put out comes back fast. If you cause others emotional pain, you will have it at some point, too, and often immediately. This is the burden of awakening your abilities. You get more, but you also must be more mindful to do the right thing. The right thing doesn't mean over extending yourself or always being available to help, because you have to do the right thing for yourself, too. You will figure it out fast because you will get your energy depleted if you don't make sure you are blessing and honoring yourself, too.

Likewise, when you help someone to feel good, you get the benefit on multiple levels. You feel good, and your higher self and neural pathways thank you with an upward cycle and spiral of more good feelings and experiences. Good builds more pathways for more good. Being in this state allows you to manifest more easily because you are in a higher and more coherent or clear frequency and in a consistent state of gratitude. Even the people who worked in the military's remote viewing program, which was (maybe still is) a psychic training and spying program, said that once you connect with the past, present and future, it makes you want to work for The Good For Humanity team, which means good for the whole ecosystem of the planet and universe.

In relationships, this plays out even better. You are with your loving partner or spouse. You do something that you know will make them feel good. You see and feel their happiness, which makes you feel good. They see and feel your happiness, which leads to them feeling even better because they want you to feel good, and they are empathizing with your feelings. Then you feel their happiness, and it's a spiral upward like a Fibonacci sequence of numbers getting higher and with more energy until you are both elevated in the experience and your lives. Then you laugh and love and feel like you are floating in the air. Enjoy it!! Write it down! What have you learned here? What is your life like with these new perspectives?

Take a minute and find deeply what you are thankful for in your life. Close your eyes and feel it, increasing that gratitude like it's the greatest gift you've ever received. Thank your inner guide, thank god, thank yourself for showing up so you didn't miss it when it was ready for you. Gratitude is the greatest of states. It's a cycle state. You are giving thanks and feeling/receiving gratitude, which is also thanks at the same time. Your heart is open. It is transmitting and receiving on high power. You send out the thanks, and you feel the thanks like a beautiful, massive cyclical engine that keeps going from mind to heart, moving so much energy. Feel it and remember it so you can use it again and again by finding, remembering or creating reasons you have to be thankful for.

2.33 Wake Up The Heart Even More.

Before we get to the next part of the book, let's WAKE UP THE HEART even more!

There are many meditations to access your heart and fill it with love and energy. A gratitude meditation is a perfect way to do that, but I'm going to give you a physical way that I discovered.

I discovered that when we see a concert or performance that we love, we want to stand up and cheer. We clap like it means the world to us. It's as if clapping is actually giving the performer our energy something, and we are.

When you clap "wholeheartedly," you are actually using your hands as antenna or radar dishes and clapping the energy of your big happy heart chakra that this person just activated for you. You are amplifying the energy of your heart through your clapping hands like a funnel and pumping it at the person you are loving at that moment. It's automatic and natural to put your hands in front of your heart to clap for a reason. There may be times you clap with your hands in your lap, but you know you don't really want to clap at that time, and you are doing it because it's kind of expected. When it's from your heart and generates excitement, your hands go to your heart level immediately. You can choose to feel happy inside and clap at any time to energize someone.

This is how you do it for yourself. When you are clapping for someone with all of that love and appreciation, close your outer palms when your hands come together. It's a little awkward to clap this way, so try it. Clap with the pinky side of your hands coming together and leave the inside of your hands open towards yourself. Your hands will look like you are holding an open book. Clap like this and feel what it feels like to have your heart energy amplified back to you. It's like using your hands as a funnel to shout through so your voice is louder. It's a very powerful feeling. It will wake up your heart and its energy field. Try it now. Think of and feel something you have deep gratitude for and remember to try it when you are at a performance to feel the difference in the strength. Send me a video about how it feels for you. I may post it on my website or social media.

Write about your experience in your journal.

2.34 Congratulations!

Congratulations on completing Part 2!

By now, you will have noticed if you did the exercises, life has already changed for you. You are noticing things that you have never noticed before, and you are having more inspiring and WOW moments as you realize that your natural born gifts, skills and abilities are showing themselves and growing.

You are likely noticing the connection between your inner messages and outer events and can see the flow of life as a clearer journey. As you look at these moments and see the path that intuitively led you to now, this very present moment, you can realize that you can trust that the same path also continues in front of you, guiding you perfectly and quietly. The messages become so much more clear and obvious as you recognize them.

You are starting to understand the meaning of "Every moment is a crystal ball" at a higher and deeper level now.

Keep up your practicing. Run through the exercises again and then again. These aren't one-off exercises. You can reinforce the new pathways that you are forming in your brain and the rest of your nervous system, bio-electrical field and your conscious mind. The training wheels are off. Now, let's go full speed.

Part 3

3.1 The Present Pre-Sent Moment.

Let's get started with using it.

The present moment has been hidden from you. Calling it the present moment makes you think it is simply the moment that you are in right now. It is. That is true, but that's not the whole story. We are taught that being in the present moment is where we can be happy. It's partially true but truer is that in the present moment, we MUST choose to be happy as much as possible. Why?

In the present moment, we are constantly creating the future. The present moment is a bridge in time to your future.

Let me explain. The moment you are now in was created from an intention and frequency in the past. I have an explanation for how it works in the physical world, but it's still being developed. This moment and this experience that you are in right now was sent to you here from the past to wait for you when you arrived here. It's like you sent yourself a package from California to New York and then hopped on a plane to fly to New York and when you arrived the package you sent from the past was waiting for you when you arrived. It was sent to you in advance based on your thoughts and feelings, intention and frequency or emotion of choice you were giving off. The moments you are experiencing are packaged as an event or a 'significant group of moments' that are happening together for what you are experiencing in your life right now. If you were in the moment or a single moment right here, there is no story because a story doesn't happen in a single moment, although change can. The story is attached when many moments come together to be grouped as a story. Just like a still photo has an image but no story, then when you add many moving pictures, you get a movie with a story.

The experience you are having now was pre-sent to you from the past. The present moment is meant to be known as the *pre-sent* moment.

This is the key to all of it. When you know that the moment you are in now is creating your future, you won't choose anger because anger will continue creating anger. You will consciously choose happiness if you know you are creating it right here and now, so it becomes your future.

So, the moment you are in now was Pre-Sent to you. It was sent in advance to meet you when you arrive. It was sent before this current moment happened. As you read this and are learning about consciousness and all of the things in this book, you planned this in the past before you actually purchased this book. You set yourself up to have the feelings you are having now.

You are pre-sending every moment you are in to your future. When you grasp this, when you see this clearly, when you hear what I am saying and understand it, you will make this moment and any moment you are aware that you are in, the most important moment of your life, because you know it is creating the rest of your life.

Every time you mani**fest** by choosing to become **fest**ive and create in the pre-sent moment with intention, you change your frequency to become closer to who you want to be. Each meditation gets you clearer. Each time you do it, you are working from a closer place to who you want to be for the next time you do it. You are starting the day closer to your goals finish line each time you do this.

The longer you hold the frequency, which is the emotion and energy of what it is you want right now, right here, the sooner it will arrive. The more you do it, the more you practice it, the more of it will show up for you. The more you practice it, the more your energy field will change to become that frequency more of the time. Like meditation, stray thoughts come in and distract you. They make you question or worry. It's natural. We are trained to do that. Meditation teaches you to train your mind to focus. Recognizing the Pre-sent moment is helped by meditation to help you train your mind's choices.

This is why some people seem to just flow through life with good things happening. They are already in that frequency because it's been experienced by them so many times. They have the opposite of PTSD. They expect good things to happen because they always do. Some people seem to have every bad thing happen to them. They also get stuck in a frequency that they want to stay in, and they think this is just the lot they have to settle for in life. Until they are ready, no one can convince them otherwise.

The solution is: Choose your emotions. Get selfish. Make it a game for yourself and choose a positive experience, then live it internally. Imagine it and feel it as if it's your life right now as a 360 degrees reality. Your frequency will change right here, right now.

I've got a library full of guided meditations on this topic on the website.

Present Pre-Sent Moment instructions for manifestation.

- Get comfortable. Breath and relax your body.
- Search for a guided meditation for manifestation on YouTube or my website.

Once you relax your body and feel yourself detach from it, bring in your intention. Make your intention real. Make your intention now. Do NOT say, I can't wait for a relationship. Imagine you have the relationship right now. Make it real right now. Next, as you do this, feel the feelings of how you feel having this experience now. How will you feel if you have it? How do you feel in this meditative reality now that you have it? Once you have it, make it as real as you can in your 5 senses. Feel the goodness and the happiness. Look over at your partner in the relationship and smile at them. Tell them how happy you are that they are here with you. Feel the love from your partner. Give them the love you have for them. Hold them. Feel it and make it real. What are you saying to them? What did they say to you? Hear it and feel how it feels.

It's natural to have conflicting thoughts, which lead to conflicting feelings. You prove this work to yourself by choosing to believe it or by doing it and living the results. You may slip out of the positive state you created and you may have an inner voice being negative. Say to that part of you, "Thanks for trying to protect me, but I'm putting you down for now while I do this work. If you are needed, I will pick you back up later. For now, this work will give me what I need. Thank you." Shut a door on it and get back to feeling the feeling fully. The more you feel it, the longer you feel it and make it real, the faster you will get the changes. You are now a giant Gong vibrating the relationship frequency. The universe has felt it through all time and space and the frequency is matching with your divine partner.

You are pre-sending this feeling and frequency as a new present moment for you to arrive at in the future, so make it exactly as you want it. Every brainwave is visible as a frequency. It's got a small electrical charge. It's a current that will find its matching current. Your heart also has a frequency with every beat that can be seen on a monitor. You are a transmitter and receiver of frequency. All of these frequencies have meaning. So create and choose the frequency of brainwaves that will manifest the future that you want in your life.

Health:

How can something like this change someone's health? This one is even easier to explain.

Think about someone who has issues around anger. They seem angry all the time. This can lead to high blood pressure, hormonal imbalance, skin issues, and faster aging. Someone who feels peaceful and happy looks happier, younger and has more happy hormones that create better health.

An example of imagining better health.

If you had trouble with your hand, and it didn't function the way it was supposed to due to a trauma, imagine yourself in this pre-sent moment moving your hands, feeling how good it feels to feel this free. Feel how happy you are to have the ability to use your hand again! You can use a spoon properly. You can pump gas, you can play the piano, or touch your partner or children. How great is it that you can brush your hair again? I'm giving you examples so you can apply it to any health issue.

You might see yourself at the doctor and see him telling you that the test can't explain it, but you are completely healed. Feel how you feel when you hear them say that to you. Go home and tell your friends and family, and show them. See your life's future in a week, a month and a year doing all the things you can do now. Do this everyday, throughout the day, and see how your body changes.

This is an example, and it's not medical advice at all, but positive thinking, along with whatever your doctor recommends can only help the situation. There are miracles that happen for people who do this every day, multiple times a day. When you change your mind and your frequency consistently enough, you are ringing a bell that can change your life in every way you can imagine.

Wealth and freedom

All of the principles are the same. Look at your checking account balance. How does it feel to see that big, exciting balance? Bring the gifts home for yourself and others and notice what it feels like to feel that proud of yourself and see how happy they are. They are happy that you brought them a gift, but even more happy that you got what you wanted. Make the feelings real. Make it now. Feel it and real it. See how your life is because of this moment when you live your future. Congratulate yourself from the future for doing this now. See yourself 1 month from now telling yourself, “I love my life. I did it. I'm finally financially free.” And, feel how that feels.

A manifestation tip.

This is a way to practice your manifesting when you feel like your thoughts are telling you that you are unworthy of having what you want.

Choose something with low stakes. Of course, you want to manifest the partner of your dreams, the money, the health, the freedom, but at times, a voice whispers or even shouts that you can’t have it, and it doesn’t make sense because there are so many obstacles.

Here is a solution. Practice. Practice with something low stakes.

Why?

No matter what, you have to learn to drop into and create an intention and then make it real in your emotions as if you have it right now. If you are having trouble feeling like you own a huge jet plane right now because you don’t believe you can have it, then build trust with your manifesting abilities by first choosing something simpler.

Decide to manifest $20 coming to you. You aren't too attached to it, so you won’t have conflicting emotions. Make it real. Feel how you will feel when you receive it. Feel how happy you are that it worked so quickly.

See and feel the feeling of many people giving you $20 if you wish.

This is a great way to build trust with Layer One of your mind's connection to the source of everything. Once you know the formulas are real, you trust the formula and understand how it works. As you have more trust, then choose something with higher stakes that you really want, so it's easier for you to hold the state you need to hold.

If you are connected to the creator, then you must have had a part in being created.

3.2 Medical Intuition

Now that you are able to see the aura let's put it to practical use to learn about health. Either find a partner or go somewhere where you can look at someone who will be staying in the same spot for a few minutes. Do a quick scan of their body with your eyes. Just give them a quick look up and down without stopping.

Now, do it again, but activate your aura vision. Do it without looking for anything specific. Just see the person's aura or have the relaxed gaze or soft eyes that lead to seeing the aura while you scan from up to down or down to up. Where do your eyes catch or feel grabbed? Notice where your eyes wanted to stop, but as you feel that, keep going on with the scan of the whole body. You may notice something catching your attention slightly off the body, as well. Make a note of it for yourself.

Your eye scan will allow you to glance over their system or body and notice something. Normally, you wouldn't notice anything because it's not a magnetic or attractive enough pull to keep your eyes there when you are busy, but now you are paying attention.

Now that you know how to pay attention using Passive Attention, allow your body to feel what it feels while you scan with your eyes.

You will notice that as your eyes catch on an area, your body, or your mind, or your breath will feel different. You may feel as if gravity has changed and you are being pulled at a different angle than just downwards. You may want to move, shift or twist your body so you can connect with the feeling, too. It is similar to when you throw a bowling ball down the lane, and as it curves toward the gutter, you turn and twist your body to get it to curve back to the middle pins.

Once you notice the feeling, your eyes catch more easily on the area waiting to be noticed. That part of the person may feel like it has some edges to it that could grab a thread on a sweater, but it's just energy, and it's grabbing your eye's attention.

Now, you are using both visual and feeling abilities, so it's easier to hone in on it. It's like seeing out in the distance with two eyes instead of one eye. Two eyes give a more accurate perspective.

What do you do with this information? Now that you are scanning the body, it's time to ask questions.

If you know someone well, you can ask questions more easily, but at the same time if you know the person well, you may already have an impression and beliefs about them. In this case, you have to drop out of what you think you know and imagine you know nothing about them. This keeps your beliefs from getting involved to not let you see rightly.

Practice doing this with strangers while taking a walk. You don't need to know what you are seeing. Just notice that your eyes are getting caught on different areas. You will quickly become aware that the health issues you have had will be the ones you notice most easily on others. The reason is because it's familiar to you. You have resonated with it in the past, so you connect to it on others.

Ask questions to know if you are correct in a tactful way. You are talking about someone's health issue that they may not even know about or that they haven't shared with others. You might say, "There is some stuck energy over here. Do you know of anything going on in this area?" They may say, "Is that where my kidney is? I have been out lately having drinks. Could that be it?"

You may notice that your eyes notice something when passing their lungs. Notice how your body feels. Tune in. Your eyes tell you to notice, so add to it now by seeing how your "feeling" system feels it. Often, the lungs can be emotional. Fear or anxiety can cause restrictions in the lungs or breath.

Practice letting your eyes scan anytime you don't have to be paying attention to activities. You will notice how often your eyes get caught on different areas. As you may have guessed, this will relate to noticing many other things besides medical intuition and lead to more synchronicity because you are spending more time consciously on the edge of your subconscious. Each skill you develop from practicing these exercises touches a skill next to it, so by learning one, you are already part of the way to learning another. It's done that way on purpose to make the next one easier and always create progress. If ever you don't practice an exercise, you may develop the new skill anyway because you started the ball rolling with the exercise before.

Caution. Do not hold the feeling of the other person's stuck energy area for long. You may be tempted to follow it deeper and learn more about the person to see what your new ability will show you. Don't do it. You don't want to resonate with it for more than a passing moment. That's all you need.

Early on, I picked up the symptoms of many patients. The reason was that if you start resonating with the symptoms at deeper, energetic levels, they may well become your symptoms. Avoid going too deep, or you can make their health concern your health concern.

3.3 Using your Medical Intuition Vision And Feelings For Becoming Aware Of Interconnectedness Of Life.

You now have your eyes trained to shift into a scanning state, and you can go into the passive attention state and let your eyes be in scanning mode at the same time.

It's time to scan as much as you want to while you are taking a walk.

If you are in a safe area that you know well, do this. It will lead you to begin to notice the interconnectedness of moments and of things. You will notice the tree and then see what its energy is connected to. "Every Moment is a Crystal Ball" will become apparent in this very receptive state as new awarenesses and intuitive messages appear.

It will be like following invisible spider webs that tie different moments and things together for you. It will also seem like you are imagining it at first. You may also feel like you have "lost track of time" if you walk like this for a while because you are in an altered state, so make sure you know your environment and come back to normal attention when crossing a street.

Touching on the edge of your subconscious while walking is similar to a style of practice in meditation, which is to meditate with eyes slightly open with a relaxed gaze a few feet in front of you on the floor. Most people are more comfortable meditating with their eyes closed because it's easier to go within when in a dark space and without visuals. You may want to begin practicing your meditation with your eyes open to see how it feels. Do it for just a few minutes out of each session. As you practice it, you will be able to shift more easily while going about your day.

3.4 Exercise: Medical Intuition

Energy Health Reading

Some knowledge of anatomy is helpful here, or you will sense something is not right or out of balance, but you won't be able to get as specific about what the issue might be. Do a web search on the skeleton and organs so the areas of the body and their names are more familiar.

If you keep seeing people who have similar health concerns to one that you have had, it's because you tend to see or notice in others what you have had yourself. It may be a 100th monkey principle, where you help people with that condition, so more come to you, knowingly or unknowingly. It has to do with familiarity to frequency and vibration. You know the tone of the injury that you have had, so when you notice that your eyes get pulled to someone's ankle or hernia, you may even feel your already healed injury having some tension. You are resonating with it, and your body remembers.

Some common examples:

- I tend to see hernias because I've had a couple.
- I tend to notice or feel irregular heartbeats because I can be prone to them.
- Hyperthyroid has a certain energy and movement.
- High blood pressure has traits that are physical and many can see, but it has an energetic state, too.
- Low blood pressure tends to have a soft feel to it, like the energy of soft spaghetti or like vessels that don't have enough pressure to move the fluids around. These are visual, too.

Each of these examples will give you ideas on how you may see or feel what you notice. As you practice this skill, you may notice that it becomes a little tiring. It's because you are accessing a part of your mind that takes effort like paying attention takes effort, and then you are exchanging information with someone and receiving some of the energy you are connecting with.

3.5 Empaths: No More Fear Of Overwhelm Going To Crowded Events

Scan and know the room.

For a sensitive empath, going out to events is sometimes very difficult. You are excited to go, and then at the last minute, you don't feel like going. You likely feel exhausted before you go. You can easily get overwhelmed and want to leave early. This is the easiest way to go forward when feeling that way. You are going to actually go and use your ability to enhance your skills, while learning how to keep it in check.

Here are the instructions. Go into your passive attention state and make this event a fun exercise.

Prepare yourself as if you are fortified and protected by a force field. You don't have to imagine there is a force field but keep your energy close to you. Don't enter in an open state yet. Walk into a room and scan it with your eyes and like with medical intuition, feel the feelings, feel the angle of energy or emotions and how it pulls on you.

Where are you drawn to? Go with it and see where it leads. Alway be mindful of safety when you do this. Not everyone is trustworthy, even if you are pulled to them. I know that because if you are in a more open state, sometimes it feels ok to be more trusting, so keep your "observer" mind active and use discernment. You are in the experience but also watching and observing the experience. For me, it is like there is ME in the experience and another ME floating above watching the experience. I'm in both at the same time. You can imagine there is a you that has no emotions, almost like a parent, floating above you and following you. You see the room from in your body and from above yourself.

Notice which couple is having a good night. Feel which couple had a fight before they arrived. Make some goals, but don't pressure yourself. Just feel. Don't say to yourself, "I am going to figure out what happened in the next room I enter." This will make it more difficult because you are taking your mind to the conscious and analytical level. No need for that here.

What you really want to do is walk into the room and let your passive attention act like a radar guiding you. Acknowledge what you notice. You don't have to know what it is yet; you just have to give yourself a small congratulations for getting a feeling or a "hit." Crawl, then walk, then run. When you got the "hit" or the "knowing" of something, you were likely feeling unattached, relaxed and in your passive state. You may have even forgotten what you were planning to do. You made space for new information. This becomes normal as you practice it more often.

Keep something to write notes in with you to transfer into your journal later. Taking notes adds to the experience and keeps you empathically safe by giving you another way to separate yourself from the others.

Remember the feeling of being in the shower with the water hitting you. Feel that feeling for a moment if you slip out of your inner state that is touching your Layer One. It's fine to slip out and back to the more conscious mind. This is normal, and it's a great practice to slip in and slip back out. You build a muscle, so it allows you to do it consciously when you want to, like opening your eyes and then deciding to close your eyes. At first, changing levels of consciousness often can cause fatigue, but after a while, it's like blinking your eyelids, and when you get tired, you can sleep it off after the event.

3.6 Exercise 1: Touch And Know

Exercise requirement: A partner.

In the Layer One Mind, The Quantum, Field or Morphic field, information has no boundary. How is it that we can get a glimpse of the future? Does it mean knowing the past is available, too? Yes, and the past is easier than the future because it has happened already. You are going to practice Touching and Knowing information through your touch.

Relax, take a deep breath, and with permission, put your hand on someone that you know little about. Don't think, don't ask to receive, just relax and get out of the way. You may get a feeling that begins to translate into an image or a sudden pop of awareness that the person ate yellow food coloring, and that's why they feel strange. You may get a sense of something and then begin to get a sense that you are close, but not exact. So, refine the feeling. It's like hanging a painting and moving it a little to the left and then a little to the right until it's just right.

This exercise is intention-based. You aren't trying to find their secrets or health problems. That's not what this is about. This is about something light and fluffy. This is seeing what comes up when you do this. You are skimming off of the top and not going deep at all. It helps you get a fast sense of someone when you first see them.

This is related to Foundational Breath, which you have practiced at least once a day by now and are using regularly without even needing to think about it. By now, you know that you sometimes don't know the answer using the breath immediately, but you have to bounce the idea back and forth in your mind, like hitting a ping pong ball between 2 rackets, bringing the rackets closer and closer until they have gone from wider apart to more specific. This is how it works with Touching and Knowing. You get the impression and then you begin to feel if it's right, or if it's similar, but not yet exact. Then, keep feeling it until you pinpoint the answer in the map in your mind.

3.7 Not Yet Reproduced In A Waking State.

One of the most unusual experiences that happened to me.

This is for your consideration only. It's just to give you additional thoughts on what is possible. This is to mention that as you spend more time in the realm of deeper consciousness exploring your innate and emerging abilities, strange things will happen, and if they seem valuable, find the energy patterns of what made it occur and map them out so you can reproduce them.

A few years ago, I had something happen for the first time and only time so far. I have been waiting for it to happen again so I can find a pattern to map it and see what state of being or frequency sets it off. I need to find the tone of it so I can drop into it and discover further. Here is what happened.

I was with a client talking about a product I loved and also sold. I had a very strong experience of Déjà vu. I said to her, "I'm having Deja vú." She said, "Oh really?" I said, "Yes, and now that you said "Oh, Really," I knew you were going to say that, too." She laughed and said something else. I kept the rest of this experience to myself as it went on because I didn't want to sound too strange. When she spoke next, I knew the words before they came from her mouth. Then I said my response, and I knew/realized that I knew that I was going to say it already.

Next was the big surprise. I got ahead of the timeline. I knew what she would say next, then I knew what I would say next, and I watched the conversation played out in my head. It was as if I had the script in my mind and I was reading ahead of the scene.

It got to the point where I saw where the conversation was going, and I knew she really needed the product, but when the price came up and we talked about the cost, she said no. The product had helped her in so many ways already, but the trial period was over. My only option was to try a different answer than the one that my mind was showing me in advance. My new answer didn't work out either, and in changing the answer that I was shown, I could no longer see into the future of what was next.

I don't know how long this experience would have lasted if I stayed with the exact words from the information I was seeing in my mind. Also interesting was that I could see the timeline playing out in front of me for as long as I stayed within the boundaries of the conversation. The moment I changed it, I was in Nowhere land. I was in the unknown, the place where any potential could be created. I didn't know that at the time, but I know it now.

Waking up every day knowing our pattern is easy, but changing the pattern that isn't serving us is a risk worth taking over and over until we find the answers. Finding a mentor, coach, or guide makes it easier, as they have been there already.

Have you had any experiences that were very unusual and have not yet been reproduced? Grab your journal and write down your thoughts. If you have had this one happen to you, I would love to hear about it.

3.8 Tai Chi, Chi Gong, Super Slow Movement

The super slow movement is a great way to slow your mind and body and develop new awareness of time, consciousness and physicality.

Adding Tai Chi or Qi Gong to your practice is even better. The reason is that you are doing a super slow movement but also working in the energetic tracks or space that energy masters discovered thousands of years ago. You are following a trail that has already been cleared for you, so you will be getting to a specific destination that was already carved out.

By doing Tai Chi and at the same time using your passive attention and energy-feeling abilities, you will dramatically enhance your practice.

Think about this: If you read the same paragraph every day that was a positive affirmation, after day 50, you know it well. After day 100, it's in your blood. On day 101, if you read it mindfully and someone changed it, if there was an added word or a word missing, you would notice it immediately.

This is the same with tai chi or super slow movement. After a short time, you will notice things you have never noticed. Changes in your body, in your mind, in energy as you do these movements. You will notice the movements get easier and smoother, and then you will notice you can do it more slowly or more quickly and find new hidden energies and also areas where the energy is blocked in your body within the movements.

I was practicing Tai Chi for a short time with Oliver in Miami. One morning, as we did some loosening exercises I noticed a new energy. I was in awe at that moment as I felt it and saw it. As Oliver would move to one side, that side of his body would turn red, as he moved back to the other side, that side of his body lit up in blue. I felt it in myself at the same time. That was awesome. Even more awesome was the awareness that this energy was new to me, but it was always there! I had to become sensitive enough to notice it. It reminded me of the infinite levels of energy there are that I don't yet know. It's like learning to see the aura. It's always been there, but you haven't been there yet to see it until you know how. Now that you are sensitized to it, you can see it anytime. It's there even when you aren't looking or seeing it, like all energy.

3.9 Advanced Intuitives And Empaths: Patterns

An advanced intuitive naturally pays attention with different parts of their body and mind.

Nothing happens by chance. If you eat something and get food poisoning, you quickly figure out that it's related.

If you have slight stomach discomfort, someone who is self-aware recognizes it's related to the food, especially if there is a pattern. Still, many won't notice it either.

If you eat meat and have pain in your toe, it may be from developing the acidic condition of gout, but a toe is a strange place for pain to show up from eating food, so one may not think it's connected.

Before you paid attention, a sore toe would have seemed unrelated to what you eat, but now you are sensitive enough to find the pattern. Pattern recognition shows relationships. It is the basis for becoming a highly advanced intuitive, empath and manifestor. Why is this? Because you learn to recognize the state of mind or state of being you are in when something good happens for you, and then you learn to access or drop into that state on demand.

An advanced empath will choose their emotional state as needed. You already know how. It's not always easy. There are times that emotions are so powerful that you can't or don't want to hold them back, but most of the time, you can change your state just by choosing to and follow some steps, which may include a good cry or punching a pillow or something that Tony Robbins does to change your state fast.

First comes choosing. Then, it gets easier. Being conscious that when you are in a "bad mood," you can also change it if you choose to is the major step. Once you can teach your mind to remember that, you have options.

Still, being conscious of your abilities is a choice, and it's not always easy.

One more tip for Empaths

Meditation will keep you and your brainwaves balanced and in your control, but it will also open you up to receiving others' frequencies much more clearly. When you better know who you are, you will recognize when the feelings you are feeling are coming from outside of you.

3.10 Exercise 1: Energy From A Distance.

You know what energy feels like now and you are feeling it whenever you put your attention on it, and sometimes without meaning to.

Place your hand on your arm. Now, lightly touch your arm. Feel the heat and the pressure of your skin against your skin. Breathe at a relaxed pace and gently remove your hand from your arm. Just a quarter inch. Move your hand side to side so you can feel movement in the form of heat, energy or magnetic pressure.

Now that you feel the energy of your arm with your hand as heat or tingling or just aware of a presence, move another quarter inch away. Do this again from this distance. Do it until you are 2 or 3 inches away. Do you feel the energy? If you don't feel it, go back to touching your arm and lifting off again. Once you feel it, move a quarter inch away and hold it there longer. If it's only heat that you feel, notice how your body feels as you feel it. Heat is a good parameter but look for something else, too. This will lead to distant healing work as you feel the difference and the changes in your body.

Now, do it again, but this time, notice the energy of your hand with your arm instead of noticing the energy of your arm with your hands. Which one is easier to do? Most find that feeling the hands or fingers' energy on the arm is much easier at first.

Write the difference in your journal and contemplate what is different, easier or less noticeable about each one.

Let's talk about energy fields. Magnetic Fields are invisible until we find a way to notice them. If you lay some magnetic filings on top of a sheet of glass or a piece of paper, they lay dormant, but there is an energy field there that you can notice with your eyes. Pick up a magnet and put it under the glass or paper. How far away can it be before the magnetic filings start to move? There is always an energy field. If you remember that, you will have a different interaction with a tree and with your cell phone and with your meditation, knowing it can reach across the world to touch and heal anyone you choose through the connection of the quantum field.

Exercise 2. Energy From a Distance. A partner is needed.

Similar to how you can't tickle yourself because your mind knows your hand is there, you can also feel your own energy more easily for the same reason. Do the same exercise with your partner's hand. It will feel very different than on your own hand.

Write about it. How was it different?

Exercise 3: Energy from a distance. Taking it further.

As you progress with your partner, let your partner touch your stomach and back. Sensory areas of the body that are already very sensitive make sense that they would also be more sensitive to feeling energy.

The famous psychic Ingo Swann wrote a book called, "Psychic Sexuality" where he explains that sexual energy was purposely called "sexual chemistry" so people wouldn't know that they were energy beings. This was done because the sexual energy is so strong and noticeable that it's easy to feel when you pass someone who has high sexual energy.

He said in his book that calling this "energy" would lead some mindful people to realize there must also be strong heart energy and strong mind energy, so the government had a hand in shaping the term "chemistry" to mislead our attention away from the fact that we are energy beings, not chemistry beings.

Remember, you aren't just feeling energy, but you are also affecting the energy. Of course, keep in mind, you are also energy that is feeling energy and affecting energy. Quantum Physics states that by observing the experiment, you are affecting the experiment. You are both doing something to each other at the same time. The person's arm can feel your hand's energy, while your hand feels the arm's energy, even if you aren't aware of it consciously, with your attention focused on the other body part.

3.11 Chemical Warning. This Will Numb Your Touch Abilities

Due to chemical sensitivity, I can pick up a paper receipt from the grocery store and my fingertips get numb immediately. I mention this to you so you will notice it, too. Heat-printed receipts have BPA, a hormone disruptor, in them. The cashiers who are not wearing gloves are getting high doses each day. I saw people working in a salad restaurant chain in NY taking phone orders and sticking the receipt with the order on it to their sweaty forearms so they could read it as they prepared the to-go orders. When the skin is wet, the BPA absorbs faster. Be careful of this. It will reduce your ability to feel, as well as affect the endocrine system's hormones.

All of the toxic chemicals in cleaner supplies will numb your abilities, too. If a bottle says, drinking this is poison, then smelling it is also poison. A wise man on the internet said, "If you can smell the poison, you are being poisoned."

Food sensitivities will misdirect your energy. You will not feel good if you have a food allergy or if you eat something like MSG, which is, to me, a toxin. With MSG, your empath skills can be strongly affected because it can cause mood swings. MSG can be called soy protein, hydrolyzed soy protein, autolyzed yeast extract, yeast extract and some other names. Please keep an eye out and read the ingredients, and then also notice how the box or bag of food feels in your hand as you reach for it. Learn the feeling so you know what not to eat. Check with your Foundational Breath so you learn the feeling. The cleaner you keep your diet, the less will get in the way of your non-physical senses.

Other food additives that may be lightly or highly toxic over time include artificial sweeteners like Sucralose, aspartame, and sugar. They keep changing the name of artificial sweeteners for some reason, so do a web search for names of artificial sweeteners. If you haven't heard of it and it sounds very flowery, look it up.

Notice how you feel after you eat too much sugar. If you are feeling hot and inflamed, it's not just your mood but your brain, vessels and organs, too. When you feel hyper-stimulated due to sensitivities, it's not as easy to be in a mindful and conscious state. You can be mindful and conscious of how you feel, but it will be harder to feel the energy that you would feel when you are in an unbothered and harmonious state of being.

3.12 Exercise: Energy In The Sky Reboot

This is a passive attention exercise that has to be done in daylight.

Go outside. Turn your face upwards and open your eyes. Don't look at anything. Just space out as you face the sky. Relax your eyes like you are spacing out, like when you see an aura. These are the eyes you need to see particles in the sky.

As you relax and look nowhere but up, you will see little particles of white light zipping around. If you blink, they go away. Relax your eyes, and they are back. Some say this is called Orgone. Mattias De Stefano says it's what makes up the first-dimensional building blocks. Have you shown anyone this phenomenon since you first learned about it?

Physical scientists say you are seeing inside of the eye. If that is true, scientists might consider saying that everything we see is in the visual cortex because nothing is seen outside of the brain and mind. Every image we see, we see in our mind. It's not in the eyeball. The eyeball is just the receiver of the vibrations or frequencies of light that make up what we see.

More on point is, the white energy dots are a phenomenon that is always there and you likely have never seen it before or even been told about it. This is a reminder that there is always something in front of you that you are not aware of. You can never put your attention on everything at once, but you can be an open door for the most important information to come in by simply asking and opening that door. Ask, "What is the most important thing I need to know right now to make my life better in "this" (financial, love, health, spiritual) way. You can also ask for something specific. Remember to do this before you go to sleep, too, where your mind is already open to your commands.

3.13 For Energy Workers: Inert Metals Analogy Part 2

Magnets and inert metals: Remember, inert metal doesn't hold a charge or feel one, as far as we know today (or it is so mild, it's not considered useful or harmful.). Science seems to be changing with non-technology in relation to magnetism, so this sentence may be outdated very soon.

Some people are not sensitive to energy, so they can't feel what you are doing. If they go to someone else with a different form of energy work, they may connect more and notice it. Not every kind of healing work works best for everyone.

Your energy work may be exactly what someone needs AFTER they go to someone who has the key to the specific blockage that keeps them from feeling your work. Then, your work can be the finishing touch that helps to complete the healing. Your work may also be perfect for them at that time, even if they won't feel it until the 10th session, but do you want to have to convince them to come back or feel like you are not appreciated for your work every time they don't feel a benefit at the end of each session? I know it depends on your system of practice. I always liked for people to have changes that were noticeable out the door.

Imagine holding a magnet next to an inert metal or piece of plastic. The inert metal and the plastic are both looking at the magnet, saying, "Nope. Nope. Nope. I don't feel it. You are not doing anything." Certain people won't feel your work in their current state of being. You must not take it personally. If anything, choose to wonder about them. You know your work works, so don't let it affect your self-awareness, except to let you know you always have more to learn.

About three percent of the people I do some simple energy work on in a stage setting don't feel it. If it was a one-on-one session, they might think I was making it up, but in a group setting, I can call up four other people who feel it, and then the person who doesn't feel it has to question why they don't feel what others are.

Interestingly, I don't know why they don't feel it. They will if they work with me a few times, but for some reason, some first-timers may fall asleep when I work on their brainwaves and mind, but they don't feel the energy physically in their body.

3.14 Exercise: Feeling And Transferring Energy

There is a good reason this exercise is in module 3 and not module 2. This exercise and technique takes the awareness you have developed until now and takes some practice to be able to do this. It takes conscious effort while remaining in a passive state to transfer the energy. Once you do it, you will know it. This was taught to me by my brother, Dr. Daniel Kalatsky.

You are going to be moving your mind to different locations in your body. In doing this, you will be able to use the energy of the mind in your hands to meet different parts of someone's body and make changes. It works especially well and quite easily with headaches and pain in general. Once you practice and learn to feel the frequency of brainwaves in the brain, you will also be able to calm brainwaves and moods very quickly as you change someone's state and even put them to sleep.

Notice your hand and notice how it feels in space right now. Notice the field around it and how it feels in relation to your hand. Your hand may feel tense or electric or something else completely. You are noticing your hand with your mind. Now, put your mind field into your hand. The way to do this is to imagine it at first so you understand the process. You will be traveling your mind down your head to neck to your arm to your hand, or you can go directly to your hand.

Then, touch someone or something and see what you feel. You will get a new kind of feedback from more ethereal mind energy. Don't overthink it. Just feel. Do this 3 times. Start and then take a break and do it again. You will start to notice the different tones or feelings of the field.

Here are the instructions.

- Please sit or lie down for this. It can make some people feel dizzy or off balance.
- Feel what your mind feels like in your head.
- Move your awareness of your mind to the left side of the inside of your head.
- Now, move your awareness to the right side of the inside of your head.
- Move it side to side and notice how it feels. Let it sit for 10 seconds on each side.
- Now, move your awareness to the front on the inside of your head and then to the back. Do it again for 10 seconds each.
- Now, move it around the side of your head like a ball rolling around from the back to the front and back around.
- Now roll the ball of your mind energy from top to bottom from your forehead down your face and back up the base of

your skull and the back of your head. Doing it 3 times. Stop if you feel at all dizzy or off balance.

- Now that you have moved your awareness inside your head, imagine you can move that mind energy down your neck, and as you do it, move it to your shoulders. Get comfortable there. Try to feel what it would feel like to think with your shoulders as if your mind's awareness was there. From your shoulders move down to your elbows and from there to your forearms and hands.
- At any time, you might slip and be back in your head. If you do end up in your thoughts in your head, slide down your neck again, to your shoulders, to your elbows, to your hands and fingers. This takes mental effort in the beginning because it's a new task.
- Once you are in your hands, touch someone that you are working with. Feel how they feel. Notice the difference in energy and the subtle feelings you may feel when your mind is in your hands.
- Now, move your mind back to your head and touch them with just your hands and hand energy. Notice the difference.

Write notes in your journal about the difference.

After doing this 10 to 20 times over a week, it will become natural to be able to shift your mind state. Your hands will be an extension of your mind's energy and awareness. Practice doing it and then feeling as if you are thinking with your mind while your mind is in your hands. Write about this in your journal, so you can compare how you do now and check your progress in the future. Once you can move your mind to your hands comfortably and stay there, then you can move your mind to the person you are touching. Then you can move it anywhere.

3.15 Exercise: Feeling And Transferring Energy Part 2

Direct the energy.

Put your hands on someone. Drop into a meditative state or peaceful state. It can even be a state of clarity. Whatever it is you want to pass on. Ease is often the best choice because it transfers so easily.

Put your hands on the person's head and put your mind into your hands. Feel the ease in your hands and allow it to connect to their mind's field. You will feel their head soften like the muscles and even the bones are melting into peace. You will be able to tell them what they are feeling. They may not notice it until you mention it unless they are sensitive to energy work.

This is very helpful for alleviating someone's stressful thoughts, insomnia, and headaches, besides giving them the freedom to have space for more energy flow and creativity.

As you practice it more often, you will feel the brainwaves moving at different speeds, and like one of the Tesla light bulbs where electricity reaches out to meet your fingers when you touch the glass, you will notice the flow of the brainwaves and then find that you can move your fingers and move the energy with them to balance it or slow it down.

You will feel it in your body and mind as they have changes. You will feel your breath change or pressure release from your own head. This is one of the ways you will know you are making changes in the other person.

As you feel the changes in yourself, ask them if they felt the same thing. You will very likely hear them say that they did. This is a favorite in a live workshop because it shows you how quickly you can make changes in someone's consciousness, which increases your own belief in your own power.

3.16 Advanced Intuition- Direct Knowing

Intuition starts with a feeling or knowing. You can use your breath to open the first door to the subconscious to allow you to access it. Sometimes, the feeling comes fast, at lightning speed, so you miss the awareness coming in, but you still got a message. When this happens, you just "know" that what came to you is correct. You can call it a "download." You can even do a Foundational Breath check to confirm it.

The answer comes without noticing that your subconscious loaded it for you. It's like an internet cable is plugged in, and a circuit is completed too fast to notice it happened. Suddenly, you have an email in your inbox that you didn't see come in. This happens as you practice the techniques, to where you no longer need the techniques.

Something that helps this happen quicker is the question, "Guess what?" It works because it activates the mind and subconscious to find an answer. Your subconscious goes to work for you. You can say "Guess what!" to yourself or to another person. The subconscious and intuition like playing games and have a curious nature, so have an intention, say "Guess What!" and let it go.

Direct Knowing can seem less fun than intuition because you don't get to use a technique and experience the process of it working. Instead, the information is automatic and injected into your conscious mind. It becomes very practical. The human body and mind are very efficient, so it makes sense that it will begin to shortcut ways of "knowing" to use time and energy efficiently instead of having to do a technique for access. Remember that the more accessible your subconscious is to you, the more you gain access outside of linear time. It seems linear because you brought the information into the physical world, but you pulled it in from a different part of the time/space continuum.

To increase intuition of knowing the future, you can shortcut the time loop. Practice imagining telling yourself from this moment to the YOU that was in yesterday or a week ago about the important things that happened today in your day, so the YOU who you were a week ago can prepare for it in advance. Don't think too hard about this. Just get in a deeper state of mind through meditation and send information back to yourself.

Close your eyes and think of something that happened today that is valuable to you. It's something that, if you knew in advance, you would have prepared for. With your eyes closed, remember a point in time a day ago or a week ago when you were doing something relaxing. In your mind, in a meditative state, go back to that time and tell yourself the information that will be happening in a week. On some level, this is what intuition, déjà vu, coincidence and the rest of these moments of natural strangeness are. If you practice this, you will have more intuition and stronger intuition because by doing this, you are training the future You to send the 'You Now" information back to the present, too. Remember, there is no linear structured time in the quantum Super Mind. It all happens at any time and all the time. It's in the physical world that time has a linear order to it. You are using the field of consciousness to add something into the physical timeline.

Try this now and write down your experience.

3.17 How To Use The Feeling Of Awe To Increase Your Ability To Access Your Subconscious Abilities.

If you watch an inspiring TV show or movie and notice a feeling of AWE or a feeling of lightness or even a tingle through your being at times when watching, you are using passive attention or being an observer while you are actively engaged in watching the program.

Most of us are hypnotized by TV shows or movies, even education programs. That's what they are made for, and that's why you watch it. It's a lot like a drug that will change your state from bored or stressed to a different emotion than one you don't feel like having right now. Of course, now you know you can choose your emotions and empower yourself. You can make up your own movie about yourself in your head and, in doing this, program the present moment for the future you want. TV and movies are doing that to you, but not for you. They are mostly made to keep you focused on something to make you see things a certain way or to sell you a physical product, belief or agenda. They are doing it by planting suggestions and leading you while you are in an emotionally available hypnotic state.

If you choose to pay attention, TV quickly opens the door to the subconscious. If there is a show that makes you suddenly feel AWE, use it! This AWE can be plugged into the formula. As you have the experience, your brain is firing in deep alpha and theta waves. Hormones are released to feel good and awaken the mind. Resonance is occurring. You are resonating with the experience from the show or movie as if it's happening to you. To your mind, it is happening to you. The feelings of awe when having an experience at any time meets your subconscious with an understanding that there is something true, good and needed happening. Use it to increase your connection to your subconscious and your abilities. So what do you do with this feeling?

When the moment comes, during any TV show or experience, and you feel that feeling, it's time. Stop and drop in. Eyes open or closed, go inside to feel it fully. Let it flow through you like water moving through sand, like electricity flowing through wires, like a thirsty plant that has been waiting for a stream of water all through a long drought. Let the feeling and energy open channels for you. Don't waste the moment.

There are secrets of manifestation and happiness in a story, and that brings on the feeling of Awe. If you pay attention to how you feel when watching it and use the emotions and feelings as tools instead of just viewing it as a story of magic, love, and learning, you will be doing two things. Enjoying a movie and using it to generate power. If you are anything like me, then you feel good when you take something meant to steal your time and make it something to better your life. Not all movies are like this, of course, but more than a few are. Now that it's been mentioned and you have the ability to use passive attention, it will jump out at you more and more.

I happen to love the idea of using my gifts to make the world better, so for me, when I find Awe-some feelings in certain shows, I make it part of my energy work, intuition practice and manifestation practice. What are some examples of TV shows or movies that make you feel Awe or inspiration?

Write them down in your journal, and when you hear of a new show that people are inspired by, write it down, too.

For me, The Truman Show, The Matrix, and The Princess Bride, are some favorites.

3.18 Exercise: Start the day with a morning cup of "Hi(gher) (Your)self."

Say hi to your higher self, and say hi to your subconscious. It will help you create a more personal relationship with those parts of your mind. It's good to do this anytime, but if you are too lazy or too busy to meditate today at least say hi and have a conversation with that part of you about what you want now in your life. Do it by visualizing it and feeling it with certainty. Then send them off to have a great day working for you, like little elves working behind the scenes to do your tasks for you. It's like putting a paper boat in the stream and letting it be carried to its destination. Just like you can put yourself in the right state before bed, as you have learned to work with more layers of your mind, you can do it while awake, too. Saying hi to your higher self lets your subconscious, intuition and higher self know that you are aware they are working with you and part of you. It helps to thin the line between the awake state and the other states that you want to access consciously.

3.19 Exercise: Pre-Sleep Exercise

Before bed, visualize and feel your DNA strands lighting up. Imagine the DNA enlightening (getting lit up), and tell your mind to activate more of your evolutionary DNA while you sleep. Activate the DNA that will give you better health, more strength, more intuition, and more manifesting abilities. You are programmed for all of it, so use it. Do it tonight.

This visualization along with making the choice to feel are commands you are giving to your subconscious. Feel the emotions of these requests and how you would feel if you suddenly had these traits active now. By connecting with your subconscious, you can control more autonomic body function.

If you were to either inhale toxins or stay in a chronically oppressed or depressed environment or mindset, you would mutate your DNA and cause damage. By making good requests like this while you are in a suggestible deeper state of mind before bed or while meditating, you can change the structure, size and shape of your brain. This leads to a fact that isn't as commonly thought about, which is if you can mutate your DNA to make it sicker, you can also mutate your DNA to make it healthier. #Upgrade.

3.20 The Surest Ways To Not Hear Your Intuition

Once you are tuned in and know how to listen, feel, see, know, or however your intuition shows itself to you, these are the factors that will make you miss it. These are the strong negative base emotions. The ones that feel addictive.

Greed. Greed makes you stop paying attention to the quiet messages of your intuition, because your want of something overrides your inner voice.

Lust. You know and feel that it's a bad idea to follow those feelings, but you do it anyway.

Other emotional states are **desperation. jealousy. pride, anger,** and **envy**. They all fit into the category of cravings, so you can flip them around and use them if you can remember in that moment to do it. It takes serious effort here.

You can choose not to have these lower-level emotions, and it's worth it for you because making that choice is the step you need to manifest what you want and more. This is mentioned late in the book because, by now, you have practice in choosing your state for manifestation, which means it's easier to call on an emotional state when you want to.

Be aware when you are in any of these states, do not tell your self that what you are thinking or feeling is intuition. Intuition has mostly closed the door here. It will be an irrational part of your mind tricking you to believe what you are thinking is intuitive. It's a good time to check with Foundational Breath and see how you feel. It will help calibrate you again.

3.21 Meditation, DNA, Enlightenment, Clues

Meditation is a key to what you are doing with all of the intuition and manifesting information. By now, you know how important meditation is for intuition, empathic, manifestation and all of the more subtle sensing abilities.

Please take some time now to do one of the meditations for five minutes or longer if you can without any rush. I do hope that by now, you are doing 20 minutes a day twice a day. If needed, take the online course and use the meditations daily or get one from the website. Even better, join me for Monday Night Meditations for Manifestation every Monday night at 7 pm. (Link on website.)

For those of you who find sitting meditation boring, difficult or uncomfortable, please do the Super Slow Movement Technique. But consider this; You perceive everything you experience inside your mind, so if you are going to the Layer One Mind, where all of your experience is perceived and created, how can it be boring? You are accessing the program's code, and it's giving you access to everything and every experience that you perceive and want to perceive. It's so juicy to have this much power over your operating system. Plant some good lines of code in there. Embed some new programs so you can make your life better starting right now. Have fun with it. You can literally make up some code while you are in a deep state of mind and put it in. Make sure to add in that this code is for my higher good, just in case your subconscious sees any double meanings in the wording. Feel the intention of what you want when you plant it, and then let it grow.

It's more valuable to do the work and feel the feelings in the present moment during your daily practice, but this has a different kind of value.

Everything you can imagine is in your mind and connected to consciousness. That's not boring. It can't be boring when you know this. A video game could be boring until you find out that each time you pick up a treasure chest, you get the treasure in real life, too. And like a video game, there are hidden clues that lift you to higher levels faster.

Meditation is one of the tools that gives you access to the clues.

3.22 Be Still and Know I Am God. The Secret Revealed.

Many years ago, I read Autobiography of a Yogi by Paramahansa Yogananda. He is most known in the West for bringing meditation to the US.

Yogananda gave one teaching on using the phrase, "Be still and know I am God." I didn't know at the time it was a passage from a biblical text, but I liked it.

He said to use it as a Mantra, which means to let it play on repeat in your mind while meditating. I meditated using the Mantra on and off for years. Then, one day, something happened. As I meditated, the mantra faded away, and I was in a place of total stillness. A voice spoke in the back of my head. It was an almost silent whisper, like a breeze blowing by. If not for the perfect stillness, I would have missed it. I knew the voice, because it had spoken to me before. It was my voice of higher self. It forced its way in when it was quiet enough, and there was stillness. It's different than intuition. It comes from somewhere else. It whispered loudly, like it was with a microphone, "Be Still and Know I am God." I heard it in my ears and in my mind. I understood the phrase. It wasn't Yogananda saying that you should repeat the phrase to yourself as if God was telling this to you. He was saying that as you repeat it, you will find that you are the one saying that you have GOD within you. He meant that in saying it in the deep stillness of your practice, you will discover that a part of you is the I AM saying I AM GOD.

There is a river flowing through all of us with this constant stream of God within us. You don't have to believe it. It may be something you discover if you use this mantra without any intention for a while. Once you know, you can't unknow, and it changes your relationship with creation and consciousness from that pre-sent moment on.

Now, with this secret revealed, it may be more difficult to get this message because you may think about wanting to hear the voice. I know that wanting can be distracting, but sharing the information is a good way to get you to use the mantra and find out. Let go of the result here if you decide to do this so that you can use it as words with no attachments. Be Still and know I am (You are) God.

3.23 Be Still and Know I am God Meditation

"Be still and know I am God." The sentence does not say, "Be still and believe I am God or believe in God."

Imagine a small straw inside a larger straw. It's a hidden straw compartment. It's a small tube within a larger tube. No one knows the inner straw is there. It was placed there long ago and the one who placed it there is no longer available now to tell you it's there. This makes the inner straw a secret compartment within the larger straw.

Imagine that the large straw has a vacuum sucking water through it. The suction goes around the inner straw without using it and the water comes up through only the outer large straw. The smaller straw inside stays empty.

The mysterious inner straw is left unused by you. Of course, there is air in the inner straw and there is space within the inner straw.

Sometimes, if it's the right angle or force happens, whatever is being sucked up by the outer straw will also pull up something through the inner straw.

The small inner straw is the place of stillness. It is the "Be Still" place from the phrase. That small straw is inside you. At some point, somehow, you may notice that secret compartment. It's not meant to be a secret. I'm telling you about it right now, so it's not a secret, but still it must be discovered. You will be aware of something much different happening to you as you pull the water through the larger straw and it also draws up through the smaller inner straw. You will know when it happens.

Now think about the Still Small Voice that you have to Be Still to hear. You have to get quiet enough and get your conscious mind out of the way. Then, the inner small voice makes itself known when you are ready. This doesn't mean when you say you are ready or think you are ready. It happens when you really are ready. It's always when you are ready and never before. Getting out of the way makes you ready. Getting still makes you ready. Once you hear the voice, you will never forget it, and you will always know it's there. This allows you to hear it more often. Hearing it more often gives you the ability to find it when you want it and trust it instead of just waiting for it.

You ask something of God or Source or higher self or whatever name you choose is most fitting for your beliefs. You ask for what you want and need, ask questions as to why things happen, or have gratitude for what you have received.

Speaking to God, or source consciousness, is a way to access the subconscious and higher self, which is God connected. Consider that the Layer One Mind is part of the everything. It feels like it starts in your head and spreads out from there because you are the magnet that holds your consciousness there, but it is everywhere, and so are you.

Does the magnet of your desire change when in a meditative state? It does because you are able to pull in more of what you want while in a meditative state. It brings you clarity and lets the vibrations that don't match fall away more easily. Then you can bring back the new state to your waking state a little more and a little longer each time.

Meditate on the phrase, "Be Still and Know I am God."

Make this your practice. Use it as a mantra for 20 minutes a day for 30 days. Expect nothing to happen because that's when it will. When that specific voice speaks up, you will never forget it and you will know exactly how close to Source you are.

This may or may not increase your manifestation ability short term, however it will increase intuition and detachment from conscious self. This means that your ability to use the pre-sent moment to manifest becomes easier. In a roundabout way, you are using it to grow your awareness, which leads to the growth of your capabilities. By now, you are likely meditating 2 times a day so that you can make one of your meditations like this and one for manifestation. Once you get good at the manifestive state, you can drop in at any time.

3.24 3rd Person Language Manifestation.

Instructions:

If I say to myself, "William, please help me." I am accessing a different part of my mind. Just as if you say, I need to help myself, or I need help, you are speaking to your conscious mind's self. By saying, "William, Please help me." I am speaking in 3rd person and accessing a light level of my subconscious mind. By asking for help, I engage the nature of intuition because that's what it's here for.

Doing this is a work-around instead of being given guidance or hypnotic instruction from someone else, and because it's from you to a part of you, it goes directly to the subconscious processing center.

If I said *"I have to help myself,"* I am speaking in the first person (instead of the third person), and so it's direct to the conscious mind, and it doesn't get into the subconscious as readily.

Talking to self in the 3rd person helps to get your subconscious mind to do things for you when you want to get something done.

3.25 Intuitive Messages Are Always Coming Through To Energy Workers And Healers That Are Sometimes Surprising To Themselves And Their Clients.

A healer, like anyone else early on, may not always know that they are getting an intuitive message. It can seem like a random thought popping up while they are working. Then, if they catch it before it dissolves away and they mention it out loud in a gentle way, they may get feedback from the client and discover that they are essentially listening in on the client's mind by becoming coherent with their brainwaves and hopping on the same train for a moment. After a while, they learn how to make the connection consciously. Science would likely call this a mirror neuron function. Neurons in the brain that will match with someone you are in sync with. It's probably happened to you, where you know what someone was going to say. Let's look at mirror neurons as little antennas for frequency and resonance.

As I mentioned, the only way for the healer to know they are receiving information from or about their client, at first, is to say the thought or feeling out loud to the patient. The healer may even say something out of the blue out loud without knowing it's related to the client or patient. After enough people let the healer know that they just said something pertinent to the patient's life, they realize that they are tuning in to the person's subtle field of awareness.

When your work is constantly to be in a meditative or calm, focused state for prolonged periods, seeing 8 patients or clients a day, 5 days a week, you will begin to access and recognize the different states of subtle consciousness without meaning to. It's a working meditation. If you have been doing this already, now you know to use this intention and to pay attention, so it will happen almost immediately, if not sooner.

The body is a bridge between the subconscious and conscious and the bridge has a two-way street on it. The subconscious outputs information to the intuition to bring it to the conscious. You can also put in an order to the subconscious for specific information or questions you want answered, which means you are programming your subconscious.

3.26 Let's Manifest Again.

What is the Present Moment?

You have manifested many times without knowing it, and you love doing it. You even say to yourself. "I can't believe it. This is exactly what I wanted!" You gave it to yourself and didn't know you were doing it. You stumbled onto the natural formula and completed it without consciously being aware of it. It's so exciting to feel like you won and the universe is in your favor. BUT it's you that did it. You were in the right state of mind, emotion and frequency. Your connection to the universe was in your favor.

Until now, your conscious awareness of this power has been stolen from you, not by anyone physically taking it, but by omission. You were never taught it. You were told it was fantasy, and it was written in the fictional fantasy books and movies to direct your mind to think it's not real. It's so subtle, like intuition, which is why you learn intuition first. Who would have thought a 100-ton plane would use the ungraspable and weightless air as a way to push against air and fly? That's making the intangible, non-physical, real by transmuting air into something that, for a purpose, becomes solid.

I know that it is easy now to know that there is a physical formula to use air to create lift for the plane if there is thrust, the wings are right and the angles are right, but until it was done, it couldn't be done. Until the formula showed itself, it wasn't possible, even though it was available.

Birds could do it, so there was an example in the physical world. The same example is available to all of us with those who are very lucky, who live in abundance, joy and health. There is a formula that must be discovered so others can repeat it. Without a specific equation to write on the board, you have been given the formula in this book based on all of the people who are doing this. It's also based on the same thing you do when you manifest. It's all the same formula and then it has to include paying attention so you know when you are doing it and when it is happening. Like any good experiment, there needs to be someone observing. After you do the work, you observe the results. Doing the work will make it easier for you to see the results in others, too. The more you see it, the more you reinforce it, which will make you crave doing it more often.

An EEG is reading the frequency of your electrical patterns or brainwaves in your brain. If you are in a bad mood, it will be different than when you feel happy. Today, scientists can use frequency reading devices to pull images out of your mind based on the frequency you are running. They can likely input frequency, too, at this point. You can input frequency by choosing your emotion. The frequency of electrical current in your mind will always attract to it the similar frequency from the quantum mind. Always. So, choose the frequency that you want and let it attract and create when you want in the 3D world!

You are creating all of the time. Creating is the upload to your downloads.

Upload the festive, and you will manifest.

When you manifest, you create what you want in your thoughts and feelings but do not know how it will come about. That's the trust factor. You call it in and then know that the universe is listening.

I remember the first time someone told me what it was like to create a product in China. He said, "You just call them and tell them what you want. You can send a drawing too. In a few weeks, they will send you a working prototype. Then you can ask them to make changes. You refine the process until it's how you want it. I almost couldn't believe it. I felt like I had a genie in a magic lamp.

I asked, "Are you sure I don't have to do anything but tell them what I want, and they know how to make it for me?" Amazing. It reminded me of our ability to manifest. It was like going into the control system's level of the mind, where we can set our desires free and release it to the universe like a giant gong that has been rung. The vibrations always find their matching frequency. Your thoughts and feelings will always find others like them no matter what they are, so make them extraordinary.

What if you are feeling depressed and stuck in a rut?

Fortunately, if you feel down or low, there are situations or people that bump you up. How does it happen? Why would these people appear when their frequency is so much higher? With people who have already healed what you are working on, they were once in a similar frequency to you, so like a scar as a reminder, their frequency recognizes yours. Their energy field and consciousness remember enough to find you and match you, and then, if you want it, their path and frequency can help lift you higher. Strong empaths that are healed will also choose to help those who want to be helped. The universe put enough of the different types of people here to make it all balance out for everyone's needs and growth.

The other way to do it is to make the choice to pull yourself out of it. It's not an easy choice, but it's not easy to stay in it either. You know you can choose your emotion, so choose a story you like and make the emotions real for yourself. It's easier said than done sometimes, but when you are ready, you will be able to do it.

3.27 Learning The Feeling In Advance. Recognize Intuition When It Comes In & Know The Future.

And as you can see, this relates to manifestation as well.

Every moment has a feeling. Now that you know how your breath responds to positive or negative and how it then bubbles up the feelings or images for you to know what it means, beyond the yes/no, good/bad, we are going to now go deeper.

This aspect will fulfill you with some Jedi-styled learning, but there is some timing involved.

By now, you are having easily recognized intuitive and empathic experiences regularly. Luck and manifesting have become much more common now that you know how to use your awareness, too.

When you have your next intuitive moment, it's possible you won't know it was intuitive until the "experience" that you felt or downloaded occurred on your timeline, meaning you got to that point in your journey through life. This can be a déjà vu moment.

When the intuitive moment does happen, just relax and think back to the moment you had the thought, feeling or vision. Feel that feeling. It may take a few times to find the feeling. You can also program yourself in meditation to give you the feeling when you are in a deeper state of mind. In your meditation, ask for the feeling or frequency of intuition to make itself known to you. Draw it in. Remember, an intuitive experience. Feel it. This will magnetize it to you. This will speed up your process. Each time you find it, tune into it and hone it further. As you become familiar with it, you will be able to notice it when it happens during the pre-sent moment on its own, and you can then create it more easily because it becomes so familiar.

I don't know if you know this, but I am color blind for a number of colors. Often, I can see that two colors are different, but I'm not sure which is red or which is green. If it's a neon color in a room that isn't well-lit, I can't tell what it is. If a color is too far away, I also can't tell what it is. But with all this, I have been able to find the tones of some of the colors, so I know them as, for example, green, even though I know I'm not seeing the same beautiful crispy brightness of the grass or a leaf because when I see it, it looks flat. But I still can tell what it is… most of the time.

So, get specific to what you need to recognize. Find the feeling that goes with the moment. For me, I was able to find a way to put the color in a category so that I could recognize it. Create a category for the feeling. What does it feel like for you? Is it a tingle? A feeling similar to Deja Vú, but not exactly the same? Maybe a feeling, like you are getting lifted up a little bit by your heart into the air. Does your breath feel lighter, like something good is happening? Find the feeling and put it in a box for yourself. Do it the same way that you can feel nauseous and know the feeling or feel happy and know that feeling. The feelings are so recognizable, but you haven't categorized them yet. I assure you it is easy once you practice it just a bit. It will be as obvious as knowing the feeling of when you are hungry.

Once you have the intuitional awareness of a passing intuitive thought, you will know at that moment that it's a foresight being handed to you from your intuition. You paid attention, so you know the feeling of intuition speaking to you. This is a very exciting time because you can sharpen this skill so precisely that you almost feel psychic.

As you can see, you first need all of the other more basic, though equally powerful, techniques we worked on until now to build sensitivity. Now, noticing with your passive attention is second nature to you.

Keep up your practice for more reasons than I can think of, from business to relationships to creating more awe in your life. I promise you that the more you do it, the more it is worth, and the more you will feel and discover that you are worthy of everything you want.

If you made it to this part of the book, you are most likely doing the exercises. If you aren't doing them and just exploring the concepts, you are missing out on the reason for this book. I know everyone is busy. You may be exhausted from working 3 jobs or from taking care of the kids or just from so much stressful news in the world. This is a gentle reminder that there is a plane of existence that we were not taught about that is so well known in fictional movies, some documentaries and to people who practice levels of spirituality and consciousness, but the teachings are not focused on in the material world of accumulation. Take the time to do the exercises.

Time is passing anyway. If they do work, you will have even more free time and energy as you build your practice and abilities.

3.28 Program Your Self for Manifestation

Use Sleep's Subconscious to Conscious Revolving Door to Plant More Seeds.

When you go to sleep there is a short time, like in practiced meditation, where your subconscious and your conscious meet. It happens when you are on your way down to dreamland. Right before you get there is that space where you are about to pass off into slumber. With practice, you can balance right on the edge, plant your seeds deeply and help them begin to create roots before dropping into the sleep state.

When your conscious self, the you that is reading this, shakes hands with the other side of the veil, you let go of your control and process your day. You refresh your mind. It's a lot like the sun and the moon in perfect balance with one moving up as the other moves down. When they meet at the midline, there is a handshake or an exchange that takes place. We don't know the depth of the energy that they exchange. When you go to sleep, the same happens with your conscious and subconscious mind, and there, you can send a message easily for your subconscious to perform a task for you. It's also the place where your subconscious hands you the dreams for you to remember; this is why people who meditate can choose to remember dreams more easily, and It's related to why people who remember dreams easily tend to find more desire to meditate.

Your inner guide knows you are on your path to fulfill your mission here. That's why it's so important. Of course, it's fun and exciting to be clued in, but the bigger picture is that it is quietly leading you to your purpose.

'When you know your true purpose, you do it, and the feeling of fear cowers. Ask any parent that runs into traffic to save their child.'

Before going to sleep, tell your subconscious mind you would like four intuitive messages in four days. Now you know to expect the messages, so you can be more conscious of when they occur.

Remember, intuitive messages are already happening often. I want to be sure you can pinpoint the feeling of the pattern so you learn and know the formula. When you have an intuition, you want to notice it when it's happening, not when you experience it in your future timeline, and then remember that you knew this already in the past. Deja Vú should be behind you for now until you get to the next level of sensitivity. Using your passive attention skills, you recognize intuition as it speaks to you. This will be equal to your phone beeping and you immediately know you have a message. You don't have to wait two weeks to know you have a message in your phone and you don't have to wait two weeks to know that you had an intuitive message that came in.

If you had the sound of a ping in your head every time your intuition spoke to you, what would that be like? Imagine that for a moment.

Read this in your phone recorder, and then sit down and close your eyes.

Think about the last time you have an intuition or a moment of Natural Strangeness. It can be Luck, Coincidence, Deja Vú, being in a flow state, or having an empathic or telepathic moment. Recall that moment and hear a ping in your mind.

Now, take a deep breath and recall that moment again, and hear the ping in your mind.

You've written much in your journal by now, and if you haven't, start writing, or you will miss out on the structure of magic that will turn these almost missed moments into skills. Read back and find all of the times and hear the ping.

Create the ping sound for yourself or a feeling. When you have the experience, the ping will be programmed to show up. Read in your journal and find any places you had great luck. Feel the feelings you had in the experience and then Ping the moment before the luck. Where did you create a miracle? Ping the day or moment before. When did you discover how to heal? Ping that moment in your mind and feeling. You are creating a doorbell to allow you to know when these moments are happening. In a live course, this would be repeated over and over and over so it becomes a part of your awareness. Treat this like a live course and you have just given yourself a compass for when you are having a breakthrough moment.

Now, recall it again and hear the ping in your mind. Feel the ping in your body. How does it feel to feel that ping? Do you have another moment of natural strangeness? Maybe a coincidence that was so surprising you are still thinking about it? Hear the ping in your mind. Feel it in your body. Make the association, so every time it happens, you have audio and physical sensations attached to it as an anchor so it's that much easier to notice it.

Soon, like a mantra, it will happen for you on its own.

3.29 The Vibrational Frequency Kiss Technique-A Bonus For Those In A Coupled Relationship

Use The Vibrational Frequency Kiss Technique to Make Someone Happily Fall for You.

I did this with a girlfriend who was very open to things like meditation, yoga and intention. This is frequency work. She was very involved in studying frequency, so I knew if I could get her to agree to do it with me when we kissed, we would both love it, and I could learn more.

I explained what I was going to do and also asked that she put any judgment aside for a few minutes for the sake of trying something a little unusual but could have a very healing pay off. She agreed. We kissed, and I started to hum as we did. Just like when you hum, you can choose where to send the vibration in your body and feel it in different places, and you can do it with a partner, too. I hummed, and energy centers started vibrating. You can aim the vibrations to different parts of each other's bodies using breath and intention. Here is how it's done.

Creating a connection with an intimate partner is a beautiful experience. This will increase your connection quickly using vibration and frequency. It will create more coherence and it will be fun and probably make both of you laugh, too. You can also choose your emotion, and the humming will transmit that frequency.

When your lips are touching, hum gently. Let it be almost imperceptible at first if you can. If you happen to be kissing someone you aren't that close with yet, then hum even more gently so you don't scare them away.

Humans tend to make sounds when they kiss anyway. The sounds are all frequencies or vibrations. If the connection is good, then they vibrate parts of the other person's body and awaken consciousness. They enhance your own experience, too. If you know the person well enough, hum louder with stronger vibrations. It will likely become funny because it is funny. It tickles. It's strange. Ask them to do it with you so they can see why you are enjoying it so much. It will also let you experience it as the receiver, too.

Ultimately, you won't be able to tell who is humming and who is receiving the hum. The vibrations will overtake different parts of you.

The vibrations will synchronize your nervous system with theirs. You will be awakening both of your awarenesses to a new level. Energetic Bonds will be made stronger.

Let me know how it goes :)

Write about it in your journal and ask your partner to write about it, too. If you don't have a partner and want one, practice, practice and practice the manifestation work.

Humming allows transmission at any time.

You can also hum while you hold an intention and emotion and touch someone's arm or back and transmit frequency too. If someone is in a difficult state of mind or emotion, you can feel love in your heart and hum gently without letting them know. And touch their arm if they are open to it. You are doing it anyway, so I don't think you need permission. If you are there for someone and hugging them, they are already asking for support or love, so add the hum to transmit more powerfully.

3.30 VERY Advanced Passive Attention

What is the most advanced level of passive attention?

You have already noticed with the Foundational Breath how your breath and feelings change based on what is right for you and what is not right for you. You are conscious of the unconscious. The door is open.

Noticing the sound of a water droplet hitting a lake while you are reading a book is a part 2 exercise.

Noticing the breeze while you are in conversation while you still stay in conversation is a part 2 exercise.

Part 3 is advanced. You have been practicing meditation and other sensitizing exercises now for at least a few weeks. You have felt energy from your hands, you have felt energy from your microwave, and you have become sensitive to auras and to the feeling of the foundational breath technique. This has led you to more intuition, more luck and more awesomeness in your life.

Are you ready to become aware of yourself as you fall asleep and notice the state when the dream starts. If you like exploring the dreamworld, would you like to become aware enough to be able to tell your partner lying next to you that you are dreaming or entering a dream and what is happening in the dream while still in it?

3.31 Dream Waking.

One of the more advanced levels of Passive Attention is being aware when you slip into the dream state and staying in part of your conscious mind without waking out of it. One foot in each world, so to speak. First, let's learn to walk the line between awake and asleep.

If you don't have to be up early tomorrow, stay awake until you are very tired and ready to sleep, then meditate in a seated position in bed instead of laying down. Pay attention as you feel yourself slipping off into sleep. Notice that the dreams are starting, and remind yourself to stay conscious. If you fall asleep, do it again the next time you can schedule it.

The next part is from an out-of-body technique that I use to make astral projection very simple. You aren't going to astral project, otherwise known as an out-of-body experience here, so don't be concerned about that. The technique is very specific. This is what to do.

Before you go to sleep, remind yourself not to move when you wake up in the morning. When you wake up, immediately remind yourself to stay perfectly still.

Meditate in this state while you are laying there. At this point, your body is still asleep. You will stop feeling it and are now in the perfect state to embody the feelings of the person you want to be. Remember, every moment is the present and pre-sent moment. Every moment you are resonating in is being pre-sent to the future. The moment you are in now was pre-sent, sent in advance, to you before you got here to be here waiting for you when you arrived, so every moment you are in is pre-sent from a different part of time, and to make it more simple to understand, I will say that it is more often sent from your past. This also means that the moment you are in is being pre-sent to the future to wait for you there. This is why you have to choose the state of creation that you want your future to be based on. You are in the future now to the 'you' that was thinking about meditating 30 minutes ago. You are always pre-sending the state you are in while in the moment you are in.

While in this body-less meditation, it is much easier to pre-send anything you want for physical healing. So imagine and feel your body and mind transforming into the person you want to be.

Do the deeply tired meditation once a week or more if you have time.

The early morning wake-up and staying frozen in place is easy to do, so do it every day for 10 minutes before waking up to do your normal morning practice.

After you do each one, write some notes in your journal about your experience.

These practices will dramatically deepen your awareness. They can also lead to OBE, Out of Body Experience, if you want it to. I won't cover that here, but in a video at some time.

3.32 Advanced Luck Guide: The Mind Field

Let's say you are now aware of at least two possibilities;

A. **Luck is random and**
B. **Luck is intuitive guidance. Aka, Your inner guide.**

What you need to know: The brain forms neural pathways and new abilities around beliefs and circumstances. If done right, this leads to massive change in your emotions, physical health and physical reality.

Believe A. Luck (or life) is just random and just happens to you, or **Believe B.** Part of your mind energy (your brain's magnetic field and electrical impulses) interact or enmeshes with the energy field and Layer One Mind of space and time around you, like other electrical and magnetic fields do.

The mind works like this, too, and because energy fields and magnetic fields interact with other energy fields and magnetic fields, your mind's field of energy follows these laws and interacts, as well, but uses your thoughts, feelings and intent as a driver. You can be the driver anytime you want, or you can end up on a bus with everyone else's group-think consciousness, which may be great for you or not, depending on which bus of consciousness you get on. If you choose the bus, take the right bus.

If you have people who are always trying to keep you in your past, find new people who allow your dreams and desires to move to the present.

Let's call on water to be an example of consciousness for a moment here. If you are in the water, you are affected by what is put in the water and the movement of the water because all of the water is one system. You feel the movement of the water, if it's fast or strong. You notice temperature changes. If you float with it and become still, you may not know you are moving at all.

You are also living in the earth's magnetic or energetic field. You are living in the solar system's field and in the universe and the multiverse's infinite fields. You get information from everything that enters the field and is in the field. You are part of the field, and you are the field.

If you could choose to believe just one of the two beliefs, A or B, which would make more sense for you to choose if you wanted to be empowered?

You have an idea or get an idea of building a table, and then you use it to create the reality of a table. You can see how you brought the subconscious to the conscious to the physical world. This also could mean there are other likely layers in your mind that you aren't paying attention to and are also going to be part of the creative process. For example, you want to get in better physical shape. This is the conscious mind thinking this. You start to walk, using the conscious mind. You start to lift weights or do yoga using the conscious mind, and you see your body changing shape, losing weight, and getting toned up. Your conscious mind is not burning the fat for you. You are working with your creation mind to make these changes. Your conscious mind plants the seeds, so your 'behind the scenes mind' can sculpt, shape and detox your body and your health. Your body is doing it, but it is running the program given to it by your subconscious mind. You are flipping the on switches to your subconscious mind by taking the steps consciously to do this.

Knowing that your energy field goes past the body and energetically can reach and connect with any frequency in the universe, you can change anything. I am inviting you at this time to take a chance with a belief that is risk free. Choose choice B; You are connected to all time and space and can create changes as you practice these exercises. See how that belief feels. See how your life changes. Become more aware of the messages you receive regularly, but now they seem louder and at a higher frequency. You don't need to believe in something for it to work, but when you do believe, it tends to give more 'voltage' to your energy field, and it works faster and stronger. It changes the way time moves. Do you remember the night before your birthday or Christmas when all the presents were waiting? Time stretched *verrrry* long. It felt like a year in the space of one night. And when you finally got to open your presents, the time changed again and it felt squeezed into a tiny space and it was over in seconds.

You control time based on your state of being. Time does not control you based on what is happening around you.

When I had new clients for energy healing work that called for an appointment, I wanted it to be from a direct referral; otherwise, there was a lot more explaining for me to do, which wasted precious time that could have been spent working on them. Even if they didn't know what I was doing, they still would have benefitted, however, hearing a story from a friend or family member about someone getting well, made them more open to the experience. Once they themselves had good changes, the client was now more open to notice the subtlety of what was happening when we worked together and excited about what they became aware of.

I always knew that just by them requesting an appointment, it meant that part of their consciousness already believed I could help them, but getting to their conscious mind's belief level made it more exciting and resonated with bigger ripples of energy in the field of consciousness. Beliefs aren't needed, but they matter until you know.

You are the one steering the boat, so keep practicing and keep meditating and you will be able to get your destination and desires so much faster.

3.33 Advanced Luck Guide: The Mind Field More

If you still have any leftover thoughts that luck may be a "random happening," then experiment for one week as you choose to change your perspective and see what works better for you.

You control subjective time based on your state of mind. Time does not control you based on what is happening around you. If you are choosing to believe luck is random and outside of you, then what will you get from that belief? You will feel like life gives you whatever shows up. Use your powerful ability to make a choice and choose to change the belief now that gives you the power, even if just temporarily, and then be aware of what happens.

You were not taught this simple principle. It's so simple, all of the teachings are so simple that they almost seem not to make sense on a physical level. But if you can see auras and feel energy, you know there is another level than the physical. You know, when you are around someone happy, you feel good. If you are around depressed people, it lowers your energy. You affect energy and are affected by it.

I'm going to take one more moment to explain while you take a breath in now and think of a time you planned on something, and it worked out powerfully. And it felt really good!

With that, add to it that you have a feeling that your luck is your intuition guiding you from behind a hidden door. It's telling you to be in the right place at the right time. Doing this will increase your Luckability dramatically. You are giving your subconscious the credit it deserves and it loves you for it, like a dog loves to be pet by you after it does something you've trained it to do.

Ever had something like this happen? You take a different street at an unusual time and notice a gluten-free bakery that you didn't know was there. Then you order a slice of blueberry pie and decide to stay for a coffee just when the person you have been thinking about comes in, and there is only one seat available in the place, and it happens to be at your table. This is certainly going to put you in a state of awe, but the awe should be pointed at the amazingness of your mind. It might be obvious at this point that you have your own inner guidance and manifestor. They work together. Your guardian angel is making sure you are going toward your success and purpose all the time, even when you don't know it consciously. Any questions?

Take a few minutes and write in your journal about luck and coincidence and your thoughts on what it really is.

3.34 Advanced Luck Guide: Coincidence

Luck, coincidence, and good fortune are all like an awesome and beautiful play in a basketball game. It looks and even more so FEELS this way, because the basketball play is so masterfully practiced in the neurology and body/mind of the player that it looks like art. It is so in the flow state that you feel it when it happens. The basketball player has had the perfect practice and belief system, knowing the proper time, place and setup for the specific play to happen.

This is how luck and coincidence work and when you know this in your circuitry, in your nervous system, your brain and mind will continuously set it up for you.

If you have some remaining beliefs that coincidence and luck can exist without the concept of intuition as the quiet voice and secret guide that directs you through the terrain to put you there, then here is one more way to perceive it.

It would be statistically impossible from the perspective of random occurrence. Any coincidence that I've ever had would mathematically be less likely than winning the lottery. The lottery has a lot of balls spinning and they have to be chosen in an order. Luck and coincidence have a location, time of day, and possibly a second person also being in the right time and at the place at the same time, with all of the second person's moments ready to match with yours at the same place and time. This is not a coincidence. Noticing the other person, thinking of the person you wanted to see the day before and then seeing them cannot be random over and over. The odds of it being random are close to impossible.

You would have missed them if you yawned and closed your eyes for a moment as you got off the elevator on the 20th floor of a building you've never been in before, as your best friend from third grade, that you happen to think of yesterday happens to be visiting NY on that day, just that day for 1 hour, and there you are. On top of that, you almost didn't go.

The possibility of this is incalculable. The timing of the elevator, stopping for gas on the way, almost missing the train. There are so many variables every time. How often do you have this kind of situation happen? Mathematically, this proves that you are doing it and not just walking into a random situation. This is happening to too many people to count every day. You are going to keep getting better at it, until you know the feeling and you know when it's going to happen.

3.35 The Third Eye (I). Open Your I

Consider that it is believed that there are 3 parts to you and your psyche. Conscious, Subconscious and Higher Self.

Many years ago, I had a dream. I was on a radio show, and I shared the dream with the host, Joey Reynolds, on WOR radio in NY. The reason I brought up the dream was because there was another guest on the show who wrote books about dreams. The dream was more of an information injection or download sent to me in my dream state.

In the dream, I saw the letter "I". It showed me the capital letter "I" with the horizontal line across the top and bottom, and it showed me the lowercase "i" next to it.

I understood that the capital I was the big I and was the ego I. The bars above and below kept it stuck where it was on the earthly plane. Nothing wrong with that. We have a lot to do while on earth.

The lowercase "i" had no bars above it or below it to hold it in. Instead, it had a little dot on top floating above it, like a spirit that could float free because the bars or ego wasn't holding it down.

But the third I is in the pineal gland, and it accesses a different level of consciousness. That is the I or eye that we are learning to access with these techniques. Much of the work comes from the subconscious, but the more you practice, the more the pineal gland wakes up.

Your Conscious mind is where you are holding attention as you read this text. You are conscious and paying attention.

Subconscious runs your systems and gives you what you need with little effort on your part. You just have to give it basic nourishing requirements. It is your servant and does what you tell it.

I call the higher self the superconscious. It's watching you like a third eye, cheering for you, throwing in a helping hand when it can, and waiting for you to bring back your experience to integrate it. It wants everyone to do the right thing for themselves while using the conscious and subconscious because that's where the learning is. It also wants to be discovered by you. It's timeless, so it doesn't NEED to be discovered, but it wants to be discovered and used.

Knowing this, do the 3rd Eye Meditation again. Connect with the 3rd Eye and Pineal gland area and all the way through your skull from front to back. Put your attention on the center of your eyebrows and imagine a tube from a roll of paper towels running through your forehead, passing at the height just at the top of your ears through your brain to the back of your head.

You are sensitive enough now to feel the energy of it. It's similar to watching a baby bird sleep. Why? You can be aware of the baby bird and be slightly in awe of its calmness and stillness. You are observing along with the calmness and stillness. By paying this gentle attention to your 3rd eye and what it notices, your 3rd eye begins to stir and acknowledge you back.

3.36 Know The Future by Being In The Present.

Can you know the future? You already often do. When touching someone and gaining information, you are feeling the vibration of the past. When sensitive, you have the ability to process the vibration, just like your eyes process the vibration or frequency of colors. Your biofield can do that, too. It's the same; although it's such a sensitive skill, it takes more practice and more quiet. You need to have reference points, just like you can tell when you are in theta brainwaves as you fall asleep if you stay conscious. It feels different. Seeing colors is something that seems external, even though it's all happening through the eyes to the brain and in the mind.

Why is it easier to know the past? It has happened already, so it has a tone or a feeling to it. The future has a feeling, too, and is often based on the most likely scenarios that could happen. You are also creating the future, so you're living with and using intention. Doing the work steers the ship. It's not too hard for a good psychic to tell you your future, because most people will choose the simplest choice or the frequency closest to what they are already doing, but you can change it by taking action.

The Kabbalah says not to put your faith in astrology or psychics, but not because they aren't real. The reasons are that it can make you forget that you have free will when someone can accurately tell you your future. You do have free will to create your life. It's an easier path to have a reader tell you what's coming unless they are willing to choose your highest path and tell you that it is the future that is waiting for you if you take the right steps. You also have to hope the psychic reader doesn't have their own trauma patterns that makes them see things in a negative or distorted way. If they have stored trauma, then that's the filter that information you will be receiving from them will be coming through. If you are very trusting, you may go towards the life they tell you is waiting for you for good or bad.

Years ago I used to see an astrologer. She was very good. I stopped going because when I listened to the recording six months later, I found that she was right about so many things that it felt like my life wasn't mine to live. When things were bad, I wanted to hear when they would turn for the better. If I heard it would take 2 years to get better, I felt helpless. When things were good, she said to save up your money and prepare now because a rough patch was coming in a month. I hated hearing that my good time was going to end prematurely. Again, she was great, and I know astrology is meant to help you prepare for things in life. It's also spiritually there to teach us to overcome and transcend natal tendencies (the tendencies shown on your birth chart), but I didn't know this at the time. I don't see any readers today, but I'm not against it. I prefer to focus on creating my life.

Back to the future: Time is not linear. Your subconscious knows or can know what's coming. You often get glimpses, so you know that's true. It is behind a veil, so you don't see it consciously most of the time. When you get a flash of a thought of someone and then they call you, you were aware of the future. You just didn't know it yet. So, let's look at random occurrences. If your subconscious and intuition are feeding you information, sometimes very loudly, you can catch it, but how much is it feeding you that's being missed?

What would it take to remove the ear muffs, buffers and blinders so you can notice the messages regularly when they occur? The flashes of insight come in the present, but they aren't attached to anything before or after the flash in that moment. You have to log or mark the information and keep it in your awareness for when the moment arrives where you confirm you had a flash of the future. Think about this. If you passed out and woke up somewhere and looked around the room, then you passed out again and woke up somewhere else. The first wake-up could seem like a dream, because you don't have a connected memory to what got you to that place. Meaning, you don't have a bridge connecting your experience from one place to another. You may have a flash of the memory about it, but it is not attached to a full story, so it floats away as a lone thought and becomes hard to find in your memories.

Because your subconscious works outside of a timeline, it decides what you should know based on another part of your consciousness giving it instruction. If you learn to passively notice and pay attention, you will consciously know the future, even if you don't yet know the insightful flash that you received is of the future. Remember that when it rarely happens, it is surprising and fun, but when it happens all the time, it becomes expected. It's still fun and awesome, but it has a feeling of inner power, too, because you know it's part of your own self you telling another part of you.

3.37 Exercise: Know The Future

Read this exercise into your recorder and then play it back and participate in this time thought experiment with me. It's also in the online course at intuitionmethod.com

Imagine your clock is on your table. Imagine you float up and rise up above the moving numbers of the clock. From that perspective, look down at it. You are quite literally above time. If you look forward, you can quite literally see a path like train tracks that go on forever. Behind the clock, the tracks go back forever, too. You can see the whole timeline moving forward forever to infinity and behind you equally as far. You can see forever in front of you and behind you from this viewing point.

The timeline train tracks stretch on and on. Float forward in time and find a spot to lower yourself for a quick stop in a different area of your timeline. Before you lower yourself, make yourself a phantom so if you see anyone, they won't be able to see you. Choose a time that is a few minutes or hours later. What do you see? Stay detached from whatever you see and just gently notice and observe. Don't interfere or get involved. Lower yourself further into the experience and mentally scoop up, grab some information like a scoop of water from a pool. Feel it in your fingers for a few moments, and then let it go. Float back up and look down at where you are now. Float back to your body and bring your awareness back to the present.

This is an easy experiment. I say it's easy because it's a visualization experiment. You are exploring states of consciousness, which may also mean exploring dimensions. You are discovering space and time in a new way and the feeling you are having when it happens.

By now, if you've been practicing, you already know how to tune into the feeling. It's a lot like turning an old radio dial until the reception is right until you connect to the feeling that you just recognize and know. Be passively aware of the information that comes in. If you are too active in getting information, your brainwaves will be too fast and in the wrong state, and you will miss the subtle, so do it from a deeper state of mind to get unexpected information.

3.38 Eureka!

When you have a Eureka moment, it interrupts whatever you are doing. It sparkles and gets all of your attention. You think you will remember it, so you may not stop to write it down. Write it down! That's what your journal is for. If you don't have your journal with you, have a place to write or record it until you get to it. Use your phone and record it if you have to. Because these Epiphanies come in from a different level of mind, they can be forgotten when you leave that level of mind if you don't write them down. These are the moments you must remember. These are the moments to have handy when you want to manifest a brainstorm of ideas or a miracle. Save these moments to your journal and use the feeling when you are meditating to manifest.

I had one of those moments when I woke up suddenly at 3 am in the morning. I had a direct injection of information into my mind. It was about my name.

My birth name is William. When I was a child, I was called Billy as a nickname. When I was in my 20's, it switched to the more mature, Bill.

One night I woke at 3 am and sat up like I was jolted with electricity. There was a message or download planted in my mind that said, "Billy translates in Hebrew to "Without." Bill is a debt or something you owe. William is the will of God. Choose the right name."

I knew I would never forget a message as powerful as this, but just in case, I grabbed my phone and put the message in my calendar for noon the next day as a reminder.

I woke up feeling good and completely blank on the memory of the information. At noon, my calendar went off and it was like I had a massive charge of energy run through me when I saw it.

I now feel that the name we are given at birth has specific properties and frequency to it and we should be using it, unless there is a good reason not to. Jewish mystics who study Kabbalah will change a person's name to a new name if the person is having health issues or problems in their life that are difficult to get through. This changes the person's vibration when they are spoken to with the new name by self or others. It will change the field around them. If you are called 'loved' and 'beautiful' all of the time, would that make you feel differently than if you were called ugly names all the time?

Words carry frequency. Words are frequency. Words direct the mind to different emotions. Language is a frequency device. Use kind and beautiful words with yourself and others and keep the bad vibes away! The dream didn't tell me which name to choose, but to me the choice was obvious. I switched to my given name that day.

By now you know that intuition covers many aspects of consciously knowing something and brings you the Eureka! You also know that Intuition can fade like a dream, so you must put it in print or record it as soon as possible, so you have the information for later.

When your intuition awakens, you have access to the most creative and inspired part of your mind, so make good use of it. The more you use it and are thankful for it, the more it will show up for you.

Sometimes I think of the subconscious as a block of moldable clay. It's there waiting to be shaped into whatever you want, once you find out it's there and able to be shaped.

3.39 Mystical Skills

It's alluring and fun to entertain yourself thinking intuition, empathic abilities, manifestation and psychic skills are mystical, but they really are not. They are not any more mystical than having a dream. It's a different part of your mind and consciousness. It's definitely exciting to think it's mystical and not coming from your mind, because you feel lucky and special that the universe is choosing you, but…

IT IS YOU DOING IT WITHOUT REALIZING IT! Remember this! It's so easy to forget.

Calling it mystical can disempower your connection to the event, unless you have the core belief that it's coming from you. Once you know it's you, call it whatever you want, but first know it is you!

It's the same way that showing a small lighter creating a flame would be mystical to a man in the year 1200. The technology hasn't developed yet, so it seems like magic. All of the things needed are available to make the lighter but the man from the year 1200 hasn't been shown the way.

I call it mystical, because like the root of the word, it's Mysterious, and it's like Mist. It's etheric and physically untouchable, but you know it's there. You know it because you can imagine it. You know it because you can feel it inside of you. You have seen it before. You have seen strange things that you can't explain, so you put it away in the back of your mind until the day comes when it happens again and you can say to yourself, "I Knew it!" Knowing it doesn't teach it to you, though. To learn, you have to work in the space of the etheric or mystical- The space of the mind. This takes training and practice and training again. It's the work you are doing here. It's the work you may be doing if you formed a study group. To make these abilities of yours consistent, you have to choose to make some small, but powerful choices for this payoff. Just like you may exercise every day or meditate every day, make time for the exercises and practice that will create the most magic in your life in the least amount of time.

I remind you of this question, "If you knew it was going to be worth it, really worth it, change your life kind of worth it, would you put in the time?"

This is the story of someone who found giving up a habit might be worth it.

There was a man who couldn't quit smoking. It was a part of his life, like his hand was part of his life. Over the years, due to health issues, he tried to stop and he failed many times until he stopped trying.

He had a cough and was feeling pressure in his head, so he went to his doctor. His doctor did some exams and said to him, "Your lungs are shot, your kidneys are shot, your blood pressure is at its limit. I don't know how to tell you this. But let me say it like this, "Do you love your family? Do you want your parents and your wife and your kids to know the pain of loss this soon? Do you want to leave your child without a father to grow up thinking about what it would have been like to have you there all of these years? Think about that, because if you have one more cigarette, your heart is going to give out, your blood vessels will constrict and you will die. We've worked together a long time. I care about you as a patient and as a friend." The doctor took a moment and wrote him a prescription and handed it to him. The man said, "The smoking medications don't work for me, doctor." The doctor said, "I know." And handed him the note.

The man read it to himself and then tears came to him. It said, "Before your next cigarette, get all of your affairs in order and take the time to write everything you need to say to your wife, your kids and your parents. Let them know why you decided to leave them sooner than you had to. Let them know it was your choice and tell them every reason you love them."

The man left the doctor's office. He didn't fully believe that he would die with one more cigarette, but also knew the doctor wasn't going to lie to him about this.

Night came and he wanted to relax, so he reached for the cigarettes in his pocket. He thought about what the doctor said to him and put them away.

The next day he was so stressed from work that he went for the cigarette. He needed it. He pulled out the prescription with it. Read it and put it down. He sat down with a pen and paper. He started writing to his wife. "Dear love of my life, you have been with me in my heart every day since the day we met and you are the one on this planet that was put here for me. I look back and know life could not have been better any other way. These years have been the best of my life. I'm about to have a cigarette. The doctor said that if I do, I will die right after. I am so sorry to do this to you."

He dropped the pen, sobbing, and thought to himself, "What the hell is wrong with me?" I gave this piece of crap cigarette so much power over my life.

He wrote his daughters name down and continued, now writing for himself, because he was able to observe the control the cigarette had over him was crumbling like an old cemented wall that was so strong for years, but somehow a small leak got in and began the process of crumbling.

"Dear sweet daughter of mine. Watching you grow up is the most beautiful thing I have ever done. Every moment has been perfect, watching you walk, talk, put on your shoes, holding you in my arms. Hearing you say, "daddy." I'm sorry I'm not here for you anymore. The doctor said if I have one more cigarette, I'm going to die and…" Immediately, the urge to smoke was gone. He realized the cigarette never had the power. It was always his choice. He took out the cigarette and broke them in half and threw them in the trash.

You may not smoke, but you have a habit that stops you from doing the work. The belief and wanting of what you desire has to overwhelm and override the programmed false belief that doing the work is not worth it.

Do you want your life to be the way it is right now in 5 years or 10 years? If you don't change it, it will be the same. If you do the work and commit to it every day, you will achieve what others call mystical, but you will call it- following a system that your body and mind are already programmed for as part of your biology.

Mysticism is ingrained in all cultures. For most, it's about focus, repetitive practice, sensitivity and paying attention. Many who developed intuitive and empathic skills and became great leaders, first went off on their own in isolation, whether they chose it or it was forced out by their community. When they returned, they had new wisdom and abilities, and new biological traits that are typically not common in mainstream society.

And why is that? Because mainstream is mainstream. Mainstream follows the herd. The herd runs without knowing where the people who are the herd drivers or leaders are leading them. The news tells them what is happening in life and desensitizes some emotions and amplifies others. If you tell a mainstream person something isn't good for them, or is good for them based on your own research, they won't look into it themselves. Instead, they will say, if it's true, then it would be on the news. You know people like this. You may have been one of them at some point.

Find your tribe until it's big enough that people call you a cult. Then do so much good for yourself and others that you become the herd.

Great leaders in history that spoke to God, or had special abilities disregarded the mainstream and listened to their passion and their inner guidance, as well as their higher self that connected them so divinely to their energy source and to their layer one mind, so much so that we know their names thousands of years later.

Just like birds know where to fly and animals know where there is water, a human with your higher intelligence can know anything, even if you don't know that you know yet. A baby bird doesn't yet know that it knows how to fly in formation either. Then one day, after taking all the steps to learn what parent birds teach a baby bird, it's flying and then flying in formation.

That's you, that's me, that's all of us who want to make our lives better by putting in the training and repetition to awaken our deeper programming.

3.40 The Real Purpose Of Meditation: Refinement And Upgrade

I wish I could tell you this earlier in the book. It's so important, but I found that without first doing the exercises and making these abilities real for you, this wouldn't matter as much. You read this far, so now I am going to share the real purpose of meditation.

The real purpose of meditation: The real purpose of meditation: It's not just mindful, it's a mind-full! Many say there are other purposes besides the one that I will talk about here in a moment, just like there are many purposes to eat foods that are sweet. Sweet foods taste good, or you may have a sugar craving, but ultimately, they are for calories to give energy.

Your brain is a super bio computer, a living consciousness computer that is always ready and waiting to be upgraded. The upgrade is done not with surgery, but with meditation getting you to the right state and attracting the right programs and frequencies. Did you see the movie, The Matrix? In the movie, they are already working in deep states of mind. They are literally behind the veil of consciousness in the movie, so they can download the needed programs immediately, by literally getting plugged in.

When you add new software to a computer, it can do new things, but the physical components, the hardware, has a limit until you upgrade it. New software code will help the computer run more efficiently, but it's still the same hardware, motherboard and circuitry. It still has the same storage capacity, and the hardware can only handle what it was built and programmed to handle.

Meditation upgrades the software. It will clear, refine and replace programs for you. It will give you the ability to notice thought viruses in your system, but it does much more than that. Doing it every day and properly with the right intention will upgrade your biological hardware.

Meditation literally reshapes and reorganizes your neurology, just like physical exercise will reshape your muscles, make fat shrink and disappear, and make your physical shape look completely different. Your brain does what your body does when you exercise it. It literally changes shape to a smarter, more calm, more inner guided and happier brain.

All you have to do is make the decision to do it and then do it.

Active intentional meditation is the easiest way to change your brain and to manifest what you want. If you commit to it fully you will turn your brain into the manifestation machine that it is made to be. It is already creating and attracting now, in this moment. To manifest by choice and get what you want, you have to put in the work and learn how to use it. Then you set it to the tasks you want it to complete.

When you order that package from amazon, you know it's coming in two days. You just know. You don't have to sit and wonder when it's coming. You don't have to give it a thought. You placed the order. That's the certainty you will develop as you build your brain and mind's ability.

In the physical world, you use your physical body to get things done, like going to get dinner. This is how it may play out. For example; To place an order in a restaurant, there are steps.

First you have to have some money, then you go to the restaurant, then you wait to get seated by a host, then once seated, you look at the menu, you ask questions of the server and you place your order.

The second time you go to that restaurant, the host may recognize you and seat you faster. You have already seen the menu, so you don't have to take as long to look at it. You may try a different order than last time, or if you like the last one, you order it again.

The third time you are there, you bring some friends, get seated quickly, and you explain to your friends what you like or didn't like on the menu. Then you all place your orders. It goes so much more smoothly than before. You have become the trailblazer and the teacher of your friends.

I was in Cancun for a meditation retreat. After the final day, I stayed with a friend for an extra couple of days. We went to Tulum and while she shopped, I walked around finding beautiful areas of the beach that were just perfect. When she was finished, I already knew where to get a smoothie, where there were bathrooms and how to get to some awe inspiring spots on the beach.

It was as if I was an expert for these 5 things. She was surprised I knew so much about where to go in just 20 minutes. In reality, I only knew what I knew. I also knew that if I found someone who lived there longer than me, I could follow them and be a master of great places to go in Tulum in a few days.

The good news is that using this book lays out the steps for you. Every angle is covered. Connect with the divine, ethereal energy of your mind. Recognize the feelings of where you are in your mind and you will achieve exactly what you really want. So make sure you are in tune with what you really want!

Learn how to get into the state to put in the order as fast as you possibly can.

Back to your brain…

Your brain actually changes size and shape during periods of daily meditation the same way your body does during exercise. Some parts shrink. Some parts grow and become more dense and other parts shrink, just like when you exercise your physical body.

The reason to meditate is not to 'feel good' or to 'be smarter' or 'make better decisions' or 'be more calm or intuitive.' The reason is to upgrade your hardware, so you can be the best possible antenna for transmission of consciousness connecting to source and receiving from source. The concept is very meta. It is levels above the reasons you might meditate, but as I mentioned earlier, all reasons we think we are meditating for are physical, emotional or mental reasons. This tends to be why we start. Part of us in some way tends to be out of balance. It will be our health, our emotions, or our mind. We are told to meditate or we are called to meditate to bring us back to balance. As we get more in higher balance, there is always a new level we gravitate towards. You can also get into a lower balance with your environment by doing unhealthy things.

When you eat healthy food, you break it down and give your body new nourishment and new information. After enough new information, your body uses it to build healthier structure. If you do the right things for your body by changing the patterns you live in, you change the software. You do it long enough and you change the physical body, the brain and DNA, the hardware. The next level up is the mind. You meditate to change the software and once it's ready and the software has been upgraded enough, the hardware in your living brain bio-super computer knows how to upgrade itself using its connection to its source. Like sunlight gives you energy, consciousness and stillness give your brain what it needs to upgrade.

It's a symbiotic relationship. You are giving back to the universe, too. The universe is alive and wants to evolve. The more you are able to vibrate at higher frequency and pull in the higher frequency, the more goodness can happen, and the less badness can happen.

If there was no obvious benefit and if there were no good feelings that came with your meditation practice, then why would you do it? If there were never any felt or personally experienced benefits, very few, if any, would ever meditate in the first place.

Becoming the greatest receiver and transmitter that you can be for all of the intuitive processes is a step on the way to becoming the perfect receiver and transmitter for consciousness and the conscious creation of your life. The changes in your brain are levels of refinement that connect you to the subtlest forms of consciousness. From this state, you know what you can do to make the world better for you and for everyone you care about. At this time in history I believe, at least part of anyone who has a craving for higher levels of awareness has the drive to make others aware of their consciousness, too. This can be in a different way for each person.

The innate abilities that I and people I know have developed are not just to help people heal. The abilities are more blatant now, because it takes seeing something happening physically to believe something is happening on a large scale. Working in the realm of consciousness to help you feel good and help clear your emotional or physical pain, needs to be seen through the media so there is a bigger awakening. We don't do the work just to help people. We also do it so more people ask questions. What is that? How is that done? Can I do that too? What if we all can do it? What else can we do? What and who are we really? Are we spirit, souls or consciousness coming into a human body? If we are simply human, how do we have access to these non physical abilities?

You made it this far in the book, so you are at minimum seriously curious, but are likely interested in developing your awareness and skills. I'm welcoming you to think about these questions. I don't recommend giving up yet on your passion and become a full-time meditator, healer or master of consciousness. You still have to pay the bills in the 3D world, but discover what your strongest abilities and skills are. The more that you do and the more that you awaken your best traits, the more we all develop a higher frequency and evolve faster.

Consider this as I tell you that the online course and offers are almost ready. If you feel called, go to intuitionmehtod.com and set up a time to come on a webinar or take the online course. I did my best to write everything as clearly as I could here in this book, but I know it is easier to learn in a class setting for many people, including myself.

All this being said, meditation is a refining and filtering process. You go from more physically dense to more still and more ethereal (less dense.) The more dense vessel is made to hold the less dense. A solid, more dense, plastic cup holds the less dense water. A solid metal tank holds a less solid gas. A solid physical body is a vessel to hold the less dense spirit and consciousness.

When you filter water, if you were to make a homemade filter using just what you find in nature, picture this. You would pour water from the top, so gravity pulls it down to the bottom. On the top level of the filter, you'd place big rocks. They remove the larger debris like sticks, dead animals and leaves. Below this, you'd have smaller rocks to catch smaller debris like twigs, small feathers, and some small leaves. Below the smaller rocks are pebbles. The pebbles catch dead insects and some contaminants. Below the pebbles, you'd have sand to capture even smaller contaminants and particles. The sand will even absorb some chemicals. Below this, there may be ground-up mushrooms or bone char to remove bacteria, toxic metals, chemicals and the smallest particles.

The water passes each layer interacting with it in different ways. Some materials let water through at a high speed to reach the finer and smaller sized materials. It passes through at slower speeds at each new level of filtration. The water slows down until it meets the sand and the mushrooms where the water exchanges information with them. It leaves behind what can't pass through the more refined, tighter level until the next refinement. Ultimately, once it's refined enough to be clean, the water is ready for drinking and integrating into even smaller and more refined cells in your body.

The brain and consciousness work in the same way. You refine and refine, layer by layer, until it can work with the finest, most subtle layers of consciousness and awareness, and your brain changes with it.

Years ago, I used a binaural meditation system that I enjoyed very much. It would entrain and lower brainwaves by about a half a hertz frequency (brainwave cycle per second) every few months. My brainwaves would be entrained and match the frequency at alpha brainwave level, then I would do it for some time before switching to the next audio file that would take me just a little deeper, until I was in theta and delta.

There came a time that I wondered about the refinement process. I wondered if I was meditating without this system entraining my brainwaves, would there be any brainwaves in between the ones they were choosing for me that my mind might want to stay in for a longer time. It's a bit like turning a channel on a radio. What if a brainwave number between 7.5 and 7.0, like 7.3 or 7.03 was the one where my mind would gain access to an important message or new skill that was waiting for me to find it? What if the brainwave being skipped was my personal key to my best life path? I stopped using that system and went back to my meditation without using technology.

The binaural beats are a great way to get into a good rhythm and also to feel what a deep state feels like. It's very good for a refresher or if you want some help. The caveat is that if it is part of a program with a formula to take you to a specific state of mind and you know this, then use it for that goal. If a binaural program holds your brainwaves in a certain level of theta brainwaves because that is the level that lets you increase intuition or lets your astral body separate from your physical body, I'm all for it. For daily usage, though, I opt for letting my inner guide be the guide of my brainwaves, unless I am looking for a specific goal that is being offered in a binaural frequency.

Talking about frequency...

3.41 Tuning Fork Diagnostics

Think of a tuning fork as a way to bounce energy off of something or someone and have it bounce back to you. If you have ever put your hand near a large music speaker, you can feel the air vibrating. You are literally feeling waves of sound, or sound waves. You feel it with your hand as a tingle or even an electric feeling. You feel it with your ears as a strong vibration or, if it's too loud, as pain. The speaker is sending out a frequency. Frequency can affect us in many ways. Another simple, yet advanced technique and refinement before we wrap up is using a tuning fork.

Learning to use tools to help with energy work or even hands on body work adds another dimension to the work. Tuning forks sound beautiful and the person you are helping will enjoy the sound and how relaxing it can be.

How to use a tuning fork for awareness training.

Get into a state of passive awareness. Run your hand over the person's body to feel areas of harmony or disharmony. Using that same sensitivity and awareness, tap the tuning fork on a hard surface like your pisiform, which is the pointed ball area on the bottom of your palm on the same side as the pinky finger. Another way to describe it would be the bottom part of the karate chop point on your hand. It's an easy place to hit the tuning fork without damaging the fork. It's not a great idea to hit it on a tabletop because you can put little dents or dings in it that will change the frequency. Tiny marks in it are like tiny shifts in your emotions when you are practicing manifesting. You want it to be the pure vibration that it is meant to be.

Once the fork is vibrating, run it above the person's body the same way that you ran your hand to feel the energy field. You will notice an area where the fork suddenly sounds flat in your ears or feels flat in your hands. It suddenly just feels deadened. It's still vibrating, but doesn't feel the same.

When you run over an area of discord or disharmony, the vibration or sound changes; it's like shouting in an open field compared to shouting into a box. The acoustics and the feeling will be completely different due to the open space or the confined space in front of you.

This is a general diagnostic. You can then use your hands to feel what you feel in that area. You can see what kind of energy your eyes see. You can touch the area to see if it feels tense or different in some way. It's something to practice and use as another tool in your tool box. If you use it enough, you will be able to know if there is a problem with an organ, an energy center, and possibly even develop a sense of sonar where you sometimes pick up an image of something in the body based on the vibrations that come back to you.

3.42 Photo Reading- An Empathic Skill And Auric Skill.

In photo reading, you are getting an understanding of the person's life based on a picture. Starting with the more physical perspective, pull up a picture of Maria Shriver for a moment. Do a quick image search on a web browser. What do you know about Maria from the picture? I won't give it away yet, but if you know her, forget her fame for now and write in your journal what you know about her from just the photo. You are opening up your feel centers now to get a sense of the person's dominant emotions and where they lead.

Now, look up a picture of Jeffrey Dahmer, the serial killer. What do you see? Now look up a picture of the president of the USA. Now someone from a beauty pageant, now Mother Teresa, now a navy seal. Now Justin Beiber when he was just starting out and another one of Justin Bieber today. Now, find a picture of me online at Instagram @William.Kalatsky.

The first thing you will notice is the tone of the muscles or their eyes. Let it process for a moment without thinking. What does the face or the eyes say to you? What about the way they hold their head forward, back or to the side? What about the wrinkle lines? It means certain expressions are more dominant. How is the jaw and the smile or lack of smile?

With these subtle cues that are easy to recognize, you will notice that your eyes will catch on certain areas of their face just like they do on someone's body. Don't think about it, but just let your mind float information to the you that is thinking about it. Then look at them further and see what you see. You will begin to see more about their life that is available in a picture. You will feel certain about it. You will start to feel something that allows you to bounce what you are picking up back and forth in your mind or heart, like tossing a ball from one hand to the other. Each toss will be a yes or a no, hot or cold, as you ask yourself questions. Did they go through this? (Abuse, break up, or a great family life.). When you get an answer, you will find your self saying, "It's similar to this, but not exactly. It's more like this." You will be feeling the weighing of these feelings in you until you suddenly know you landed it and you will have the certainty that you are correct. Now, don't just have unfounded certainty, but practice with a relaxed group of friends so you can get real certainty. Have friends show you pictures of friends that they know but you don't know, and practice doing analysis. If you get good at it, it will help you if you consider doing healing from a distance for others.

3.43 Field Of Consciousness Clearing. Migraine Clearing and More.

As I finish the last edit of Intuition Method, I must mention the work that I have developed working with migraines and other headaches over Video calls.

In the energy healing work that I have been doing, I was asked at one point, if I could do it over a distance. I tried it. It worked. I then did a 2 week study with people suffering with migraines and other headaches and had an over 90% percent success rate in helping them heal. For most of them, their pain was gone in less than 30 minutes in the first session.

This work isn't about treating migraines, but it is about clearing the patterns in the field of consciousness that just sit there creating tension and constriction in your physical and emotional self in some way. It can show itself in many ways. For many people, it's a migraine headache. The headaches are one way for someone to know they are out of balance. Before the headache, always comes the patterns and constrictions associated with past stresses or trauma that was never released. I now clear these patterns and am giving workshops so others can learn to do it, too.

There is much more to this method. The first part is clearing the pain and calming the mind. Once out of suffering and with a more peaceful mind, we expand the activity of the brain so you feel better, and have more brain function. You will feel their mind wake up, feel more bright and alive during the session. Then comes the part for those who want more out of life, the high performers and achievers and those who want to be in that category.

Now, we do work to expand your field, so you have more energy and information available to you. We are increasing the size of your atmosphere or field of consciousness of your world. Your antenna becomes bigger. You can choose to pull in and store more information and also have a bigger buffer zone to keep out information that you don't want.

Finally, there is installation of new patterns into your field. It's a shortcut to helping you get what you want.

For more information about the headache aspect of this work, go to Headachesheal.com and subscribe for the free ebook.

3.44 Finale: Is There More?

Yes, there is more.

Part of the more will come from the private group on the web where there will be open discussion of experiences and topics. Each conversation leads to new awareness.

As you continue to do these exercises, you will far surpass where you are right now. You will have "consciousness pops," or evolutionary bursts of consciousness. Because you are already open and receptive, and you commit to your stillness and meditation practice, you will be achieving levels that feel like mastery in a shorter time. Then, they will become a new normal until the next level is achieved. The truth is that it gets better and better, but it's an upward spiral that keeps on going, and I don't think it ends. This means endless opportunities if you want them or take a break at any time you feel you have gotten the tools and formulas to get what you want.

The new awarenesses and insights that have come up for me while editing this book are more than I can add to the book without going back and doing a rewrite. For now, I am going to wait and share it in videos and public presentations until the next edition.

Mastering these techniques and skills will take you to a personal place (which will be different for each person) similar to the end of part 1 of The Matrix, where Neo is walking through a busy city street. You will notice you are observing everyone and everything, aware of your separateness from it, but also aware of your connection. You may see someone and immediately notice they need help emotionally, physically, spiritually (or consciously), and you bridge your energy to theirs to give them a quick lift in perspective or health. You will watch them have a shift in their step, and they don't even know they are suddenly feeling a bit better. You get a karmic contact of goodness off of this and feel instantly better, proud to be able to help your fellow human. The only person you can tell is someone who gets it, and it's likely someone in our social media chat group or someone who knows you well. Find interested friends to share this with. You want people who you can talk to about it. You will want people to share with you and you will be excited to share with them. Ask the questions. Learn the shortcuts.

The more you share, the more ideas are generated and the more instantaneous "WOW" or "Eureka's" transmit to everyone who is reading and listening.

3.45 Thank You

Thank you for reading this book and allowing me to share with you one of the reasons I feel I am here.

Thank you for being one of the people on this planet to upgrade your consciousness and, by doing this, resonating your brainwaves and frequency at a higher levels setting the stage to make it easier for others to resonate with it and get clearer and in more harmony, as well.

As you go through this book again and if you decide to take the online course or live in person training, I hope to be able to teach you and learn from you in person, because the magic that happens in larger groups lifts us all so much higher so much faster.

May you create everything you want and may you only want what brings you your best life.

If you have any questions or would like to expand your consciousness further, please contact me here:

William @ IntuitionMethod.com

Subscribe to the mailing list for the newsletter, tips and to get your questions answered. @ IntuitionMethod.com

Instagram @william.kalatsky

Facebook.com/William kalatsky

Other Books By Dr. William:

Piranha Yama and The Art of Non-Biting

and his Ebook

Headaches Heal:Migraines Goodbye. *Relieve Your Migraines in 1 session. Heal them in 90 days. HeadachesHeal.com*

New Books Coming Soon:

The Healers Chronicles.

Miraculous healings are only miracles because most aren't following the necessary protocols taken by the one who experienced the miracle. Find out what they did and do it. Then you can experience a miracle, too.

For Kids

ToothFairy Hunter: She Wants Her Teeth Back

Made in the USA
Columbia, SC
07 June 2025

58924342R00165